The Sacred
Heritage

The Sacred Heritage

The Influence of Shamanism on Analytical Psychology

Edited by
Donald F. Sandner
and
Steven H. Wong

ROUTLEDGE
New York • London

Published in 1997 by
Routledge
29 West 35th Street
New York, NY 10001

Published in Great Britain by
Routledge
11 New Fetter Lane
London EC4P 4EE

Copyright © 1997 by Donald F. Sandner and Steven H. Wong

Printed in the United States of America on acid-free paper.

*Library of Congress Cataloging-in-Publication Data is
available from the Library of Congress*

In memory of
Poul Andersen

Contents

Foreword

Linda Schierse Leonard

Several years ago I was invited to participate in the first of a series of unique meetings to be held every spring near the Continental Divide, high in the Rocky Mountains. The focus of these discussions was the connection between the ancient curative arts of shamanism and the contemporary means of healing practiced by Jungian psychotherapists.

Just as the waters at the Continental Divide flow down from the mountains in two directions—east and west—so the majority of therapeutic approaches used in the modern western world have moved from the ancient wisdom of aboriginal cultures toward more impersonal, rational, and technical methods of treating patients. I was grateful for this opportunity to discuss ways to bridge the chasm between the healing arts of traditional tribal cultures and modern psychological methods at the very physical juncture where the waters themselves part on the American continent.

Ever since I trained in Jungian psychoanalysis in the late 1960s in Zurich, I have been fascinated by shamanic cultures from various parts of the world. In 1982, on a trip led by Don Sandner to study shamanism in Bali, I consulted a Balian shaman who went into a trance, then described exactly a series of events that had occurred and told me how to deal with this difficult situation. After following her advice, I was able to transform this problem on both the external and internal levels. Throughout the years I have been spiritually inspired to visit Aborigines in Australia, hill tribe people in Thailand, and Sami the reindeer people in the Arctic.

Shamanic motifs have appeared in my own dreams as well as in the dreams of some clients. Moreover, I have seen shamanic themes emerge in contemporary culture through Australian films such as *The Last Wave,* directed by Peter Weir, and *Walkabout,* directed by Nicolas Roeg, the Norwegian film *The Pathfinder,* by Sami director Nils Gaup, and the Mexican film *Chac,* directed by Rolando Klein. Influences from shamanic cultures—for example, the underlying paradigm of crossing the border between the visible and invisible worlds and the conflicts between shamanic and technological cultures—appear in films by Russian directors such as Andrei Tarkovsky (*The Sacrifice*) and Nikita Mikhalkov (*Close to Eden*), the Japanese director Akira Kurosawa (*Dersu Uzala*), and the German directors Ulrike Ottinger (*Joan of Arc of Mongolia*) and Wim Wenders (*Wings of Desire* and *Faraway, So Close*). American films such as Robert Redford's *The Milagro Beanfield War,* Michael Apted's *Thunderheart,* and Michael Cimino's *The Deer Hunter,* show such shamanic motifs as well.

Films often reveal unconscious attitudes, values, and viewpoints that an entire culture needs to bring to consciousness and to integrate in order to maintain balance and harmony in living. To me this indicates that the need for shamanic wisdom is emerging on a multicultural level, too. So I was eager to find out whether other psychotherapists who were working with dreams and deep experiences emerging from the human psyche had discovered links between the healing rituals of shamanism and their own practice of depth psychology and how they were applying this material in their clinical work.

Because I was away in the Arctic with my partner Keith Chapman, M.D., researching the shamanic practices of the people who follow the reindeer in the far north, I was unable to attend the first exploratory meeting, held in 1990. But at the 1991 meeting held in Winter Park, Colorado, I learned about the different ways that contemporary psychotherapists are utilizing shamanic practices such as waking visions, archetypal dreams, imaginal work, body experiences, and even entering into an altered state of consciousness themselves as they dive with their clients into the deep waters of the psyche.

Some of these therapists are exploring personally the ways and rituals of other cultures, such as those of the Lakota, Polynesian, Navajo, Andean, Pueblo, Ecuadorian, and Balinese native peoples. Others use their own visions, dreams, Kundalini body experiences, art, and imaginal work to help heal themselves and their clients. In this book you will find stories of their personal journeys to heal and find meaning in maladies and traumas such as breast cancer, surgery, death of a child during birthing, abuse, addictions, depression, anxiety, and our cultural loss of soul.

In 1993 and 1994, as a group under the guidance of Pansy Hawk Wing, a Lakota (Sioux) pipe carrier and spiritual teacher, we focused on Lakota rituals and ways of healing. Together, in a ceremonial ritual directed by Pansy and her son, Bo, we built a sweat lodge ourselves. After entering this sacred enclosure on our knees, we sat on the ground around the steaming stones in the center and prayed for healing for ourselves, our relatives, our friends, and all peoples of the earth. For me, this was an especially sacred event because I was suffering from despair about the approaching death of my mother. Prior to this experience, I had never participated in a sweat lodge ceremony. I was anxious and apprehensive that I would faint from the heat or would have to leave the sweat lodge. At the same time I was partly skeptical. But the experience of having met Pansy earlier at a women's conference on healing and Jungian analysis, together with the sincerity and community of our group, gave me the confidence to venture into the ritual.

Inside the sweat lodge, sitting on the earth, feeling the drops of perspiration from my sisters and brothers all huddled close to each other, praying to the four elements and directions of the cosmos, inviting healing nature spirits inside to help us, I experienced a humility that cleansed and released me from the resentment and anger I was feeling about my mother's dying. I experienced both death and rebirth, giving me a new sense of hope.

At our meeting in 1994 we shared more experiences centering around shamanic healing and continued to learn more about the Lakota rituals, and in 1995 we focused on the Blackfoot tradition.

My own exploration of shamanism was furthered by the following dream of my partner, Keith Chapman, M.D., who also participated in these meetings.

I was in a cold white room with other physicians and their wives. Immediately I felt alienated. All of the people at this gathering were formal, stiff, and staid and were dressed as though they wanted to show off their wealth and prestige. Everywhere I turned I heard only small talk and these professionals' attempts to impress each other with their importance. I was uncomfortable, and looked around to find something genuine or a way to escape. I saw a white piano in the room and walked toward it, wanting to sit down and play. But the atmosphere was so cold that I couldn't create. I felt a lack of soul in the room, and I knew I had to leave. I suddenly saw an exit at the back of the room and walked rapidly toward it. When I crossed the threshold, I entered into an amazing space. All of the doors and windows of this new room opened out onto a vast wilderness. I was astonished to see a woman, her hair blown by the wind, suddenly run into the room from the forest. She wore deerskin clothing. In amazement I asked, "Who are you, and where have you been?" She answered, "I've just returned from a journey. I have run for months with a herd of pregnant reindeer."

This dream, which shows the contrast between healers focused on outer, material possessions and the natural woman from the wilderness, so alive with the mysterious connection to the pregnant reindeer, reminded me of the concluding reflections in my first book, *The Wounded Woman*. The image of the mysterious Reindeer Woman seemed relevant for fostering the female spirit grounded in nature.

Keith's dream inspired us to travel to encounter the reindeer people of the Arctic—in both Lapland, where the Sami people live, and Siberia, where many shamanic cultures still thrive. In 1992 we journeyed to the province of Yakutia in the northeast sector of Siberia. We traveled there in a cargo helicopter once used by the Soviet military. Sitting on sacks of potatoes and other goods with a few of the native people, we wondered where we were going as we flew over the vast mountainous wilderness near the Arctic Circle. Suddenly the helicopter swooped down between two mountain ranges and landed in a dry riverbed. Members of the Even tribe, nomadic people whose lives revolve around the reindeer, came running to meet us with gifts for the pilots. As the helicopter left, our eyes followed its flight through the sky, and we wondered whether it would return. Russia was in turmoil and gas shortages and plane breakdowns were common. The clan members led us up to a high valley where we met their elder, a short, round man of seventy who emanated the wisdom and serenity of the Buddha. He grinned and pointed into the distance, and we saw over a thousand reindeer running toward us with some of the tribe members astride them. We were so inspired to see the Even people riding the reindeer across the tundra that we forgot our worries. We were mesmerized by the reindeer's sea of antlers, which looked like birch branches moving in the wind.

The elder told us that on the earthly level, the Even people follow the reindeer across the tundra on the animals' annual migration to give birth. Spiritually, they revere the reindeer as a holy animal that travels between the earthly and spiritual realms to carry shamans who journey to the spirit world to bring back healing for the community. The Even people, he said, believe they were created to ride the reindeer.

Atop the reindeer, they balance themselves and guide their mounts by touching the earth with a large stick. The pole is said to be the world tree that unites the three planes of reality—the upper (spirit) world, the mid-world of earth, and the underworld. The riding pole is more than an ordinary stick, and the balance they achieve transcends sheer physical balance. The pole gives them a supernatural center of balance, through which they experience an ecstatic state of serenity. Riding the revered antlered animal is a spiritual experience for the Even, who still live a shamanic life. "The reindeer is a child of the sun," one of the Even teachers told us, "and turns into a great swan or wild gander as it flies to its home. A golden reindeer pulls the sun across the sky. When we ride the reindeer, we fly like birds. To us, the reindeer is like a great spaceship, a great bird that is always in the air."

The elder told us that the Even people need the reindeer, just as the reindeer need them—the souls of the reindeer and those of the Even are interrelated and interdependent. The Even have an "I-thou" relationship with the antlered animals that they cherish. The elder looked at us and said, "If the reindeer perish, so will we." Each Even person has a special relation to a particular live reindeer that is his or her spirit guide. He pointed to a nearby tree and told us that this earthly tree was an embodiment of the world tree, and that the antlers of the reindeer composed its branches. When an Even dies, the corpse is placed in a coffin and hung high among the branches of a tree along with the antlers of that person's special spirit reindeer. In the leafy cradle of this transforming "tree of life," the Even believe, the souls of humans and reindeer together return to the spirit world, where people and reindeer still ride as they do on earth.

As we sat together around the campfire, Keith shared his dream of the Reindeer Woman and a vision of her that he had earlier that day. The people nodded, then told us that they revere a Reindeer Goddess whose name, *Khinken*, means "without stress." Whenever they dream of her, they know they will receive her guidance, protection, and help.

On the day that we left the Even people and the reindeer the Siberian elder gave us a parting gift. Knowing that Keith was a doctor, the elder had asked him a favor. The elder was concerned because he had suffered a heart attack several years earlier; now he was in the wilderness, far away from medical facilities, and he was worried about some recurring symptoms. Since the Soviets had, as far as we know, killed all the Even's shamans, he had no native healer to help him. Keith offered to listen to his heart. He put his ear to the elder's chest, tapped his back, touched the old man's wrist gently to feel his pulse, and found his heart to be in good condition. The elder was grateful for Keith's help, and in thanks he gave us a necklace of bear gallstones, along with a vial of bear blood and a paw. "Bear are sacred," the elder told us. "Wear this necklace, which circles the heart, to remember us and to protect the heart and its health." Caring—the heart's task—was the pivotal gift that we received following the reindeer, meeting their people, and looking into the eyes of these holy animals.

By following the dream of the Reindeer Woman, I encountered directly the shamanism of the reindeer people of the Arctic, was inspired by their

"I-thou" relationship to the animals and the earth, and experienced the way dream and reality intertwine as one great whole. I have recounted the meaning of these adventures for me and my understanding of their relevance for healing and for an ecological, spiritual, and creative way of life in my book *Creation's Heartbeat: Following the Reindeer Spirit.*

Jung once commented that the spiritual plight of Western civilization—the loss of soul—stems from its alienation from the rest of the world. In this volume you will discover many fascinating accounts of the way the practice of Jungian psychotherapy can emerge from the varied and ancient heritage of shamanistic healing to revitalize our sense of wonder, renew our faith as we search for meaning and to help heal the broken relationships and the alienation we suffer when we try to separate ourselves from our ancient heritage or any part of the cosmos.

Acknowledgments

We wish to gratefully acknowledge the Colorado Group for the study of shamanism and analytical psychology. This includes those who have contributed essays to this book and those who haven't. It took everybody together to inspire and support this effort.

We especially wish to thank Sharyn Cunningham, who undertook the prodigious task of getting this manuscript into one piece; Pansy Hawk Wing and her son, Bo, for leading us and sharing with us many sweats, Lakota rituals, and teachings; the staff of Woodspur Lodge of Winter Park, Colorado, for taking care of us so well; Hunter Whitney, for editing above and beyond the call of duty; Mary Sandner, for being something of a midwife to the birth of this book; and Lydia Lennihan and our many other friends, who gave constant help and encouragement along the way.

Editors' Preface

The material in this book is neither strictly about shamanism nor strictly about analytical psychology. It is a close look at how shamanism has influenced analytical psychologists in their work and in their lives.

The first section, "Beginnings and Meanings: The Shamanic Archetype," is an overall look at the definitions and boundaries of shamanism and analytical psychology: how they intersect and interact. A major part of this is a discussion of how Mircea Eliade's work, an overview of worldwide shamanism, influenced Jung, and a survey of the many ways Jung's life pattern mirrored the life pattern of a typical shaman. The final essay in this part touches on one of the deepest symbols in shamanism, the book of knowledge, which ties in with our modern psychology.

The second part, "Shamanic Medicine: Explorations in Healing," gives a vivid picture of how analytical psychologists use shamanic techniques and theories in their clinical work with modern patients. This is an area that to my knowledge has never been explored.

Part Three, "Dark Encounters: Personal Transformations," the most dramatic part of the book, tells how analytical psychologists have used shamanic methods to cope with dire threats to their lives and to their work from illness, injury, pathological childbirth, surgery, and the spirit world. All of them experienced strong contact with what psychologists would call the deep unconscious, and what shamans would call the other world. In these essays both of these worlds come together.

The fourth and final section, "The Numinous Web: Cultural Connections," describes how analytical psychologists have visited, observed, and taken part in the shamanic activities of other cultures where shamans are still part of the indigenous culture. This has been for these psychologists a transformative personal experience.

Part I

BEGINNINGS AND MEANINGS: THE SHAMANIC ARCHETYPE

Chapter 1

Introduction:
Analytical Psychology and Shamanism

Donald F. Sandner

The art and practice of psychotherapy is in its infancy compared to the mil-
lennia-old history of shamanism. There are caves in southern France containing twelve-thousand-year-old paintings of shamans in trance states.
Extending not only in time but also in space, shamanic practices have been
found throughout the world, from Patagonia to Siberia. It should not be
surprising, then, that Jung realized that his most profound conceptions of
healing had much in common with shamanism. He wrote, "The [shaman's]
ecstasy is often accompanied by a state in which the shaman is 'possessed' by
his familiars or guardian spirits. By means of this possession he acquires the
mystical organs which in some sort constitute his true and complete spiritual personality. This confirms the psychological inference that may be
drawn from shamanic symbolism, namely, that it is a projection of the individuation process" (Jung 1967, 341). Jung realized that in spite of their apparent differences, both shamanism and analytical psychology focused on
the healing and growth (individuation) of the psyche. Inspired by this work,
some therapists have continued exploring shamanism in order to enhance
and perhaps even redefine the ways they treat patients. Many examples of
their work will be found in the essays in this volume.

Both historically and in the present, there have been several different
forms of healing. The gathering of herbs and the task of preparing them for
medicinal use is performed by the native herbalist; exorcistic and blessing

rites with songs, prayers, dances, and incantations are often performed by a medicine person. But the heart of the healing effort for those groups that still practice shamanism is the shaman's trance, a journey into another reality outside time and place. Here he may plead with the spirits or higher powers to send good weather or good hunting conditions for his people. Or he may be able to diagnose the nature and bodily location of a patient's illness and be given songs or rituals to cure it. He may be able to see into the future and locate lost objects or people. Often he is told by the gods and spirits what the people must do to atone for broken taboos or for neglect of sacred shrines. But in the oldest traditions, his journey was to locate the out-of-body soul and return it back to the patients's nearly dead body.

Siberia appears to have been the homeland of shamanism. The word *shamanism* itself comes from a northern Siberian tribe, the Tungus, and shamanism until recent times was practiced there in its basic form. An observer, Waldemar Jochelson, described a soul retrieval in the late nineteenth century:

> Suddenly the shaman commenced to beat the drum softly and to sing in a plaintive voice: then the beating of the drum grew stronger and stronger, and his song—in which could be heard the sounds imitating the howling of a wolf, the groaning of the cargoose, and the voices of other animals, his guardian spirits—appeared to come, sometimes from the corner nearest to my seat, then from the opposite end, and again from the middle of the house, and then it seemed to proceed from the ceiling. . . . The wild fits of ecstacy which would possess him during the performance frightened me. (Jochelson 1907–8, 49)

In these ecstatic states, which occur not only in Siberian shamanism but in various cultural guises throughout the world, the shaman makes his journey. His many kinds of animals, his helpers, the cosmic tree he climbs to the world above, the costume he wears (made up of iron bells, mirrors, and animal motifs), and the drum carrying him on his way are all parts of a complex of symbols that is found in a recognizable pattern across the globe, despite cultural differences. The point of this book is that the basic shamanic pattern is not a manifestation of a certain culture but rather is, as Jung pointed out, an archetype—a constant and universal part of the human psyche, manifested more in some persons or places than others but always there and ready for use. Jung saw this pattern as a projection of individuation (the inner psychic process of development) and shamanism as part of the heritage of analytical psychology.

Jung and his followers, analytical psychologists, are not shamans; they do not conduct their healing functions in an altered state of consciousness or ecstatic trance. They are considered rational psychologists in a society in which a premium is placed on focused attention and conscious rationality. But in addition to their healing intentions, Jungians have other important features in common with shamanism: They seek direct experience with an inner world (in shamanism it is the world of spirits, and in analytical psychology it is the collective unconscious) by encountering imaginary inner beings (spirit helpers, or archetypal figures) who are regarded as subjectively real. Perhaps one of the strongest and most subtle connections between shamanism and analytic psychology is this firm insistence on the reality of a separate space to which the psyche has access. Shamans would see this as a world of spirits that is a mythic part of their cosmology. An analytic psychologist would see this space as a part of the deep unconscious that is collective and partially personified by such archetypal figures as the hero, the trickster, the Great Mother, and others. These figures are seen in dreams and visions and form the individual counterpart to the mythic world of shamanism.

Instead of the wild shamanic trances described by Jochelson in Siberia, Jung developed the modern method of active imagination. In this method the patient empties his mind, much as in meditation. Then he allows an image to form in the field of inner attention and focuses on it, regarding it closely. This image may move or become part of a scene. Finally he must give it some form of creative expression: recording it, painting it, sculpting it, and so on.

Given the differences in perspective, the two disciplines follow a remarkably similar pattern. It might be said that in the archetypal processes of analytic psychology the patient experiences the dynamics of shamanism. The inner journey, encounters with magic animals, the ease of movement through time and space, the magical control of elements, and the death and rebirth experience are all part of the inner experience of the modern analytic patient.

Jung underwent such an experience himself during a period of intense self-analysis after his break with Freud. At that time Jung let himself sink into the unconscious background of his psyche. Once he went into this inner realm, he found an abundance of visions and images.

> I did my best not to lose my head but to find some way to understand these strange things. I stood helpless before an alien world. . . . Then I let myself drop. Suddenly it was as though the ground literally gave way beneath my feet, and I plunged down into the dark depths. Before me was the entrance to a dark cave, in which stood a dwarf with leathery skin, as if he were mummified. I squeezed past him through the narrow entrance and waded knee deep through icy water to the other end of the cave where, on a projecting rock, I

saw a glowing red crystal. I grasped the stone, lifted it, and discovered a hollow underneath. At first I could make out nothing but then I saw that there was running water. In it a corpse floated by, a youth with blonde hair and a wound in the head. He was followed by a gigantic black scarab, and then by a red new-born sun, rising up out of the depths of the water. . . . I was stunned by this vision,"I realized that it was both a hero and a solar myth, a drama of death and renewal. The rebirth was symbolized by the Egyptian scarab. (Jung 1962, 178–79).

But it was many years before Jung regained his psychic equilibrium and fully grasped the meaning of the experiences that had befallen him. His story, as fully told in *Memories, Dreams, Reflections*, is remarkably close to Joan Halifax's description of the shamanic process: "The initial call to power takes the shaman to the realms of chaos, the limen where power exists in a free and untransformed state" (Halifax 1982, 9). The beginning of the mastery of that power can be ecstatic. Jung regarded the unconscious material that burst forth and nearly swamped him as "the primary material for a lifetime's worth of work" (Jung 1982, 9).

The shamans themselves corroborate these perceptions. The Caribou shaman Igjugarjuk told the Artic explorer Knud Rasmussen that all true vision "is only to be attained through suffering. Privation and suffering are the only things that can open the mind of man to those things which are hidden from others" (Halifax 1982, 9).

Both shamans and analysts are wounded healers. If they have a true vocation (and there are many counterfeiters), analysts as well as shamans must find their way through many painful emotional trials to find the basis for their calling. They have all taken their own long analytic journeys. Dreams, visions and fantasies made conscious have allowed them, at considerable cost, to penetrate the depths of their unconscious. The material produced in this process is sometimes so intense that it brings about a temporary loss of orientation that is experienced as death or dismemberment of the conscious ego. A sacrifice of childish self-aggrandizement and immature impulses must take place before deep healing can occur. To be able to bear expanded consciousness, a stronger and more resilient ego must arise from this sacrifice. All of these workings go on within the therapeutic relationship between the patient and the analyst, much as the shamanic candidate must completely depend on his mentors to guide and protect him through his painful initiations.

Andreas Lommel, an early authority on shamanism, reminds us that "the concept of the helping spirits is naturally difficult for modern man to understand. It is an image that stands for a definite psychological event—an increase in psychic power" (Lommel 1967, 59). These spirits often take the form of animals, but they may be in other forms. Such magical animals are an integral feature of shamanism and are also quite common in the dreams and visions of analytic patients. The shaman recognizes magic animals such as the bear, the wolf, the tiger, the otter, the owl, and many others as allies and helpful spirits and knows how to make use of them. But of all spirit animals the snake is one of the most common in shamanic mythologies and in the dreams and visions of modern people. This is rather remarkable in that urban people rarely see a snake in nature, and if they do, it is usually at a distance and of little danger. But the image of the snake carries a great fascination and its meaning goes deep; it stands for healing (on the doctor's staff) and for poisonings. It inhabits the lower regions most often as a denizen of the earth and a companion to the goddess; it might be said to stand for the unconscious itself in its cold blooded, inhuman aspect.

In northern Australia, a shaman gains power through the snake. In one account a man has a vivid dream about a snake at the bottom of a water hole. After he awakens, the man travels far and wide to find the same water hole he saw in his dream. When he finally finds it, he lies down and sends his soul down deep into the water. He feels that he is dead but goes on anyway. He enters a cave where the sun is shining and finds a great snake there. The snake speaks to his soul and gives it medicine. Then the soul rises out of the water and once more enters the man, who then feels strong and alive. A shaman who has had this experience with the snake never loses his power. He can always heal (Lommel 1967, 59).

It could also be said that almost all long term analytic therapy, the snake puts in at least one appearance in the patient's dreams. Many times this is not just a walk-on role, but a dream vision of such power that it is good for a lifetime. For example, in the visions of a modern young woman named Christiana Morgan, Jung's patient in the late 1920s, she saw a gothic cathedral and in it "the priest knelt chanting 'Forgive us, O Lord, for we have sinned.' A snake with a black hood over its head silently glided up the steps to the altar and wound itself upon the cross. I went up to the snake and asked it why it was there. The snake answered, 'I am he who has taken the place of Christ'!" (Jung 1976, 204). In Christian iconography the snake has been represented as the dark brother of Christ. In other cultural traditions it is also an associate of the Great Mother (think of the statue of the Cretan goddess with the wide skirted dress holding aloft two snakes, one in each hand) and lord of the underworld. There is a Greek statue showing Hygeia, daughter of Aesculapius, holding a thick-bodied serpent in one hand and feeding it an egg with the other. Because the snake has the ability to shed its skin periodically and thus seemingly be born anew, it is regarded as a prime agent of healing and renewal. As such it finds a place on the doctor's staff.

I have given so much attention to the snake because it is the primary animal link between shamanism and modern psychology. Much shamanic symbolism has been repressed or denied in modern life, but not the snake. It is too powerful to be denied. We have tried very hard to banish it from our conscious lives, but it has withdrawn to the underworld (unconscious) and deals with us in our dreams. Many of the more powerful dreams I have had contain the snake. In my early thirties, when I was in analysis and just starting my practice, I had a vivid dream of a hand held aloft unfurling a large flag. On the flag was the image of a coiled, threatening rattlesnake and underneath the motto "Don't tread on me!" This is an actual early flag used in the American Revolution. From this dream, I knew that, like the early American colonists, if I was trodden upon by some power-seeking authority, I would not submit; I would retaliate like the serpent, and would sting!

In a final point of comparison between shamanism and analytic psychotherapy, both have imagined that the deep psyche is androgynous. In analytical psychology, the anima is a personified image of the feminine in men's psyche, including all those feelings, moods, intuitions of the irrational, and deep capacity for love (including the sexual) that are associated with the feminine. The anima also represents the soul in its role as gateway to the deeper psyche. The animus is a corresponding deep presence of the masculine in women, cherished for its aggressiveness, intellectual powers, and spiritual insight. It appears in women's dreams as an intruder, a dark and mysterious man, or in waking life as the voice of inner authority, sometimes to the point of tyranny. Both anima and animus are thought of not only as images but also as entities (complexes) with an autonomous existence in the psyche.

Mircea Eliade, author of the definitive classic *Shamanism: Archaic Techniques of Ecstasy* (1964), reminds us that male Siberian shamans will often ritually assume the dress and behavior of a woman. They may even take a husband. In Japan and China, female shamans may sometimes marry their spirit husband (or animus). These rituals are performed to uncover a hidden wholeness. They symbolically represent the inner marriage not only of male and female but also of matter and spirit (Eliade 1964, 258). Similarly, in analytical psychology the anima/animus represent the gateway to the deeper psyche, to wholeness.

This inner marriage is beautifully represented by a Navajo sand painting showing Mother Earth and Father Sky side by side, connected by a line of pollen (the most sacred substance) from head to head and a rainbow band from tail to tail. Sand paintings, with their vivid images, are made by Navajo medicine men on a floor of the ceremonial hogan by running a stream of fine, colored sand between the thumb and the forefinger onto the smooth

sand floor. They are made as part of the long, elaborate healing ceremonies, and they represent the cosmos in miniature, halfway between the
macrocosm of nature outside and the microcosm of the psyche inside.
Through chanting and prayer, healing power from the gods is directed into
the figures in the painting. Then the patient sits on the sand painting and
receives healing power with the help of the medicine man.

In the sand painting just described, Mother Earth is a large blue-green
oval figure with a square head, jointed arms and legs coming out from the
sides, and a rounded tail. In her middle, a round black hole of emergence
leads down to the lower worlds. Around this opening are the four holy
plants: corn, beans, squash, and tobacco. She represents the great earth
goddess of the Navajo, offering fertility and shelter for all of her creatures.
Father Sky, a large black oval figure with a square head, arms, legs, and a
tail, represents the night sky. He displays many of the constellations as well
as the Milky Way stretching across his chest. The sun is also represented,
wearing his horns to show his power. Interestingly, the Navajo always show
the sun as being turquoise blue. The image of the moon depicted on Father
Sky, however, is white. These are the cosmological forces that influence human destiny. On the other side, Father Sky is connected by another hole of
emergence to the spirit world above. In this sand painting, the feminine
and masculine forces are exactly equal; they are in balance, connected by
pollen and the rainbow. Also, the tail of Mother Earth is the black color of
Father Sky, and vice versa. Each one contains part of the other. Here we
have a symbolic representation of the shamanic tripartite cosmos: We live in
the middle world between Mother Earth and Father Sky. Below Mother
Earth is the underworld and above Father Sky is the spirit world.

This image of the cosmic marriage of Mother Earth and Father Sky res-
onates with the earthly marriage of a man and a woman, and with Jung's
idea of an inner marriage of the anima (feminine part of a man) and the
animus (masculine part of a woman). This union at every level is what Jung
called the *mysterium coniunctionis*, and he placed it as the central idea of his
psychology. During a long convalescence after a nearly fatal heart attack in
1944, he had many vivid images of this inner marriage. In the last of these,
he was walking up a wide valley that brought him to a classical amphitheater, "and there, in this amphitheater, the hierosgamos was being celebrated. Men and women dancers came on-stage and upon a flower-decked
couch All-father Zeus and [All-mother] Hera consummated the mystic marriage" (Jung 1962, 294).

For Jung, this vision became the prefiguration of his final great work, *The
Mysterium Coniunctionis*, which discussed the final transcendental unity at
the core of his psyche. "The living mystery of life is always hidden between
Two, and it is the true mystery which cannot be betrayed by words or de-

pleted by arguments" (Jung 1973, 581). For Jung, it is the eternal monocosmos that is split apart, as in this Navajo sand painting, into Mother Earth and Father Sky, then united again and again in the embrace of the man and the woman. In both shamanism and analytical psychology, this unification represents a state of wholeness, both within and without.

Shamanism and analytic psychology, so outwardly different and so inwardly similar, have something to teach each other. Analytical psychology contributes its skill in self-reflection, conscious analysis, and self criticism. The old shamans badly needed these qualities of the modern mind. There were certain ways in which they claimed to regularly influence outer reality: changing the weather, influencing the fortunes of the hunt, healing known illnesses, and so on. They were very effective as long as the influence operated within the aboriginal environment. But when, this was no longer the case—as in North America, for instance, when the Europeans introduced the hard outer reality of the steam locomotive, the modern rifle. and the devastating scourge of smallpox—the shamans had very little effect. They did not consciously know their limits, and this contributed in large part to their loss of credibility and status. In spite of the most potent shamanic magic, the ghost-dance shirts used by the Plains Indians did not deflect rifle bullets. In the triumph of the focused mind that produced powerful machines, shamanism all but died.

But now, interest in and practice of a new shamanism, born out of the ashes of the old, reasserts itself. Why does this new shamanism seem so important to the modern world? I think it is because it brings relief for the modern mind, which is always so focused on some minute detail of outer reality. Shamanism unfocuses the mind, loosens the ego from its rigid outward ties, and allows it to descend into the other, inward reality of the core psyche. This experience restores to us the depth, richness, and perspectives of an open universe populated by animal and human forms that are found not on earth but only in the inner psychological reality of myth. In this wealth of symbolic forms (and only there) can the meaning of life be shown, not intellectually or dogmatically but experientially and metaphorically. This is also, as Eliade so correctly perceived, a "technique of ecstasy." Ecstasy gives us the strength and the will to follow, apart and alone if need be, our own path through life and into death, gratefully and willingly.

As Jung said of his almost fatal illness in his late sixties: "On the whole, my illness proved to be a most valuable experience, which gave me the inestimable opportunity of a glimpse behind the veil. The only difficulty is to get rid of the body, to get naked and void of the world and the ego-will. When you can get rid of the crazy will to live and when you seemingly fall into a bottomless pit, then the truly real life begins with everything you were meant to be and never reached. I was free, completely free and whole as I

never felt before" (Adler 1953, 60). This to my mind is a modern experience of shamanism with its meaning and its ecstasy; it is also the goal of individuation.

But let us recognize pride of discovery in the old shamans as represented
by Maria Sabina, the Mexican Mazatec shaman, who said: "There is a world
beyond ours, a world that is far away, nearby and invisible. And there it is
where God lives, where the dead live, the spirits and the saints, a world
where everything has already happened and everything is known. That
world talks. It has a language of its own. I report what it says" (Halifax 1979,
130). But this shamanic world is unknown to those of us who do not participate in traditional shamanic cultures, because we have destroyed all routes
of communication with it. In restoring that communication I realize that we
are, as Joseph Campbell said, "participating in one of the very greatest leaps
of the human spirit to a knowledge not only of outside nature, but also of
our deep inward mystery" (Campbell 1988 xviii). For this we need the wisdom of the deep psyche, such as has been held in trust for us during the
long history of shamanism. Tribal societies such as the Navajo, the Hopi,
the Huichol, and others are now returning this wisdom to the greater collective world and to the conception of a greater healing that includes both
the scientific and the shamanic. That process has just begun, and we, the authors of this book, hope to further that progress, and through the many descriptions and illustrations presented here, be a part of it.

REFERENCES

Adler, G., ed. 1975. *The Selected Letters of C. G. Jung*, Vol II *1909–1961*. Princeton:
    Princeton University Press.
Campbell, 1988. *The Power of Myth*. New York: Doubleday.
Eliade, [1954]. *Shamanism: Archaic Techniques of Ecstasy*. Bollingen Series LXXVI. New
    York: Pantheon.
Halifax, J. 1979. *Shamanic Voices*. New York: E. P. Dutton.
———. 1982. *Shaman: The Wounded Healer*. New York: Crossroads.
Jochelson, W. l907–8. *Religion and Myths of the Koryaks*. New York: American Museum
    of Natural History.
Jung, C. G. 1975. *Letters, 1951–1961*. Princeton: Princeton University Press.
———. 1962. *Memories, Dreams, Reflections*. New York: Pantheon. New York.
———. 1967 [1954]. "The Philosophical Tree." In *Alchemical Studies*. Bollingen Se-
    ries XX: The Collected Works of C. G. Jung, vol. 13. Princeton: Princeton Uni-
    versity Press.
———. 1976. *The Vision Seminars*, Vol. 1. Zurich: Spring Publications.
Lommel, Andreas. 1967. *Shamanism: The Beginning of Art*. New York: McGraw-Hill.

Chapter 2

"What Was All that Rustling in the Woods?": Quotes from C. G. Jung

Compiled by Meredith Sabini

Meredith Sabini has compiled major quotations from Jung in which he explicitly mentions or touches on the main principals of shamanism as they relate to his own work. The title is particularly apt. If, as rational minds would have it, there is no truth in all this talk of spirits and shamans, then, as the boy in the tale asks his father, "What was all that rustling in the woods?"

Jung spoke passionately and poetically about the loss of sacred tradition:

Through scientific understanding, our world has become dehumanized. Man feels himself isolated in the cosmos. He is no longer involved in nature and has lost his emotional participation in natural events, which hitherto had a symbolic meaning for him. Thunder is no longer the voice of a god, nor is lightning his avenging missile. No river contains a spirit, no tree means a man's life, no snake is the embodiment of wisdom, and no mountain still harbors a great demon. Neither do things speak to him nor can he speak to things, like stones, springs, plants, and animals. He no longer has a bush soul identifying him with a wild animal. His immediate communication with nature is gone forever, and the emotional energy it generated sunk into the unconscious. (Jung 1976, para. 585)

He discovered, however, that this tradition never completely dies out but lives on in the deep psyche:

Every civilized human being, whatever his conscious development, is still an archaic man at the deeper levels of his psyche. Just as the human body connects us with the mammals and displays numerous relics of earlier evolutionary stages going back to the reptilian age, so the human psyche is likewise a product of evolution, which, when followed to its origins, shows countless archaic traits. (Jung 1933, 126)

Dreams and creative fantasy provide bridges to the lost tradition:

The symbol-producing function of our dreams is an attempt to bring our original mind back to consciousness, where it has never been before, and where it has never undergone critical self-reflection. We *have been* that mind, but we have never known it. We got rid of it before understanding it. (Jung 1976, para. 591)

For Jung, this imaginal world became a separate, objective reality:

Philemon and other figures of my fantasies brought home to me the crucial insight that there are things in the psyche which I do not produce, but which produce themselves and have their own life. Philemon represented a force which was not myself. In my fantasies I held conversations with him, and he said things which I had not consciously thought. For I observed clearly that it was he who spoke, not I. He said I treated thoughts as if I generated them myself, but in his view thoughts were like animals in the forest. . . . It was he who taught me psychic objectivity, the reality of the psyche. . . . Philemon represented superior insight. . . . To me he was what the Indians call a guru. (Jung 1961, 183)

Through introspection, we may be able to perceive basic archetypal or phylogenetic patterns:

As animals have no need to be taught their instinctive activities, so man also possesses primordial psychic patterns, and repeats them spontaneously, independently of any teaching. Inasmuch as man is conscious and capable of introspection, it is quite possible that he can perceive his instinctual patterns in the form of archetypal representations. As a matter of fact, these possess the expected degrees of universality (cf., the remarkable identity of shamanistic structures). (Jung in Adler 1975, 152)

Shamanism and alchemy are examples of the natural process of spiritual development:

This confirms the psychological inference that may be drawn from shamanistic symbolism, namely that it is a projection of the individuation process. This inference, as we have seen, is true also of alchemy, and in modern fantasies of the tree as it is evident that the authors of such pictures were trying to portray an inner process of development independent of their consciousness and will. The process usually consists in the union of two pairs of opposites, a lower (water, blackness, animal, snake) with an upper (bird, light, head, etc.) and a left (feminine) with a right (masculine). (Jung 1967a, para. 462)

Suffering is an integral part of this process, not as punishment but for transformation:

Since all mythical figures correspond to inner psychic experience and originally sprang from them, it is not surprising to find certain phenomena in the field of parapsychology which remind us of the trickster. . . . His universality is co-extensive, so to speak, with that of shamanism, to which the whole phenomenology of spiritualism belongs. There is something of the trickster in the character of the shaman and medicine-man, for he, too, often plays malicious jokes on people, only to fall victim in his turn to the vengeance of those whom he has injured. For this reason, his profession sometimes puts him in peril for his life. Besides that, the shamanistic techniques in themselves often cause the medicine-man a good deal of discomfort, if not actual pain. At all events, the "making of a medicine-man" involves, in many parts of the world, so much agony of body and soul that permanent psychic injuries may result. His "approximation to the savior" is an obvious consequence of this, in confirmation of the mythological truth that the wounded is the agent of healing, and that the sufferer takes away suffering. (Jung 1969c, para. 457)

The numinous experience of the individuation process is, on the archaic level, the prerogative of shamans and medicine men; later, of the physician, prophet, and priest; and finally, at the civilized stage, of philosophy and religion. . . . The shaman's experience of sickness, torture, death, and regeneration implies, at a higher level, the idea of being made whole through sacrifice, of being changed by transubstantiation and exalted into a pneumatic man— in a word, of apotheosis. (Jung 1958, para. 448)

Jung summarizes the stages in the evolution of consciousness, and concludes with a description of our modern dilemma:

Since, at the present level of consciousness, we cannot suppose that tree demons exist, we are forced to assert that the primitive suffers from hallucinations, that he hears his own unconscious, which has projected itself into the tree. If this theory is correct—and I do not know how we could formulate it otherwise today—then the second level of consciousness has effected a differentiation between the object "tree" and the unconscious content projected onto it, thereby achieving an act of enlightenment. This third level rises still higher and attributes "evil" to the psychic content which has been separated from the object. Finally, a fourth level, the level reached by our consciousness today, carries the enlightenment a stage further by denying the objective existence of the "spirit" and declaring that the primitive has heard nothing at all, but merely had an auditory hallucination. Consequently the whole phenomena vanishes into thin air—with the great advantage that the evil spirit becomes obviously nonexistent and sinks into ridiculous insignificance. A fifth level, however, which is bound to take a quintessential view of the matter, wonders about this conjuring trick that turns what began as a miracle into a senseless self-deception—only to come full circle. Like the boy who told his father a made-up story about sixty stags in the forest, it asks, "But what, then, was all the rustling in the woods?" The fifth level is of the opinion that something did happen after all: even though the psychic content was not the tree, nor a spirit in the tree, nor indeed any spirit at all, it was nevertheless a phenomenon thrusting itself up from the unconscious, the existence of which cannot be denied if one is minded to grant the psyche any kind of reality (Jung 1967b, para. 248).

This is how he thought analytical psychology could help restore our original wholeness:

> People live as though they were walking in shoes too small for them. That quality of eternity which is so characteristic of the life of primitive man is entirely lacking. Hemmed round by rationalistic walls, we are cut off from the eternity of nature. Analytical psychology seeks to break through these walls by digging up again the fantasy-images of the unconscious which our rationalism has rejected. These images lie beyond the walls; they are part of the nature in us, which lies buried in our past and against which we have barricaded ourselves behind walls of reason. Analytical psychology tries to resolve the resultant conflict not by going "back to nature" with Rousseau, but by holding on to the level of reason we have successfully reached, and by enriching consciousness with a knowledge of man's psychic foundations. (Jung 1969a, para. 739)

The realm in which transformation takes place is ultimately a paradox:

> The place or the medium of realization is neither mind nor matter, but that intermediate realm of subtle reality which can only be adequately expressed by the symbol. The symbol is neither abstract nor concrete, neither rational nor irrational, neither real nor unreal. It is always both. (Jung 1968, para. 400)

> Just as the archetypal is partly a spiritual factor, and partly like a hidden meaning immanent in the instinct, so the spirit, as I have shown, is two-faced and paradoxical: a great help and an equally great danger. It seems as if man were destined to play a decisive role in solving this uncertainty, and to solve it more-

over by virtue of his consciousness, which once started up like a light in the murk of the primeval world. (Jung 1969b, para. 427)

REFERENCES

Adler, G. (1975). *C. G. Jung: Letters, 1951–1961*. Princeton: Princeton University Press.

Jung, C. G 1933. *Modern Man in Search of a Soul*. New York: Harcourt Brace Jovanovich.

————. 1958. Transformation Symbolism of the Mass. In *Psychology and Religion: West and East*. Bollingen Series XX: The Collected Works of C. G. Jung, vol. 11 Princeton: Princeton University Press.

————. 1961. *Memories, Dreams Reflections*. New York: Random House.

————. 1967a. The Philosophical Tree. In *Alchemical Studies*. Bollingen Series XX: The Collected Works of C. G. Jung, vol. 13. Princeton: Princeton University Press.

————. 1967b. The Spirit Mercurius. In *Alchemical Studies*. Bollingen Series XX: The Collected Works of C. G. Jung, vol. 13. Princeton: Princeton University Press.

————. 1968. Religious Ideas in Alchemy. In *Psychology and Alchemy*. Bollingen Series XX: The Collected Works of C. G. Jung, vol. 12. Princeton: Princeton University Press.

————. 1969a. Analytical Psychology and *Weltanschauung*. In *The Structure and Dynamics of the Psyche*. Bollingen Series XX: The Collected Works of C. G. Jung, vol. 8. Princeton: Princeton University Press.

————. 1969b. On the Nature of the Psyche. In *The Structure and Dynamics of the Psyche*. Bollingen Series XX: The Collected Works of C. G. Jung, vol. 8. Princeton: Princeton University Press.

————. 1969c. On the Psychology of the Trickster Figure. In *The Archetypes of the Collective Unconscious*. Bollingen Series XX: The Collected Works of C. G. Jung, vol. 9, part 1. Princeton: Princeton University Press.

————. 1976. Healing the Split. In *The Symbolic Life*. Bollingen Series XX: The Collected Works of C. G. Jung, vol. 18. Princeton: Princeton University Press.

Chapter 3

Eliade, Jung, and Shamanism

Bradley A. TePaske

Mircea Eliade, one of the great historians of religion in our time, wrote a book, entitled *Shamanism: Archaic Techniques of Ecstasy* in which he integrated the many world-wide tribal variations of shamanism into one unified concept. In this essay Bradley TePaske shows us the ways in which shamanism, as defined by Eliade, has many points in common with Jung's archetypal psychology. Indeed, it sometimes appears that archetypal psychology is a modern offshoot of ancient shamanism.

The vital contributions to contemporary thought made by the historian of religions Mircea Eliade and by C. G. Jung, the founder of analytical psychology, lend themselves to ready comparison for many reasons. These include the cross-fertilization of their ideas through personal acquaintance and a shared concern for dreams, visionary states, and the phenomena of religion, as well as their specific use of technical terms such as *archetype* and *symbol*. The writings of Mircea Eliade enjoy considerable popularity in Jungian circles. Jung himself refers to Eliade, along with Heinrich Zimmer, Erich Neumann, and Karl Kerenyi, as a significant contributor to our understanding of the archetype (Jung 1976, 529). Eliade's *Shamanism: Archaic Techniques of Ecstasy* (1974a) offers an especially rich point of comparison, however, for it is the sole work by Eliade to which Jung refers in his *Collected Works,* and this in a number of important contexts to be examined here. Virtually all of Jung's references to Eliade appear in three essays, "Transformation Symbolism in the Mass" (Jung 1976b), "The Visions of Zosimos," (Jung 1976a), and "The Philosophical Tree" (1976b), where the transformation of personality and specific problems of psychic phenomenology are discussed.

Eliade documents shamanism as an archaic and global religious complex, while Jung focuses on certain special features of shamanism that parallel features of the psychological individuation of the modern individual. Specifically, these are typically recurring personifications of psychic contents that Jung terms *shadow, anima,* and the *Self,* and dynamic inner processes such as dismemberment, sacrifice, and a coming to psychic consciousness that is comparable to the shamanic flight. In light of the fact that there are numerous varieties of shamanism and that any individual shaman may fulfill the roles of psychopomp, priest, mystic, or poet as well as healer, it is important for the psychologist to remain mindful of shamanism's full complexity. While Eliade recognizes the value of psychological approaches, he warns that it is "inacceptable to assimilate shamanism to any kind of mental disease" (Eliade 1974a, xi–xii). The warning is important, for it is also imperative that the psychologist realize how little is understood through the category of psychopathology.

The shaman is initially a sick individual, personally experiencing epileptoid seizures, nervousness, extraordinary dreams, trance states, and displaying a number of aberrant behaviors. He is a person innately disposed to extreme introversion, whose unique inner experiences effect a radical separation between him and his fellows. (While most shamans are male, there are also many female shamans. The masculine pronoun is used here for the sake of simplicity alone.) So distinguished as a special personality, he is tortured and dismembered by various demons and spirits, yet receives the aid of his familiar and helping spirits. He may be disemboweled, flayed, cooked, and have his skeleton separated bone by bone, yet he undergoes a regeneration and an ecstatic flight by which he comes into his own as a "technician" of the sacred. Indeed, he becomes a personification of the sacred. The shaman's passage through these ordeals and the knowledge he attains in this entrance into the realm of the sacred develop his ability as a healer.

Jung considered shamanism to be among "the great religions," and he saw shamanic experience as exemplifying the individuation process on an archaic level (Jung 1973, 294). The shaman as the healed one may thus be taken as paradigmatic of a human being who has been transformed by sickness in a meaningful way, as one who has contacted the very source of life and been created anew. Jung considers shamanism within the broader context of rebirth. He, like Eliade, sees not only a restoration of physical health and psychological equilibrium but also a spiritual opening, an awakening to religious experience. An examination of the deep connection between the shaman's psychological turmoil and the knowledge and expertise which he gains in the initiatory process provides the modern psychologist with extremely important insights into the fundamental nature of psychic life.

The shaman, like any personality, is not of his own making; rather, he is an individual seized upon by autonomous psychic forces in the most spontaneous way. It is this spontaneity that is understood by his fellows as the surest sign of an authentic "election" to the role of healer. The shaman initiate is at first a passive object of the sacred, singled out from the rest.

> What is important to note is the parallel between the singularization of objects, beings and sacred signs, and the singularization by "election," by "choice," of those who experience the sacred with greater intensity than the rest of the community—those who, as it were, incarnate the sacred, because they live it abundantly, or rather "are lived" by the religious "form" that has chosen them (gods, spirits, ancestors, etc.). (Eliade 1974a, 32)

No one can fail to be impressed by the purity and directness of the shaman's experience of the unconscious. Typically one can see in oneself and in one's patients the strong role of personal complexes and histories, which in addition to their obvious importance in therapy also veil many transpersonal contents emerging from the collective unconscious. Eliade's broad cultural examples document shamanic experiences of the collective unconscious rather than the personal complexes of the individual. In any case, the power of the autonomous psychic complex, be it personal in nature or more spiritual archetypal experiences, can have a similarly intense impact on the individual, prompting a disruption of consciousness, conflicts in emotional life, or any number of psychosomatic symptoms. In any event, the feeling of singularization, of being cut off from the community and one's intimates, forces the individual to deal with the unconscious as a personal problem. From his perspective as a historian of religions, Eliade sees the unity of humankind in terms of the *homo religiosus*. Accordingly, he speaks of the experience of the sacred by individuals who "are lived" by a religious "form." The psychologist recognizes as well that the development of the personality springs not from the ego alone but also from the finalistic dynamism of a more comprehensive superordinate personality, the Self. The continual tendency of the Self toward regulation and transformation may therefore be considered as that simultaneously instinctual and spiritual "form" by which we are lived and through which the highest religious experience is mediated to human consciousness.

Shamanism confronts us with the fact that sickness and vital visionary experiences have always been intimately interrelated. This constitutes an important challenge to the superficiality and excessive positivism of popular attitudes regarding "mental health" and "psychopathology," which view sickness and the possibility of meaningful religious experience as mutually exclusive opposites. The medical model of psychiatry, for example, characteristically seeks to diagnose, treat, and eliminate pathological symptoms with a pharmacological regimen. In many instances this has the insidious effect of merely repressing the psyche's emerging contents and obscuring transformative possibilities born within the symptoms themselves. The failure to recognize sickness and health as wholly relative, inclusive opposites not only entails many unexamined assumptions on the part of the healthy doctor but sustains a more essential split in the archetype of the wounded healer. This archetypal figure may be imagined as Christ, as Aesculapius or as the initiated shaman but must be understood and embraced by any practitioner claiming to work holistically or psychologically in depth. The greatest danger exists in allowing this figure to be forgotten, for the therapist who is out of touch with his own psychopathology will tend to identify with one pole of the archetype and fail to invoke the healer archetype within the psyche of the patient. As Eliade points out, and as Jung would certainly agree, psychiatric interpretation of the shaman's "psychosis" does precious little to aid one in understanding the psychological and religious significance of an individual's experience.

The meaning of sickness and suffering may well be beyond the purview of modern medicine, remaining rather a question for the religiously sensitive, the philosopher, and the depth psychologist. As to the question of what a religious experience might consist of, or in what sphere it might be had, Eliade offers a broad framework. He outlines an "archaic world" that knows nothing of profane activities and in which every activity with a definite meaning participates in the sacred (Eliade 1974b, 28). As the study of shamanism testifies, sickness and suffering are preeminent among these latter "activities."

In viewing the given world, as in confronting the powerful forces emerging from the unconscious, another observation of Eliade's may likewise be borne in mind: "Like the sick man, the religious man is projected onto a vital plane that shows him the fundamental data of human existence, that is, solitude, danger, hostility of the surrounding world" (Eliade 1974a, 27).

From a psychological perspective, these "fundamental data of human existence" include typical intrapsychic figures which are central in individuation of the personality. Jung terms them the *shadow*, the dark and ostensibly negative aspects of the personality, the *anima*, the psychic personification of a man's feminine side (the anima is a corresponding psychic representation of a woman`adf`s masculine side); and the Self, the superordinate personality and ultimate identity of the individual.

The shaman is equipped to penetrate the darkness of the soul and battle disease precisely as a result of having encountered the shadow in his own initiation. The shadow is generally the same sex as the individual and is capable of appearing in numerous guises. In the confrontation with the shadow lies not the demise of the personality but the potential for psychic equilibrium, enhanced consciousness, and spiritual power. The polarity of this darkness with the light of the soul is exemplified in Eliade's description of black and white demigods of the Buryat people known as the Khans. A fierce enmity exists between the two types. ``Black'' Khans are served by "black" shamans who are particularly adept as intermediaries between humans and these archetypal shadow figures. While psychiatry is generally not interested in the specific contents of the psyche, contemporary religious creeds also offer scant celestial mythology, much less a differentiated infernal one, by which the "black" forces within us might be ritually apprehended as meaningful. Imaginatively confronting and, in some measure, integrating these forces within the personality is the task of the individual, and it is a task forced upon one in the periodic downward cycles of the individuation process.

While the anima problem is an issue of much lesser importance in indigenous shamanism, Jung cites one highly specific example of the ritual union between a young shaman and his "celestial wife" in the ritual mythology of the Buryat and Teleut peoples of Siberia. There the spirit of an ancestral shaman takes the initiate to meet the gods of the Center of the World, particularly Tekha Shara Matzkala, the god of dance, fecundity, and wealth. Amorous relations with the god's nine wives are a prelude to the shaman's meeting his own future celestial wife.

> Before this ceremony the candidate travels through all the neighboring villages and is given presents that have a nuptial significance. The tree that is used in the initiation, and that also resembles the one put in the house of a newly married couple, represents . . . the life of the celestial wife; and the cord that connects this tree (planted in the yurt) with the shaman's tree (in the courtyard) is the emblem of the nuptial union between the shaman and his spiritual wife. (Eliade 1974a, 75)

Jung frequently describes the anima/us as a figure that mediates between consciousness and the unconscious. The shamanic material does instance this very clearly, particularly in the shaman initiate's sexual intercourse with the wives of a deity so intimately associated with the Center of the

World. In the shamanic cosmos, Eliade states, the celestial wife plays "an important but not decisive role," serving as no more than the shaman's helper and inspirer. Nevertheless, for the other members of the shaman's community, these liaisons constitute "another proof that he shares to some extent in the condition of semidivine beings, that he is a hero who has experienced death and resurrection and who therefore enjoys a second life, in the heavens" (Eliade 1974a, 77).

In his references to Eliade's work, Jung shows a central interest in the shaman's initiatory dismemberment and the mystical experiences that accompany this symbolic death, and he cites the entire process of dismemberment and reconstitution as an example of the act of sacrifice taking place on an archaic level. The symbolic sacrifice of Christ in the Catholic Mass, the self-sacrifice of the central visionary figure in Zosimos, and the shamanic dismemberment are cited as manifestations of the same essential transformative process, culturally discrete though these examples may be. In each case the individual (in the Mass, the responsive believer) is seized upon by a divine force that effects, through symbolic death and rebirth, a passage to spiritual awareness. Psychologically, each example may be considered in terms of the relationship between an ego still tangled in naive and literalistic identifications with the body and the world, and the higher spiritual personality and agent of individuation, the Self.

Jung presents an especially striking and instructive parallel to the initiatory dismemberment of shamanism with the dream visions of the third-century Greek natural philosopher and alchemist, Zosimos of Panopolis. Having fallen asleep, Zosimos beholds an inner figure who stands upon an altar and describes his transformation into a spirit.

> "I am Ion, the priest of the inner sanctuaries, and I submit myself to unendurable torments. For there came one in haste at early morning, who overpowered me, and pierced me through with the sword . . . and mingled the bones with the flesh, and caused them to be burned upon the fire of the art, til I perceived by the transformation of the body that I had become spirit. And that is my unendurable torment." And even as he spoke thus, and I held him by force to converse with me, his eyes became blood. And he spewed forth all his own flesh. And I saw how he changed into the opposite of himself, into a mutilated anthroparion, and he tore his flesh with his own teeth, and sank into himself. (Jung 1976a, 60)

In this and an ensuing sequence of visions, the sacrificing priest and the sacrificial victim display their identity as opposing aspects of one archetypal process. The spiritualized priest and the fleshly anthroparion (homunculus) symbolize opposites that stand in a fierce dynamic tension. In shamanism, the dynamism of autonomous psychic forces is experienced directly, as though the initiate were a veritable sacrificial victim offered up by the denizens of another world. Jung observes that

> What is performed concretely on the sacrificial animal, and what the shaman believes to be actually happening to himself, appears, on a higher level, in the vision of Zosimos, as a psychic process in which a product of the unconscious, an homunculus, is cut up and transformed. By all the rules of dream interpretation, this is an aspect of the observing subject himself; that is to say, Zosimos sees himself as an homunculus, or rather the unconscious represents him as such, as an incomplete, stunted, dwarfish creature . . . and thus signifies the "hylical" man. Such a one is dark, and sunk in materiality. He is essentially unconscious and therefore in need of transformation and enlightenment. For this purpose his body must be taken apart and dissolved into its constituents, a process known in alchemy as *divisio, separatio* and *solutio,* and in later treatises as *discrimination* and *self-knowledge.* (Jung 1973, 272)

Here Jung emphasizes a progressive psychization of forces within the psychosoma as central to the individuation process. Personal experiences corresponding to those of the shaman initiate entail a profound and disquieting upheaval of unconscious psychic contents. The remarkable intensity of such experiences only underscores how crucial the sustained integrity of an observing ego is to any successful unfolding of the personality. Through a series of similar experiences in time, these disruptions anticipate a radical transformation and expansion of consciousness. Thus with the greatest interest does the psychologist consider the structure, dynamics, and diverse inhabitants of the "mystical geography" that opens itself to the shaman in his initiation and ecstatic flights, for the great sphere he enters, and in which he performs his searches and transactions, reflects the self-regulatory phenomenology of the Self in full flower.

Eliade describes how the essential realms, structures, and personages of an indigenous shamanic cosmos reveal themselves with great constancy through time and in the experience of tribal shamans. "There are three great cosmic regions, which can be successively transversed because they are linked together by a central axis," he says, and goes on to observe that

> This axis, of course, passes through an "opening," a "hole"; it is through this hole that gods descend to earth and the dead to the subterranean regions; it is through the same hole that the soul of the shaman in ecstacy can fly up or down in the course of his celestial and infernal journeys. (Eliade 1974a, 259)

In this cosmological imagery is a celestial realm of the spirit that in the psyche informs fantasy, ideation, and intellect; a subterranean realm that, though already psychic, may be correlated with the bodily and instinctual sphere; and the intermediary and specifically psychic sphere. As a personification and technician of the sacred, the shaman moves adeptly within this imaginal world. One may note the overall image of psychic polarities (archetypes) that create a *complexio oppositorum* at a central axis—this being another Jungian characterization of the self. In introducing his discussion of "The Philosophical Tree," Jung observes:

> An image which frequently appears among the archetypal configurations of the unconscious is that of the tree or the wonderworking plant. When these fantasy products are drawn or painted they very often fall into symmetrical patterns that take the form of a mandala. If a mandala may be described as a symbol of the self seen in cross section, then the tree would represent a profile view of it: the self depicted as a process of growth. (Jung 1976b, 253)

Through a process that begins in complete spontaneity, sickness, and ego death, the shaman's capacity to enter the realm of the sacred at will gradually emerges. His personality steadily builds up a reservoir of extraordinary strength, craft, and insight based upon a sustained receptivity to the teachings of formerly strange and overwhelming forces. This change may be most graphically discerned in the contrast between the shaman initiate, who experiences his own body as a sacrificial offering, and the initiated shaman, who has the ability to pursue the errant soul of a sick person, escort the dead as a psychopomp, or accompany the souls of sacrificial animals within the spiritual world.

The tree, stretching above and below, is perhaps the most familiar symbol in the shamanic cosmos, and it is the prime avenue on which many journeys and crucial transactions are made by the shaman healer. In light of Jung's remarks concerning the tree and the mandala as symbols of the self, the shamanic activity of preserving psychic equilibrium may be imagined horizontally, vertically, or on any plane passing through the central axis. The shaman's entranced ascent or descent amounts to an interaction between human consciousness and the varied archetypal and transpersonal elements of the collective psyche.

While not generally identified as the primary sacrificial priest, the shaman is he who plays the more spiritual role in sacrifice, conducting the soul of the animal to the appropriate deity in exchange for the errant soul of the patient. In indigenous shamanism, the individual is frequently conceived as consisting of as many as seven souls, some of which may have fallen into the possession of a demon or spirit. Psychologically, one of these single souls may be considered as a functional component of the personality that, however rightly belonging to the human personality, is but a part of "a precarious psychic unity, inclined to forsake the body and easy prey for demons and sorcerers" (Eliade 1974a, 182). Through acts of exchange and retrieval with various archetypal personages, equilibrium is reestablished. Significant in regard to healing, to the vitality of the shaman, and to tribal life, as well as in the process of psychological individuation; sacrifice, and the ritual interactions with the transpersonal forces which accompany it, are guarantors of the general sustenance and renewal of life.

Why these sacrificial processes should have such efficacy in healing may not be immediately apparent, since it involves the special nature of the realm of the sacred (as Eliade would describe it) or the numinous nature of the archetypes and the collective unconscious (in a more psychological description). Eliade points out that "one does not repair a worn-out organism, it must be re-made; the patient needs to be born again; he needs as it were, to recover the whole energy and potency that a being has at the moment of its birth" (Eliade 1973, 48). The archetypal processes thus far examined result in a remaking, a rebirth from the very source of psychic life. Jung emphasized this source in discussing shamanic flight, the tree symbol, and the mysterious replacement of the initiate's natural viscera. Eliade documents as an experienced phenomonom many instances of the shaman initiate being disemboweled only to be refilled with crystals of quartz, each a bit of "solidified light" from the vault of the celestial sphere and each possessing its respective indwelling spirit. Psychologically, the discovery of such "mystical organs" amounts to nothing less than a progressive realization of the Self through a dawning awareness of the luminous multiple aspects of the subtle body. The symbol of the crystals in shamanism is paralleled by the diamond body in Chinese alchemy and the philosopher's stone in the Western tradition and may stand as the source of psychic life par excellence and a final symbol of the spiritual Self.

The inner development of the modern individual may involve psychic experiences as intense, varied, and exotic as those known to indigenous shamanism. Absent for us in our Western industrial culture, however, is the traditional fabric of *representations collectives* by which traditional cultures recognize the shaman's experiences of the sacred as valid and collectively meaningful. Contemporary notions about mental health as well as inadequate popular conceptions of religion and of the sacred are but two of the factors that tend to isolate an individual facing the objective psyche. Even the most sophisticated interpretation cannot convey a true impression of the strangeness and immediacy of certain psychical experiences. They must be had or simply imagined. A work such as Eliade's *Shamanism: Archaic Techniques of Ecstasy* provides the most differentiated itinerary for the latter course. It offers to the psychologist, or to anyone concerned with the role of religious experience in healing, the most provocative insights into the nature of the individuation process on an archaic level, and a new appreciation of the religious forms by which we "are lived."

REFERENCES

Eliade, Mircea. 1973 [1943]. *Myths, Dreams, Mysteries.* New York: HarperCollins.

————. 1974b [1951]. *Shamanism: Archaic Techniques of Ecstasy.* Translated by Willard R. Trask. Princeton: Princeton University Press.

————. 1974b [1954]. *The Myth of the Eternal Return.* Princeton: Princeton University Press.

Jung, C. G. 1973 [1942]. Transformation Symbolism in the Mass. In *Psychology and Religion: West and East.* Bollingen Series XX: The Collected Works of C. G. Jung, vol. 11. Princeton: Princeton University Press.

————. 1976a [1938]. The Visions of Zosimos. In *Alchemical Studies.* Bollingen Series XX: The Collected Works of C. G. Jung, vol. 13. Princeton: Princeton University Press.

————. (1976b) [1945]. The Philosophical Tree. In *Alchemical Studies.* Bollingen Series XX: The Collected Works of C. G. Jung, vol. 13. Princeton: Princeton University Press.

————. (1976c). [1954] Foreword to "Von den Wurzeln des Unbewusstseins." In *The Symbolic Life.* Bollingen Series XX: The Collected Works of C. G. Jung, vol. 18. Princeton: Princeton University Press.

Chapter 4

C. G. Jung and the Shaman's Vision

C. Jess Groesbeck

In this essay Jess Groesbeck enumerates and evaluates the many ways Jung's life and work were similar to those of shamans throughout the world. Many of the single comparisons may seem fortuitous, but when they are taken together, the point is clear. From the standpoint of this essay, Jung was a powerful healer and the nearest thing to a great shaman our Western culture can provide.

The study of Carl Jung's life has become of great import because of his contributions to the healing disciplines. His primary concerns are related to understanding the healing process within the psyche as well as his more expanded concept of individuation, that is, the idea of an individual realizing the full potentialities of his life. While it is true Jung was officially a psychiatrist and a physician, he has also been examined from religious, philosophical, and anthropological perspectives; recent biographies have shown him in these different modes. While many of these frames are undoubtedly helpful, the total picture of the man still remains a mystery. One student and analysand of Jung's, Joseph Henderson, recalled the following:

> There was, however, another aspect of Jung's character which refused to conform to European cultural patterns because it seemed to come totally from

outside any culture. It seemed to burst upon him from an absolutely foreign but absolutely compelling primitive level of being. I think of it today (thanks to some of his own formulations) as the shaman which made Jung at times into a man of uncanny perception and frightening unpredictability of behavior. This was the side which could never endure boredom and managed to keep him in hot water with someone all his life. Yet one always ended by feeling the beneficent ultimate effect of this spiritual tornado. This same shamanistic tendency, freed from any tricksterism, was an essential part of the psychological doctor who came to the rescue over and over again during analysis, placing the healing fingers of his intuition upon our symptoms. He diagnosed and cured them frequently before we ever had a chance to describe them or even complain of them. (Henderson 1963, 221–23).

Henderson's remarks occasion consideration of Jung as "the shaman." Shamans were the original medicine men, practicing the oldest system of healing known to the world. This essay will examine Jung's life and experiences as a healer in the context of the shamanic complex or archetype and shed light on the implications of Jung's work for modern-day treatment methods and methodologies.

THE SHAMANIC COMPLEX AND ARCHETYPE

A detailed review of shamanism in its classic form has been carried out by Eliade (1964) as well as by a number of other important investigators, including Hultkrantz (1973).

Eliade noted that the shaman's role and function is first and foremost involved with techniques of ecstasy. He goes into ecstasy or trance and has direct communion and contact with the spirits involved with illness or danger to the individual or community. He can actually communicate with the dead, demons, and nature spirits without being taken over by them. Most significant is that the the shaman's spirit can leave his body and go to "other worlds," where he then seeks out the lost soul of the patient and restores it to him. The shaman is able to deal with the most serious form of primitive illness—soul loss.

Hultkrantz noted that a more expanded definition of shamanism really was in order if the data from shamanic cultures was to be viewed in its totality. He suggested that the shaman is also a part of the social order who, by means of his guardian spirits, goes into a state of ecstasy in order to treat his patients (Hultkrantz 1973).

Thus, healing in its most fundamental form is that procedure in which the restoration of psychic integrity can take place, whether it be soul restoration, ridding a person's body of an evil or foreign spirit, removal of some object that was inside the body, removal of some curse, or resolving guilt over having broken a taboo. All of these procedures attempt to restore the balance and harmony of the soul.

The shamanic complex with its archetypal pattern has the following dimensions: first, those who become shamans have a serious illness early in life. The illness is experienced in the form of a calling; an individual's life order is disturbed to the point that in order to be cured he himself, will have to become a healer. He will have to face the most strenuous of all ordeals, the initiatory rites necessary to obtain the powers of shamanism. This initiation involves a profound experience of death and rebirth with experiences of altered states and ecstasy in which the spirit leaves the body and comes into direct contact with the other world. Part of the profound initiation process may be dismemberment, which could include visualizing and experiencing oneself as a skeleton.

The candidate then goes through the process of obtaining certain kinds of important personal powers. A shaman often gains the powers of telepathy, psychokinesis, and precognition and the ability to defy certain physical laws, such as walking on fire or performing tremendous feats of endurance. Most important, he can have the uncanny power of seeing into the other world and seeing into the body and soul of the patient to detect and rectify the cause of illness. In addition, he has helping spirits or agents who aid him in the healing quest. Shamans often become closely aligned with a special animal, which gives its power to the shaman and which he can call upon for healing energy. Also, the shaman often has a celestial wife who aids him, serving as a guide or a muse (Eliade 1964, 67).

Out of these experiences, the shaman evolves a myth of healing involving symbols usually related to the cultural context in which he lives, and with it theory and techniques that would define as well as alleviate illness in all its forms. From this myth of healing comes a transcendent relationship to celestial worlds and gods belonging to the shaman's culture whereby health can triumph over illness and a vision of harmony can be achieved by the person who seeks the shaman's services.

Of particular significance in many shamanic ideologies is the idea of the world tree, a tree that reaches between the three worlds noted in shamanic cultures; The underworld of the demons, where the dark and the evil exist; the mortal world, the world of men in the here and now; and the upper world, where only the gods reside. The shaman can ascend or descend to all three worlds via the world tree.

C. G. JUNG'S SHAMANIC ILLNESS

In his very early years Jung suffered from eczema, which coincided with his parents' separation. He spoke of having had suicidal urges at that time, and once he almost slipped off a bridge before he was caught by the maid who took care of him. He described having had vague fears of the night and fantasies and thoughts of hearing people drown, of seeing bodies swept over rocks, and of a cemetery nearby. He would often see men in black boots and coats, and he heard women weeping (Jung 1963, 8–9).

At age three or four Jung had his first remembered dream, a profound one that preoccupied him all his life. In the dream he saw a magnificent throne. Standing on it was a tree trunk twelve to fifteen feet high and one and a half to two feet thick. It was made of naked skin and flesh; on top of it was something like a rounded head with no face and no hair. At the very top was a single eye gazing upward. He felt terrified and imagined it would creep toward him. He heard his mother's voice say, "Yes, just look at him. That is the man eater!" He awoke sweating and sarced to death (Jung 1963, 11–13). For Jung, this fleshy column was a ritual phallus that stood for Jesus (associated with the Jesuits near his home), who might devour him. The phallus in its cave was also associated with death and the grave; the eye might have signaled the advent of Jung's emerging consciousness, which would in fact take up (swallow) his life. The phallus was a subterranean god, a god so profound that it kept him from fully accepting Christian doctrine.

During his prepubescent years, Jung had symptoms of a disturbing nature. He suffered suffocation or choking fits, and he recalled being held by his father at night and seeing images of persons with detached heads. He had marked anxiety episodes. He felt alienated and isolated from his peers. He became preoccupied with a little mannikin that he invested with profound meaning and power. He later identified it with stone images that were seen in Aesculapian temples in Greece and that were used as amulets of healing. This is another example of childhood illness with hysterical symptoms that have a shamanic quality (Jung 1963, 18–20). Eliade noted that often stones become sacred objects invested with powers that will later be involved with healing (Eliade 1964, 124–25).

Later Jung received a head injury, which caused him to have fainting episodes. These fainting spells occurred for more than six months and apparently were partially feigned so that Jung could get time away from school to develop his inner life, close to nature. He was later thunderstruck when he overheard his father discussing this condition with another man; speculating that perhaps young Carl had epileptic seizures or fits and would be unable to earn a living. Jung became upset at this prospect, took control of his life, and overcame his illness.

This incident is a good example of what later became the foundation for Jung's moral theory of neurosis, the individual's conscious involvement with his symptomatology. His father's fears of what might happen to him brought him up short and forced him to play a part in correcting and dealing with his own condition. He later spoke of neurosis as the refusal to bear legitimate suffering. Thus, he thought, the cause of neurosis was to be found mostly in the present and not in the past.

Not long after this, Jung came to the startling realization that he was "two persons." He described his "number one" and "number two" personalities. Number one was interested in the intellectual, rational endeavors involved in everyday life, seeking out the meaning of things directly. Number Two was an old man, skeptical, mistrustful, remote from the world of men, close to nature, earth, sun, moon, and all living creatures. This could best be described as the mystical, intuitive Jung (Jung 1963, 33–35, 44, 45).

One of the most striking personality criteria of the shaman is his capacity to dissociate. At the core of the shamanic experience is the dissociative quality that leads him into altered states of consciousness and ecstasy. Eliade believes this to be essential to the shamanic experience (Eliade 1964, 88–89). Though Jung denied that he was a dissociative personality in the clinical sense, it is my opinion that during Jung's later years, when he had depressions and suffered his "creative illness," he underwent a dissociation of profound proportions. His description of his number one and number two personalities suggest the very dissociative ability that he saw as the source of his creativity as well as the source of many of his and his parents' pathological conditions (Jung 1963, 63). He noted, for example, that the number two personality led him to into illness and depression.

Along with or allied with this dissociative trait, Jung had an uncanny ability to see things in telepathic and visionary ways, much as shamanic personalities are noted for doing. He also had a deep connection to animals and felt in touch with their souls (Jung 1963, 67).

These are a few of Jung's early life experiences, which started him on the path of initiation, much like the shamans of old. Even more profound experiences were to come.

JUNG'S SHAMANIC INITIATIONS

Jung's intense involvement with Freud between 1913 and 1916 presaged what was to be one of his most powerful descents into the unconscious. This period was heralded by a profound dream he had on the boat with Freud during the Clark University trip (Jung 1963, 169–70). On this trip both Freud and Jung had been invited to speak in the United States for the first time in their rapidly expanding professional careers. In this dream, he saw his house with several floors or levels, and at the bottom level he saw bones and skulls. This was the first inkling of what he saw as "a diagram of the psyche." His later formulations concerning the personal and collective unconscious came directly out of this dream. Though there were many personal complexes involved in the dream, of greatest significance was the final imagery concerning the two skulls. This may have foreshadowed the shamaniclike initiation as a healer that both he and Freud would need to experience in order to understand healing in its ultimate sense (Groesbeck 1982, 26–28).

Jung went into a profound withdrawal after his break with Freud; in the next few years he functioned almost not at all, maintaining contact with the world primarily through his family. Many have thought of this as a schizophrenic break; others, a psychosis; some, a creative illness; some, a neurosis; but to me it represents a profound hysterical dissociation, an illness of immense proportion with precursors noted from early illness episodes suffered in childhood. As one reads the annals of shamanic initiatory experiences, this has a familiar ring (Halifax 1979).

His visions during World War I have a prophetic quality to them. In the autumn of 1913 he became more depressed and had visions. In one he saw a flood overflowing all of northern Europe, particularly Switzerland. He saw a catastrophe with dead bodies that had drowned and thousands dying; the sea was turning to blood. He was nauseated, ashamed, and perplexed. He concluded that perhaps he was being menaced by a psychosis.

However, later in 1914, he had a dream of the Arctic cold destroying all human life. Later in 1914, he had another dream of a frightful cold. Then he had a vision of a "leaf-bearing tree, but without fruit (my tree of life, I thought), whose leaves had been transformed by the effects of the frost into sweet grapes full of healing juices. I plucked the grapes and gave them to a large, waiting crowd" (Jung 1963, 175–76).

Here again, the imagery of the tree and its shamanic connotations amplify a deeper understanding of Jung's experience during this time. Jung was virtually in a trance during these years and suffered from what was happening in the collective psyche: World War I with all its suffering.

In some of his visionary experiences, Jung came into touch with figures from the collective unconscious. Elijah, Salome, and later Philemon were all significant figures who became his aides in reorganizing his view of the world (Jung 1963, 180–183). These were like the helping spirits that often come to shamans when needed (Eliade 1964, 88–89). At this time it was as if Jung was suffering loss of soul, much as is described in the shamanic literature. Also, at this time Jung formed his relationship to Philemon, an alter figure from the unconscious.

C. G. JUNG AS SHAMAN AND HEALER

Accounts of Jung as a healer are noteworthy for the unusual style they reveal. He himself recounts cases, undoubtedly special ones, in which he exercised telepathic and precognitive abilities in dealing with patients and particularly in handling transference issues. In one case, for example, prior to seeing a young woman he had a dream that outlined her total psychology (Jung 1963, 138).

James Kirsch, another student and analysand of Jung (Kirsch, personal communication), recalls that there were analytical sessions with Jung in which Jung spoke the whole time and never received a single response from Kirsch. During some of these times, Kirsch stated, he wondered what in the world Jung was talking about, but toward the end of the session he recognized that Jung was in fact talking about him, Kirsch, in a symbolic and indirect way, discussing Kirsch's private, unexpressed concerns. Kirsch and others have said that Jung was the only analyst who could analyze dreams without hearing them. This is certainly a shamanic attribute (Kirsch, personal communication; Henderson, personal communication).

Henderson (personal communication) described a case that Jung discussed with him in which an old woman, unknown to Jung, was involved. Upon analytic exploration, two men who had serious, symptomatic illnesses of a psychosomatic nature were found to have the same grandmother. Jung telepathically sensed that this grandmother was a "witch" and would need to die if these men were going to get better. In the treatment of these two men Jung performed some mental exercise at a distance (best described as shamanic power) in detaching this grandmother's hold upon the two patients. When that transpired, she, in fact, died strangely and the two men were cured. This is a rather startling description of a shamanic cure in which one shaman battled with an opposing shaman, unknown and unseen. This may be considered a form of curing by means of foiling the witch, sometimes called counterwitchcraft or white witchcraft (Eliade 1964, 298).

There is a documented case in which Jung was able to diagnose a brain abscess in a patient by simply reading the patient's dreams, knowing nothing about the patient. This became the source of some attention by a British neurologist and later by British psychiatrists and psychoanalysts (Jung 1976).

In another case history, Jung differentiated an organic illness from a hysterical one by utilizing the patient's dream. This again drew a great deal of attention because of its uncanny, shamanic quality (Jung 1966a, P343). Clearly these modes of diagnosis and therapy are highly unusual and outside the standard patterns of psychotherapeutic expertise.

In what some have considered a most profound statement on psychotherapy, Jung stated:

> As a doctor, it is my task to help the patient to cope with life. I cannot presume
> to pass judgment on his final decisions, because I know from experience that

all coercion—be it suggestion, insinuation, or any other method of persuasion—ultimately proves to be nothing but an obstacle to the highest and most decisive experience of all, which is to be alone with his own self, or whatever else one chooses to call the objectivity of the psyche . . . if he is to find out what it is that supports him when he can no longer support himself. Only this experience can give him an indestructible foundation (Jung 1963, 27)

There is a shamanic ring to this viewpoint that needs more elaboration.

JUNG'S SHAMANIC MYTH OF HEALING

When Jung formulated his theory of the psyche with complexes and archetypes as its central aspect, and with the collective unconscious lying below the personal unconscious, he made some parallels to the oldest system of belief known in the world, animism. This system is intimately connected to shamanism with its reference to a natural world that is alive and vibrant in its own right. Jung correlated the shamanic illnesses of soul loss (the most common world-wide illness) and spirit intrusion (or spirit possession) directly to his theory of psychopathology related to the personal (complexes) and collective unconscious (archetypes). Depression and schizophrenia figured prominently in his formulations (Jung 1963, 175–99).

Concerning psychotherapeutic and analytic methodology, Jung described four different methods that he saw as the basis for all psychotherapies, including his own (Jung 1966a, 114–74). These are confession or abreaction, elucidation or interpretation, education, and transformation. He identified forms of religious treatment with the confessional and abreactive approaches; Freud's classical psychoanalytic approach with interpretation; Adler's socialmethodologies with education; and finally, his own symbolic analytic approach with transformation, considering it analysis proper.

Each of these four methodologies has some relation to shamanism. Confession and abreaction are methods of purification that are used in shamanic rituals. Shamans at times function as teachers and/or physicians. In their journeys they often collect a wide store of herbal and other non-shamanic medical knowledge. But it is in the method of symbolic transformation that Jung and his methods come closest to shamanism.

When Jung speaks of the methodology of transformation, he speaks of a psychotherapeutic relationship in which the psychotherapist as well as the patient is transformed and in which the Jungian model of dialectical exchange is significant. It is this methodology that can come closest to the shamanic experience the healer can have *direct* contact with the patient's illness and perhaps go as a shaman into the other world and war with the powers of darkness to free the patient from his malady. In this process, the archetype of the wounded healer is at the very core. My own studies of this archetypal pattern have led me to the conclusion that this *is* the core archetypal pattern of healing at a deep level (Groesbeck 1975). The shaman and the Jungian analyst are wounded healers par excellence. Because they have the wound, they *know* the wound and can bear it with the patient (Groesbeck 1988).

The priest, the medicine man or physician, the teacher, and particularly the shaman form a very interesting cadre of healers. Shamanism, the oldest form of healing, is the prototype out of which the other forms of healing are derived. Jung put this at the core of his theory of healing. Further, it is to be emphasized that the basic shamanic experience of healing is so powerful and so dangerous that anyone who functions in that realm does not abide it for long. Their energy diminishes and they often wear out. In shamanic cultures, the roles of priest, physician, or teacher rapidly evolve and take over mediation of the healing experience via ritual, medical techniques, or education to avoid dealing with illness on the intense, direct plane of the shaman. Returning now to Jung's life, one might ask how he evolved his own myth of healing. My opinion is that Jung's myth of healing evolved out of his own personal difficulty with his parents and his efforts to heal the split between them as well as that between them and himself. His mother represented the primal nature of the psyche as she and her ancestors were connected with ghosts, demons, and parapsychological phenomenon. Because of her family history she introduced these things to Jung at an early age. It was this ghostly, intuitive, mystical side that Jung had to wrestle with and which appeared in his dreams and early life experiences. On the other hand, his father was more rational; yet Jung had difficulty making an emotional connection to his father and struggled with the opinion that his father never solved the problems of his Christian religion in an intellectual way (Jung 1963, 1–113).

In one remarkable, shamanic like experience, he described his interaction with his father. He noted that he had not dreamed of his father since 1896, the year of his father's death. For many years he wondered why he never had contact with his father through his dreams, and then in 1922 he had a dream of his father. His father came to him and asked him a great deal about his work, specifically about dealing with couples who had marital problems. Jung was mystified but curious. Not long after this, his mother died unexpectedly. Jung concluded that his father, who had died many years before, had been able to avoid dealing with the conflicts of his marriage while his wife was still in the mortal world. However, when he came to know that his wife would soon be coming to the other side to meet him, he recognized that he now needed help to resolve that difficulty. Jung saw himself as being called upon in his dreams by his father to help him prepare to meet with his wife in the other world (Jung 1963, 315). This rather unusual personal interpretation suggests, again, a shamanic orientation to Jung's life.

As Jung evolved his myth of healing in shamanic style, he experienced the great strains and tensions in an attempt to bring together the disparate aspects of his world view. There was the mystical and occult, represented by his mother, as well as the rational and religious, represented by his father; but in addition there was the struggle with the death of the spirit of Christianity and the issue of apostasy from the Christian church. Science, too, created for Jung tremendous contradictions and conflicts. There was a death of meaning on virtually all sides. This paralleled his great difficulty in attempting to resolve his father complex, which was something he did not do until the end of his life (Jung 1958; Groesbeck 1982.)

His relationship with Freud was also part of this struggle. With Freud in particular, Jung tried to identify with science and materialism, which represented his rational side, Jung number one. Yet he could not accept it, for in the end it seemed empty and illusory. On the other hand, the mystical almost swept him away and made him lose touch with his own moorings.

Jung, in the fashion of a shaman of old, had to go in between and evolve a believable myth of healing that attempted to unite both science and mysticism (Zinkin 1987). Jung eventually evolved his own world view, emerging with deep personal truths that have encouraged many. At times the contradictions seemed overwhelming; indeed, they were never fully resolved. He was criticized by theologians for psychologizing God, and he was ridiculed by scientists for being too mystical and irrational. But somehow he was able to weld together his theories of complex archetypes and the collective unconscious with primal views of the world related to animism and shamanism. In fact, if one is looking for a mirror image of animism, Jung's theory of the psyche is a good candidate. In almost dialectical form Jung number one and Jung number two fertilized each other, evolving a myth of healing of creative proportion. Like a shaman, he was always on the edge of human understanding, and like a shaman, there is a trickster-ish quality involved in his writings; sometimes he contradicts himself. It is my opinion that the most important thing to understand when reading Jung is that Jung number one and Jung number two are always in opposition, battling, but in the end are synthesized and transformed to a new level of paradox. It is only with this orientation that one can make sense out of all he tried to do.

JUNG'S SHAMANIC POWERS

Jung's powers as a healer became well known. Over time it has come to light that he relied heavily on his cousin, Helene, as well as upon Sabina Spielrein and finally Toni Wolff. These three women, along with his wife, Emma, played a crucial part in the development of his feminine side, or anima. In a sense, they became helpers in shamanic fashion—"celestial wives"—to help him in his great journey of healing. The history of Jung's relationships with significant women has been confusing, and some, such as Bruno Bettelheim, have even stated that virtually all of Jung's theories have come from Sabina Spielrein and are not original to Jung himself (Bettelheim 1983). A much deeper exploration of all of this certainly needs to be made (Groesbeck 1983).

What is seldom appreciated is that Jung functioned as a shaman in a whole series of dreams in 1916 in which he tried to persuade the German kaiser to make peace. He felt that the collective unconscious may have been operating in a way that would allow him to have an important part in resolving the world war (Hannah 1976, 132).

James Kirsch, an analyst trained by Jung, had a shamanic experience in connection with Hitler (Kirsch, personal communication). Kirsch had a dream in which it was stated that at the end of World War I, one man should have died who did not. Later Kirsch correlated this with what in fact happened to Adolf Hitler in World War I. While in the trenches, Hitler allegedly received a premonition that something was going to happen to him. He suddenly jumped out of the trench, and moments later a grenade blew up there. It temporarily blinded him, for a short time and then he had a hysterical reaction of blindness for longer. He was saved by his premonition. It is interesting that Hitler became involved in the occult and allegedly was a member of a secret order in which he was chosen to lead his people. Baynes has described Hitler as a shaman, a "black shaman" as it were, who attempted worldwide domination (Baynes 1941).

Jung wrote of a visit he made to the United States and the Pueblo Indians in which he looked at the underlying, collective psychic contribution of the American Indian to the present-day American. He later formulated the idea that American patients would have as one of the deepest manifestations of their souls the American Indian and his psychology. This idea has been important in the lives of a number of analysands, as confirmed by analysts and pupils of Jung, such as Joseph Henderson (Henderson, personal communication). Jung observed that sometimes the deepest layers of influence upon a collective psyche are those of the culture that has gone before in the land in which the dominant culture resides (Jung 1963, 246).

Finally, it must be noted that Jung, in resolving the issue of Hitler and the German phenomena, analyzed the German psyche by reviewing the Scandinavian mythology related especially to Wotan, the storm god, and his influence upon the Germanic people. His analysis of Friedrich Nietzsche also played a significant part in his understanding of this (Baynes 1941).

C. G. JUNG AND THE SHAMAN'S WORLD VISION

The East was the area of the world with which Jung had the greatest difficulty intellectually, emotionally, and spiritually. Finally one needs to go to one of the final phases of his life when his myth of healing involved an experience of transcendence that led him to a world vision (Jung 1963, 289–91).

During this period, Jung had some serious setbacks. He broke his foot and then had a very severe heart attack. Barbara Hannah describes this as the period in which he made his greatest step in the process of individuation (Hannah 1976, 134–36, 275–84). During his illness he had a visionary experience in which he flew high above the earth and saw Ceylon far below. Also, his gaze focused upon India. It was as though Jung saw a map of the whole world as it would be if he were far above the earth, an experience similar to a shaman's "soul flight" (Jung 1963, 291–293).

> It seemed to me that I was high up in space. Far below I saw the globe of the earth, bathed in a gloriously blue light. I saw the deep blue sea and the continents. Far below my feet lay Ceylon, and in the distance ahead of me the subcontinent of India. My field of vision did not include the whole earth but its global shape was plainly distinguishable and its outlines shone with a silvery gleam through that wonderful blue light. I knew that I was on the point of departing from the earth. (Jung 1963, 289–90)

With this vision, Jung completed a celestial, shamanic climb of the world tree that had begun with the first dream of the tree phallus underground (Jung 1963, 11).

It was in this series of visions that Jung experienced perhaps the deepest secret of healing. He had an experience, related to his own doctor, in which he saw the magnificent healer Aesculapius. Out of that he understood the divine truth of Aesculapius, that only the wounded physician can heal. This touched upon Jung's own archetype and showed him that the shaman was, in fact, the wounded healer (Jung 1959, 256, 457).

Jung also saw that shamanism was a form of the individuation process (Jung 1969, 306). His vision of being high above the earth was a clear example of the shaman whose spirit leaves his body and goes on a soul flight to other worlds to perform a transcendent function in recovering and understanding the secrets of healing for the community. In this case, the world was his community.

The next series of visions involved the *coniunctio* (Jung 1963, 293). These allowed him to unite some of the core healing myths of Judaism, Christianity, and the Greeks. All have powerful images of the hierosgamos, the sacred marriage. More specifically, when Jung wrote his treatise on transference, he noted that at the core of transference was the need for Eros in the archetype of the *coniunctio* (Hannah 1976, 279–80). In the other portion of this vision the concept of individuation and "an objective view of reality" emerged. This experience confirmed his relationship to life and death (Jung 1963, 295). In some ways, it rivals the vision of Black Elk, a Lakota medicne man and visionary, and his shamanic vision for his culture, as well as the whole world (Neihardt 1979). It calls to mind Eliade's mention of the necessity of having one man who can communicate with the other worlds and bring back reliable information for an understanding of life by his people (Eliade 1964, 509).

It is important to underscore that it was after this series of visions that Jung wrote his most creative works, including "The Psychology of the Transference" and "Answer to Job."

SUMMARY AND CONCLUSION: IMPLICATIONS FOR MODERN ANALYSIS AND PSYCHOTHERAPY

We are now into the second generation of followers of Jung, and it is with this backdrop that one may pause to reflect. It is clear that Jung himself performed the functions of a shaman in how he affected a culture and its power to deal with the elements of healing. He fused science and religion (or the rational and the irrational or mystical) in a remarkable synthesis. However, this is a time of great questioning from every quarter in Jungian circles as the initial light and power emanating from his personality are on the wane and as those who knew him are now beginning to pass on. As that light begins to fade, many questions arise as to what will be the meaning of the movement he represented. What is emerging is that different schools and different approaches to treatment and healing process are evolving.

At the present time, it could be said that there are eclectic or modern Jungians, who utilize dreams. There are also classical Jungians, who have almost ritualistically tried to re-create what he represented. They evoke the numinous and archetypal in the healing process, much like priests. There are the physicianly Jungians, who have fused psychoanalysis and other traditions, such as the work of Klein, Winnicott, Bion, Langs, Kohut, and others, and who are expressing Jung in a technical, scientific form. Finally there are those few who might be called true Jungians, who are very different from the other styles of Jungians today; they function as shamans, much as Jung did in the therapeutic process, directly dealing with the patient's illnesses and/or producing a transformational experience in healing.

The great difficulty is that there are *very* few who can be shamans and work the way Jung did. As is revealed to us in the shamanic literature, shamanism is a very dangerous occupation and one that few can survive for a long period of time. Therefore, the natural pull is to function in one of the three other larger categories.

As the Jungian movement proceeds, the perspective on Jung as a shaman, such as has been outlined here, needs to be taken into account and to be experienced so that the natural evolution of Jung's thought and work can continue. Unfortunately, what may be on the horizon is only a sense of division, alienation, and disparity. Yet, ultimately, that diversity is exactly how Jung would have liked it. After all, did he not say that he was the only "Jungian analyst"? The rest of us are who we are.

REFERENCES

Baynes, H. G. 1941. *Germany Possessed*. London and Toronto: Jonathan Cape, Ltd.

Bettelheim, B. 1983. "A Scandal in the Family." *New York Review of Books.*, vol. XXX, No. 11, 39–44.

Eliade, M. 1964 [1954]. *Shamanism: Archaic Techniques of Ecstasy*. Bollingen Series LXXVI. New York: Pantheon.

Groesbeck, C. J. 1975. Archetypal Image of the Wounded Healer. *Journal of Analytical Psychology* 20(2): 122–45.

———. 1982. A Jungian Answer to "Yahweh as Freud." *American Imago* 39(3):239–254.

———. 1983. When Jung Was the Analyst." Review of *A Secret Symmetry*, by Aldo Carotenuto. *Psychological Perspective* 14(1): 89–98.

———. 1988. The Archetype of the Healer. Unpublished manuscript.

Halifax, J. 1979. *Shamanic Voices*. New York: E. P. Dutton.

Hannah, B. 1976. *Jung: His Life and Work*. New York: G. P. Putnam and Sons.

Henderson, J. 1963 C. G. Jung: A Personal Evaluation. In Michael Fordham, ed., *Contact with Jung*. Philadelphia: J. B. Lippincott.

———. 1967. *Thresholds of Initiation*. Middletown, Conn.: Wesleyan University Press.

Hultkrantz, A. 1973. A Definition of Shamanism. *Temenos* 9.

———. 1958a [1952]. Answer to Job. In *Psychology and Religion: West and East*. Bollingen Series XX: The Collected Works of C. G. Jung, vol. 11. Princeton: Princeton University Press.

———. 1959 [1954] On the Psychology of the Trickster Figure. In *The Archetypes and the Collective Unconscious*. Bollingen Series XX: The Collected Works of C. G. Jung, vol. 9, part II. Princeton: Princeton University Press.

———. 1963. *Memories, Dreams, Reflections*. Edited by A. Jaffe. New York: Vintage.

———. 1966 [1953]. Introduction to the Religious and Psychological Problems of Alchemy. In *Psychology and Alchemy*. Bollingen Series XX: The Collected Works of C. G. Jung, vol. 12. Princeton: Princeton University Press.

———. 1958 [1952]. Foreword to White's *God and the Unconscious*. In *Psychology and Religion: West and East*.

———. 1976. The Tavistock Lectures. In *The Symbolic Life*. Bollingen Series XX: The Collected Works of C. G. Jung, vol. 18. Princeton: Princeton University Press.

Neihardt, J. (1979). *Black Elk Speaks: Being the Life Story of a Holy Man of the Oglala Sioux*. Lincoln and London: University of Nebraska Press.

Zinkin, L. 1987. *The Hologram as a Model for Analytical Psychology. Journal of Analytical Psychology*, vol 32, no1, p 1–22.

Chapter 5

The "Book of Knowledge" in Shamanism and Mysticism: Universal Image of the Source

Meredith Sabini

This paper by Meredith Sabini concerns one of the key motifs of mysticism and shamanism: the inward vision or dream of a book of knowledge. It seems to be the living source from which shamans and mystics derive their special wisdom. As the divine messengers said to the great healer and shaman Maria Sabina: "Everything is in it. Everything written in it is yours. Take it so you can work."

When Teresa of Avila was deprived of books during the Inquisition, Christ appeared to her and said, "Do not be distressed, for I will give thee a living book." He then became that "book." The Mazatec Indian healer Maria Sabina, during her initiatory shamanic vision, was handed a book of wisdom in which "everything was written, everything needed to do your work." Over the years, I have known of similar images of a sacred text or ancient tome in the dream and visionary material of psychotherapy clients as well as professional colleagues. What is this book of knowledge or book of wisdom, and what does it mean that individuals from vastly differing cultures and times would be shown such a text as part of their interior education as shamans, mystics, and healers? In this essay I will present examples of this image, which I believe represents the *living source* to which shamans and mystics are granted access and from which they bring forth what Jung called "something like 'absolute' knowledge" built up over the history of our species and accessible under certain unusual conditions.

An exploration of this image or symbol eventually led me to the origins of the various religious traditions, when prophets were also shown or given revelatory texts: the tablets of Moses, the Egyptian Book of Thoth, the law books of the Veda, the Cumaean Books of the Sybil, Joseph Smith's Book of Mormon, the scroll with seven seals given to St. John the Divine. This image takes us into the heart of the wisdom traditions and enables us to find the link between shamanic and mystical experiences. Material drawn from these traditions appears after a presentation of the dream and visionary material of four noteworthy individuals: St. Teresa of Avila, Maria Sabina, Dr. Anna Kingsford, and C. G. Jung. Interwoven are similar examples from the dreams of contemporary persons.

The appearance of this motif in different cultures and at different periods in history means that it is an archetypal image or "mythologem", a term Jung defined as " 'portions of the world' which belong to the structural elements of the psyche . . . constants whose expression is everywhere and at all times the same" (Jung 1966, para. 207).This mythologem can be cataloged alongside others Jung recognized as being part of the individuation process as portrayed in both alchemy and shamanism: loss of soul, dismemberment, descent into a lower world, ascent into an upper world, and union with a spirit spouse.

I first came across this motif many years ago while reading Anna Kingsford's *Dreams and Dream Stories*, published in 1908. A physician and mystic, Kingsford lived in England at a time when the Theosophical movement had introduced Eastern philosophy to the West, and seances with trance mediums were commonplace. (In addition to this book of her dreams is a two-volume biography of Kingsford by Edward Maitland and several volumes of her visionary experiences, carefully recorded by Maitland; this body of work constitutes an unusual chronicle of the activation of the collective unconscious in a modern individual.) Her dream "The Wonderful Spectacles" contains a passage that stunned me:

> *John the Baptist delivers to Kingsford a letter from Maitland telling her that he had gotten hold of "the earliest and most precious book extant, written before the world began," and could she please obtain for him the spectacles of Swedenborg's that Spinoza had made. She replies that they are available in London but they haven't been worn for years and need cleaning, and she will do this.*

A book written before the world began? Spectacles made by Spinoza and worn by Swedenborg? Here were references to the actual history of Western philosophical and mystical tradition. Was Maitland to continue this tradition with Kingsford's help? I was chilled by the magnitude of this imagery and felt I had come upon something quite unusual. The whole of Kingsford's dream will be recounted in the material that follows.

The spontaneous appearance of this particular symbol allows us to study the unfolding of a religious motif and its roots in the collective unconscious, which is variously known as the Dreamtime, the pleroma, the implicate order, the realm of the ancestors, nonordinary reality, and a separate reality. Jung's psychology of archetypes is especially valuable in interpreting this material because of its grasp of the relationship between the conscious mind or ego and the nonpersonal contents of the unconscious. The shaman is a go-between who has learned, through intense personal suffering and initiatory ordeals, how to transit between the explicate world of ordinary reality and the nonordinary realm, whatever it is called. In the latter realm, the shaman often has access to some source that provides knowledge in general and aids clients in particular. The mystic may experience a similar source of wisdom available in rapture or ecstatic moments but does not necessarily draw upon that source in order to perform healings for others. By looking at the way this mythologem presents itself in dreams and visions, we can see the various roles that individuals are given: medium, seer, scribe, prophet, dream interpreter, healer. In traditional cultures, one individual may be gifted at visionary perception, another at artistic portrayal, and another at translation into cultural or psychological terms.

I would like to begin with the dream material that is simple in structure, in the hope that this allows the complexity of archetypal imagery to unfold. There is no implication that a more complex dream or vision is of more value, for that is simply not the case. The first example comes from a woman naturally inclined to the religious life. In this dream, an important relative shows her a special tome:

> *I was in my grandfather's house. He didn't speak to me, but had this big book, perhaps three or four inches thick. We sat together and he turned the pages, one by one. Some contained writing; others had beautiful pictures and geometric designs. When I awoke, I had a numinous feeling of mystery. But it also bothered me that I couldn't remember what the book said.*

The dream was the first of many about her paternal grandfather that took place following his death, when she was thirty; she had been especially close to him, as her father had died the year she was born. In this dream, he was very serious and his eyes had a numinous intensity. The book was short and thick and looked like a tome from the Middle Ages. It seemed odd to her that her grandfather didn't speak, but he did convey the importance of the book with his eyes. Reflecting on it some years later, she said "it was as if I were given over the opus of the deceased in some way." She and her grandfather shared an interest in philosophy and mysticism, and she went on after his death to have visionary and shamanic-like experiences as part of her preparation for working as a healer, or psychotherapist. Following the grandfather's death, there were other dreams in which he appeared, offering wisdom in fundamental matters.

This dream contains all the elements that we will see in this mythologem: the text or book is large; it may have words but more often has symbols and pictures; there is an air of awe or mystery surrounding the discovery of the book; it is presented by an ancestor, actual or spiritual; the understanding of it may be nonverbal and immediate. These elements characterize a sacred object that seems to emanate from somewhere beyond the known world.

This particular individual did feel awe upon waking, as if something of great value had been shown her; but she also felt disappointed not to be able to recall the text. Here the grandfather performs the initiatory function of presenting this sacred text to his heir; he is the psychopomp who may develop into a spirit guide for shamanic journeys. For those who do not hold with the view that the implicate order, or spirit world, is a separate entity, the object relations perspective is adequate for explaining the function of the grandfather: he is an introject who represents the dreamer's own capacity for wisdom. His death is the occasion for his appearance in the interior life of dreams, since he was no longer available to her in the ordinary, or explicate, world. From this perspective, we could speak about ego consciousness calling upon a self-object or subpersonality for guidance, just as a shaman might call upon a particular ancestral spirit.

The next example is St. Teresa of Avila. Born in 1515 in Spain, she lived at a time when most women had two choices: marriage or convent life. Her mother died when she was young, and her father encouraged her to enter a convent. At eighteen Teresa did this; but due to illness—palsy and cataleptic fits—she was in and out of the convent between 1536 and 1542. A crisis took place in 1539, when she was so ill that the nuns gave her up for dead, put wax on her eyes, and had a grave dug. But Teresa recovered from what appears to be a shamanic illness; indeed. Ier entire religious conversion bears many similarities to shamanic training, including ecstatic trances, levitations, and betrothal to a mystical figure. At age forty-four, when the Inquisition was well under way and books were banned, she wrote that she was "very sorry books in Spanish were taken from us, for reading gave me pleasure and I could no longer continue this as I had them only in Latin." She then had this singular vision: "The Lord said to me, Be not distressed, for I will give thee a living book." She wrote in her diary that she could not understand why this was told to her; but a few days afterward wrote:

I came to understand it very well, for what I saw before me gave me so much to think about and so much opportunity for meditation, and the Lord showed me so much love and taught me so much, taught me by so many methods, that I have had very little need of actual books. His Majesty Himself has been to me The Book in which I have seen what is true. Blessed be such a book, which has impressed upon us what we are to read and what we are to do in a way that is unforgettable. (Peers 1960, 247)

Soon after this, her major visionary experiences began.

The parallels between her experience and that of the Mazatec Indian healer Maria Sabina are quite striking; two women from different cultures and different eras in history with almost identical inner experiences related to their vocation. We know of Maria Sabina from two sources: Gordon Wasson, the famous ethnomycologist who came to Maria's village near Oaxaca, Mexico, to study mushroom usage, and recorded her chants; and from Alvaro Estrada, an engineer and journalist who came from Maria's village, spoke the language, and took an interest in her work. He recorded an oral biography of her in 1975.

Maria Sabina was born in 1894 and lived her entire life in the small Indian village of Huautle de Jimenez; she became known throughout Mexico for her healing ability. It was on the occasion of her shamanic initiation that the book of wisdom was given to her. She dated the event "some years after becoming a widow for the first time." She was very worried because her sister was ill and the efforts of local curers had been of no avail. Maria knew that her people took mushrooms, variously called "the Saint Children" and "the blood of Christ," to help in healing; she gave her sister several and took many herself. During the trance, her hands were guided to her sister's abdomen; she massaged where her sister reported pain and sang words the Saint Children told her. Eventually, her sister hemorrhaged, and then the bleeding stopped and she fell asleep, appearing to recover. But Maria could not sleep and had this singular vision:

Some people appeared to me who inspired me with respect. I knew them to be the Principal Ones, of whom my ancestors had spoken. They were seated behind a table on which there were written many papers. I knew that these were important papers. I knew that it was a revelation that the Saint Children were giving me. I heard a voice, sweet but authoritative . . . say, "These are the Principal Ones." . . . I felt an intimate happiness. On the table appeared an open book that went on growing until it was the size of a person. In its pages were letters. It was a white book, so white it was resplendent. One of the Principal Ones spoke to me, and said, "Maria Sabina, this is the Book of Wisdom, it is the Book of Language. Everything is in it, everything that is written in it is for you. The Book is yours. Take it, so you can work." I exclaimed with emotion, "That is for me, I receive it." The Principal Ones disappeared and left me alone in front of the immense book. I knew it was "The Book of Wisdom." I knew I was reading the sacred language. I had attained perfection and was no longer a simple apprentice. (Estrada 1981, 47)

With this example, we come to an image of the book explicitly identified as a book of wisdom, containing "everything." Again, it is a huge tome and is given to the dreamer by the ancestors, a council of elders. The language of the book is sacred language. As Maria looks at it, it grows into the size of a person: that is, it comes to life, as did the "book" Christ promised to Teresa of Avila. This change in shape, it seems to me, signifies the transubstantiation of two-dimensional knowledge into three-dimensional, living wisdom that pertains to the human world. Like Teresa, Maria accepts the book, knowing that this acceptance entails the responsibility of her avocation. In talking with her biographer, Estrada, about a later period in her life, Maria commented that the book no longer appeared to her, because she already had its contents in her memory.

How are we to understand this image of a book when it appears in a culture that has no written language? In researching the history of sacred rites among the Mazatec, Gordon Wasson discovered that the term for book, *amoxtli*, had appeared three centuries earlier in a similar context. A text written by a Spanish historian in 1629 points out how the "Nahuatl Wise One stressed the amoxtli, 'book,' as a means of arriving at the secret knowledge he uses" (Estrada 1981, 16). The Nahuatl are an antecedent people whose culture forms a continuous link with the Mazatec of Maria's time. Wasson commented that although there would have been a Bible and other liturgical books in the village parish church, "there has also evolved in the mind of Maria Sabina a mystical 'book' that belongs specifically to her and that may come down to her from the amoxtli of pre-Conquest times" (Estrada 1981, 17).

With her scholarship regarding fairy tales, M.-L. von Franz furthers our understanding of this image as it appears in nonliterary traditions. Such tales also contain references to a magical book used by seers, magicians, druids, and priests. Reminding us that in folk cultures "there is an oral tradition of stories and known facts, knowledge which is handed down through the generations," she interprets the knowledge from this book as "some kind of tradition, a knowledge of psychic laws and events which have already been codified to a certain extent and handed down" (Van Franz 1974, 247). This interpretation would be in agreement with my contention that the book of wisdom represents the possibility of access to knowledge in the collective unconscious, which we can understand as a storehouse of the accumulated wisdom of our species.

Turning now to Jung's own experience, we find three instances in his autobiography of a dream or vision in which a special book appeared. In one dream, Jung wrestled with a regal youth until he agreed to translate a Manichaean text; in a waking vision, a friend of Jung's, who had suddenly died, led Jung to his library and pointed to a leather-bound book titled *The Legacy of the Dead* (Jung 1961, 243, 312). Jung said that between the ages of forty-five and fifty, he had many dreams about a wing of his house that had always been there but was unfamiliar to him; finally he dreamed of reaching that wing, where there was a special library:

> I discovered there a wonderful library, dating largely from the 16th and 17th centuries. Large, fat folio volumes, bound in pigskin, stood along the walls. Among them were a number of books embellished with copper engravings of a strange character, and illustrations containing curious symbols such as I had never seen before. (Jung 1961, 202)

Jung commented that at the time, he did not understand what the symbols referred to and only much later did he recognize them as alchemical: "In the dream, I was conscious only of the fascination exerted by them and by the entire library." (Jung 1961, 202). This element of fascination—the emotional pull exerted by the books and library—is an important signifier of the presence of the numinous. Jung spent more than a decade researching and reading alchemical texts and eventually acquired a library much like that in the dreams. He came to understand alchemy as the lost mystical aspect of Christianity; with this momentous discovery, he was able to establish the uninterrupted intellectual chain back to Gnosticism. Here again, a book of special value was brought to the dreamer, who accepted the task it entailed. The alchemical symbols were a central part of his initiation into the mystery of the process of transformation.

A contemporary psychotherapist was also led toward the alchemical tradition by a dream that took place early in his training as a healer. This dream again contains the themes of being offered a gift of great value and recognizing the import of its acceptance:

> *I am kneeling at an altar. From my right side, a man appears and walks toward the center of the altar, where a book is on a stand. He lifts the book and brings it to me. He offers it to me and bows. At that moment I look up and take the book in my hands. As I stand up I realize that the book is full of golden pages. On each page there are Chinese characters in relief. When I look at the man again, I see it is Richard Wilhelm and that the book is* The Secret of the Golden Flower. *I then feel the presence of people behind me, thousands of them, all weeping.*

The figure in the dream, Richard Wilhelm, is the scholar who translated *The Secret of the Golden Flower,* an ancient Chinese alchemical text. In a sacred setting in front of an altar, the dreamer is bequeathed a text full of golden pages. As the ceremony concludes, there is weeping on a massive scale, as if to mark the import of the event. Over many years, the dreamer underwent the classic stages of shamanic initiation and eventually studied Chinese medicine. The metaphor of being handed a sacred text containing ancient wisdom is an apt one for the gifts that this person has been given; and he does consult an unseen source for guidance in his practice as a healer.

Now we come to the dream of Anna Kingsford, which likewise mentions historical sources. Dr. Kingsford was ardently devoted to her dream and visionary life, and her lifelong companion, Edward Maitland, himself a visionary, made sure that her experiences were fully and accurately recorded. The dream that follows is the first of many in which a special book is mentioned:

> I am walking alone on the seashore. The day was singularly clear and sunny. Inland lay the most beautiful landscape ever seen; and far off were the ranges of tall hill, the highest peaks of which were white with glittering snow. Along the sands by the same sea came toward me a man accoutred as a postman. He gave me a letter. It was from you [Edward Maitland]. It ran thus:
>
>> "I have got hold of the earliest and most precious book extant. It was written before the world began. The text is easy enough to read; but the notes, which are very copious and numerous, are in such minute and obscure characters that I cannot make them out. I want you to get for me the spectacles which Swedenborg used to wear; not the smaller pair—those he gave to Hans Christian Anderson—but the large pair, and these seem to have got mislaid. I think they are Spinoza's make. You know he was an optical-glass maker by profession, and the best we ever had. See if you can get them for me."
>
> When I looked up after reading this letter, I saw the postman hastening away from across the sands, and I cried out to him, "Stop! How am I to send the answer? Will you not wait for it?"
>
> He looked round, stopped, and came back to me. "I have the answer here," he said, tapping his letter bag, "and I shall deliver it immediately."
>
> "How can you have the answer before I have written it?" I asked. "You are making a mistake."
>
> "No," he said. "In the city from which I come, the replies are all written at the office, and sent out with the letters themselves. Your reply is in my bag."

"Let me see it," I said. He took another letter from his wallet and gave it to me. I opened it, and read, in my own handwriting, this answer, addressed to you:

> "The spectacles you want can be bought in London. But you will not be able to use them at once, for they have not been worn for many years, and they sadly want cleaning. This you will not be able to do yourself in London, because it is too dark there to see well, and because your fingers are not small enough to clean them properly. Bring them to me, and I will do it for you."

I gave this letter back to the postman. He smiled and nodded to me; and then I perceived to my astonishment that he wore a camel's-hair tunic round his waist. I had been on the point of addressing him—I know not why—as Hermes. But now I saw that he must be John the Baptist; and in my fright at having spoke with so great a saint, I awoke. (Kingsford 1908, 31)

An essay could be devoted to this one dream alone, so rich and complex is it. The details in it give hints about the visionary capacity and its cultural history, referring to this in terms of a special pair of glasses that are used and a special book written before the world began. The spectacles needed in order to read this particular text can be found in London but will need cleaning, which Kingsford will do so Maitland can perceive the margin notes. The messenger delivering the letter is not the Greek god Hermes but St. John the Baptist; and indeed, the content of Kingsford's visions was largely Christian, in the mystical tradition of Swedenborg. London was a center where the mystical tradition had been revived; but often the capacity to perceive the other world was used for parlor games and to provide superficial contact with the dead, and was frequently misused. What Kingsford perceived were large-scale visions, not ones like those a writer of fairy tales such as Anderson might have had. The dream clarifies that Maitland was the actual owner of the special book, and Kingsford his assistant. A modern reading of her biography verifies that she remained primarily a trance medium, or channel, and he was the one more capable of integrating the material. Though she was able to report on the archetypal pantheon, there is no indication that she ever developed her ability as a seer to aid in her work as a physician the way a shaman would. The visionary material she channeled was of a grand, impersonal—and often grandiose—scale. She tended to exteriorize and concretize it in ways that did not serve it or her well. And though she too had a shamanic-like illness, she did not benefit or recover from it, but remained chronically ill and died at a young age.

I would now like to recount briefly some instances in which the book of knowledge image has appeared in established religious traditions.

Examples of this mythologem are listed in *The Encyclopedia of Religion and Ethics* under the headings "Celestial Books" and "The Book of Life." The author of the latter entry, Alfred Jeremias, states that the notion of a primordial Divine wisdom inscribed in books is found generally amongst the peoples of antiquity.

The Egyptian Book of Thoth contains a chapter in which the history of the text is traced back to a time when it was transcribed "in the handwriting of the god"; the priests, as bearers of revelation, were considered "scribes of the book of God." The twenty-third Ode to Solomon, from early Christian times, mentions a celestial letter descending from on high like "an arrow which is violently shot from the bow"; it was "a great Tablet which was wholly written by the Finger of God." In the Ethiopic Acts of Peter, Peter receives a book from Christ "written from His own hand." St. Nino was a fourth century-Georgian who had a vision of a book brought by a divine visitor; the contents of this revelation were incorporated into the Gospels.

The Mormon faith is based solely on the divine revelation to Joseph Smith, in 1829, of inscribed tablets. An angel came and told Smith that there was a book, written upon gold plates, giving an account of the former inhabitants of this continent and the source from which they sprang. Like Anna Kingsford, Smith was shown special "glasses" by which the tablets were to be read: they were called "Urim" and "Thumim" and were two stones buried with the gold plates. He was told that those who had possessed them in former times were seers. Smith was to use these for the purpose of translating the gold plates. What he translated became the Book of Mormon.

Both the Old and New Testaments contain many references to divine scrolls, books, and tablets, on which revelation was given. Most relevant for our purposes are those of St. John and Ezekiel. Ezekiel recounts his vision:

> And he said unto me, Son of man, stand upon thy feet, and I will speak unto thee. And the spirit entered into me . . . [and said] And thou shalt speak my words . . . And when I looked, behold, a hand was sent unto me; and lo, a roll of a book was therein. (Ezekiel, 2:1,2,9)

Then Ezekiel is told to eat the scroll:

> Moreover, he said unto me, Son of man, eat that thou findest; eat this scroll, and go speak unto the house of Israel. So I opened my mouth, and he caused me to eat that roll. And he said unto me, Son of man, cause thy belly to eat, and fill thy bowels with this roll that I give thee. Then did I eat it; and it was in my mouth as honey for sweetness. And he said unto me, Son of man, go, get thee unto the house of Israel, and speak with my words to them. (Ezekiel 3:1–4)

Very similar instructions were given to St. John after he had been witness to the opening of the seven seals. A voice tells him to seal those up and write them not.

> The voice from heaven spoke unto me again and said, Go and take the little book which is open in the hand of the angel which standeth upon the sea and upon the earth.
>
> And I went unto the angel and said unto him, Give me the little book. And he said unto me, Take it, and eat it up; and it shall make thy belly bitter, but it shall be in thy mouth sweet as honey.

And I took the little book out of the angel's hand, and ate it up; and it was in my mouth sweet as honey; and as soon as I had eaten it, my belly was bitter.

And he said unto me, Thou must prophesy again before many peoples, and nations, and tongues, and kings. (Revelations 10:8–11)

What does this image of eating a book or scroll signify when it refers to the act of prophecy? It means that they are to "chew on" and digest the archetypal material before proclaiming it. Whereas Joseph Smith primarily reported what he saw, these men were instructed to digest the vision and then go forth with its message. The original divine vision of the seven seals was not to be spoken of; in its place was something that could be made humanly palatable. The adjectives *bitter* and *sweet* are often associated with prophecy in the Bible; though the experience of the revelation or vision may initially have a sweetness to it, the task of carrying forth a vision often entailed a bitter fate, such as St. John's exile. The task that each of these religious prophets were given was a very large one, affecting the destiny of their cultures.

I will close with a dream of my own, which allows me to emphasize the importance of the human stance in relation to archetypal material. This dream stands as a counterpoint to the preceding material, which was enormous in scope. Here, the book is not identified as sacred, but rather as a resource book in which symbols can be looked up; the process turns into an organic one that is nourishing, not academic:

> *I am in a library. There is a reference book on "Jungian . . ." where one can look up ideas and see where they are written about. I am pleased and surprised. I open it and start at the beginning. The page is A and the listing is* apricots*—only they are real ones! I take several onto my plate for eating. They were dried, then stewed with onions and spices—unusual and very good-tasting. A man who is with me looks at the next entry, B. This is* beans *and again they are actual ones. He takes some out. He asks me how many apricots I took; I say, "twelve," and mention that women are more familiar with*

*estimating according to weight. I estimate that I took a quarter pound of apricots. Then
I estimate how many beans he took, by weight.*

This dream occurred before chaos theory in physics had become popularized. It seems to present a similar idea, namely that there is an inherent
order in the implicate world or collective unconscious, here signified by the
alphabetization. The contents of this book are ordered, and the task is to
"begin at the beginning." This sense of implicate order came into play with
a particular client of mine, who dreamed that my task was to assist her in
learning how to use a reference book—by showing her it was alphabetized.

This dream portrays the archetypal symbols being transformed through
the alchemy of cooking, eating, and digesting. Drying is a traditional
method of preserving food; perhaps this detail hints at the way in which
knowledge is stored in the collective unconscious. The addition of water, or
aqua vitae, revitalizes the raw ingredients; cooking and adding the "spice of
life" makes dream and visionary material "palatable." The dream emphasizes the process of counting out—weighing and measuring—the portions
that can be digested on a daily basis. Maria Sabina indicated that she took
from her book of wisdom only what she needed. Jung's task of translating
alchemical texts and reinstating alchemy to Christian mystical tradition was
certainly a large one, but nevertheless specific and circumscribed in scope.
Likewise the study of Chinese alchemy for the dreamer mentioned earlier;
the amount he was given to read was humanly possible.

Among the examples presented here, only Maria Sabina lived wholly
within a folk culture whose spiritual practices were historically continuous.
In this respect, she serves as a prototype with which to compare the experience of contemporary healers; her vision of the book of wisdom is a culturally pure portrayal of the source to which a shaman turns for information and guidance. The vision itself has the elements of an initiatory rite:
She appears in front of a council of elders; she is given a task and the assistance to perform it; and she acknowledges the elders, the task, and the
assistance.

At the beginning of the initiatory ceremony, Maria was "inspired with
respect" for the Principal Ones, or ancestors. Some powerful emotion is
present in most of this material—awe or delight upon discovering the
book, weeping over its presentation, disappointment at not being able to
read it, fascination with its arcane symbols. Jung noted that this emotion is
a crucial element:

> It represents the value of an archetypal event. This emotional value must be
> kept in mind and allowed for throughout the whole intellectual process of
> interpretation. . . . Psychology is the only science that has to take the factor of

value (feeling) into account, since it forms the link between psychic events on the one hand, and meaning and life on the other. (Jung 1955, para. 596)

This, then, is why channeled material may seem compelling at first but soon becomes boring, like reading an encyclopedic account of creation: cosmic though the content may be, the feeling or "spice" that gives it meaning and relevance for human life is absent.

Let me now summarize some of the other themes that surround the book of knowledge mythologem. First, the book is often old and what it contains is timeless. The language is often archaic, strange, or somehow "foreign." Rarely located in the dreamer's own library, it is usually elsewhere, as if to indicate that there is a spiritual journey involved in discovering it. And though the dreamer may be handed the book to read and use, there is no sense that it ever comes into their private possession; it remains an Other that they are granted the privilege of seeing. The contents of the book are not depleted by its use but remain enormous far beyond the human capacity to integrate and understand.

One of the most intriguing themes in this material is that the book comes to life when it comes into human hands, as if a quickening takes place when knowledge crosses from the unseen or implicate world and enters the seen or explicate. What was flat or dry when stored becomes enlivened by the entry into the human realm, where it can be used for healing, understanding of suffering, and the broadening of experience that accompanies shamanic and mystical experiences. Once across that boundary, the knowledge is no longer two-dimensional, but rather living knowledge of a deep reality.

I have not gone into detail about the nature of the foreign languages the book is written in, the sort of glasses worn in order to perceive the invisible world, or the types of knowledge obtained from the book. My purpose here was to introduce this image and identify it as integral to the type of spiritual development that may take place among mystics and shamans, both contemporary and historical. I believe that the book of wisdom or knowledge is a symbol of the knowledge actually contained in the implicate world of the collective unconscious. Jung spoke a few times about this type of knowledge; just before his death, he said, "True, the unconscious knows more than consciousness does; but it is knowledge of a special sort, knowledge in eternity, usually without reference to the here and now, not couched in language of the intellect" (Jung 1961, 311).

Why would the source of knowledge represent itself as a book rather than, say, as an animal that could speak or the voice of a wise elder? It *is* represented in these and other ways; but the book of knowledge stands alone as a particular class of mythologem that seems to signify the building up of knowledge over time and its storage in a modality that is accessible to humans. It seems to me that the unconscious is conveying the manner in which this "knowledge of a special sort" is held and contained.

Jung once wrote about access to it, in a letter to a colleague who had had an experience of clairvoyance:

> Surveying the sum of experiences of this kind, you come to the conclusion that there is something like an "absolute knowledge" which is not accessible to consciousness but probably is to the unconscious, though only under certain conditions . . . the unconscious seems to have access to this "absolute knowledge" (Adler 1975, 18)

We have seen some of the "certain conditions" under which access to this knowledge takes place: when the curtain between the visible and nonvisible worlds opens during ecstatic states, shamanic trances, spontaneous waking visions, and night dreams.

If this knowledge already exists in some other dimension of reality, why must it be discovered and rediscovered by a visionary or shaman or healer in culture after culture? I will allow Jung to speak to this mystery, in what is one of my favorite passages from his writings:

> In order to find valid answers to these questions, a complete spiritual renewal is needed. And this cannot be given gratis, each man must strive to achieve it for himself. Neither can old formulas which once had value be brought into force again. The eternal truths cannot be transmitted mechanically; in every epoch, they must be born anew from the human psyche. (Jung 1970, para. 443)

The increasing appearance of this mythologem at this present point in history may signify the revitalization of our human connection with archetypal wisdom after having lost this connection through the overdevelopment of linear, rational consciousness. This material enables us to witness the process of eternal truths being born anew in the psyche of humankind.

REFERENCES

Adler, G. (1975). *C. G. Jung: Letters, 1951–1961.* Princeton: University Press.

Estrada, A. (1981). *Maria Sabina: Her Life and Chants.* Santa Barbara, Calif.: Ross-Erikson.

Franz, M.-L. von (1974). *Shadow and Evil in Fairy Tales.* Dallas: Spring Publications.

Hastings J., ed. 1908. *Encyclopedia of Religion and Ethics.* New York: C. Scribner and Sons.

———— 1960. Review of Complex Theory. In *The Structure and Dynamics of the Psyche*. Bollingen Series XX: The Collected Works of C.G. Jung, vol 8. Princeton: Princeton University Press.

———— 1961. *Memories, Dreams, Reflections*. New York: Random House.

Jung, C. G. 1955. Healing the Spirit. In *The Symbolic Life*. Bollingen Series XX: The Collected Works of C. G. Jung, vol. 18. Princeton: Princeton University Press.

————. 1966. Medicine and Psychotherapy. In *The Practice of Psychotherapy*. Bollingen Series XX: The Collected Works of C. G. Jung, vol. 16. Princeton: Princeton University Press.

————. 1970. After the Catastrophe. In *Civilization in Transition*. Bollingen Series XX: The Collected Works of C. G. Jung, vol. 10. Princeton: Princeton University Press.

Kingsford, A. (1908). *Dreams and Dream Stories*. London: John Watkins.

Peers, A., ed. (1960). *The Autobiography of St. Teresa of Avila*. Doubleday. New York: Doubleday.

Part II

SHAMANIC MEDICINE:
EXPLORATIONS IN HEALING

Chapter 6

An Integrated Approach to Soul Possession: Applying Shamanistic and Jungian Techniques

Steven H. Wong

Steven Wong brings us a sample of true shamanic healing. People are always amazed that Jung sometimes knew what was wrong with a patient even before a word was uttered. Similarly, through his visionary gifts Steven knows the inner condition of many of his patients and how, with focused intent, they can be helped. This is a glimpse of shamanic healing from the shaman's point of view and rare case histories of the shamanic mind at work.

From a Jungian perspective, soul loss is a condition in which the ego has become listless, morose, and depressed. There is a loss of both vital energy and consciousness. In terms of possession, Jung sees possession of the ego on many levels. The ego or soul can be possessed by a complex, persona, inferior function, shadow, and anima/animus. But there is another level, of which most Jungians are unaware, and that is the realm beyond the transpsyche. This is a very complex issue. In 1919 Jung explained parapsychological events as exteriorizations of the psyche in which ghosts and spirits are projections of complexes onto outer events.

I for one am certainly convinced that they are exteriorizations. I have repeatedly observed the telepathic effects of unconscious complexes and also a number of parapsychic phenomena, but in all this I see no proof whatever of the existence of real spirits, and until such proof is forthcoming I must regard this whole territory as an appendix of psychology. (Jung 1969, para. 600).

Jung had a most peculiar experience in London in 1920. After a long series of lectures he stayed at a friend's rented country house.

> During the nights he experienced various increasingly violent ghostly phenomena like knockings, evil smells, sounds of rustling and dripping. They aroused in him a feeling of suffocation and a sensation of growing rigidity, and culminated in the apparition, or hallucination, of a solid-looking half of a woman's head lying on the pillow about sixteen inches away from his own. Its one eye was wide open and staring at him. The head vanished when Jung lit a candle. He spent the rest of the night sitting in an armchair. He and his friend later learned what was already known to the whole village: the house was haunted and all tenants were driven away in a very short time.
>
> Jung interpreted some details of his experience as exteriorizations of psychic contents in the unconscious. But what remained an insoluble puzzle was the fact that the haunting took place solely in that house, indeed, in one particular room of the house. (Jaffe 1984, 9)

In 1948 Jung recanted his previous statements and suggested parapsychological phenomena cannot be explained only psychologically.

> After collecting psychological experiences from many people and many countries for fifty years, I no longer feel as certain as I did in 1919. . . . To put it bluntly, I doubt whether an exclusively psychological approach can do justice to the phenomena in question. Not only the findings of parapsychology, but my own theoretical reflections outlined in "On the Nature of the Psyche" have led me to certain postulates which touch on the realm of nuclear physics and the conception of the space-time continuum. This opens up the whole question of the transpsychic reality immediately underlying the psyche. (Jung 1969, 318 [footnote])

Most Jungian analysts and Jungian psychotherapists now would say that the transpsychic realm is the collective unconscious. The collective unconscious is not only the reservoir of all archetypal patterns needed for the propagation and transformation of all life forms, but it also has absolute knowledge which appears in the form of precognitions, dreams, and visions.

But, following in the pioneering spirit of Jung, some analysts have taken a more critical stance on what the transpsyche might be other than the collective unconscious. The major criticism is that the collective unconscious may not be able to explain every phenomenon experienced by human consciousness—that is, paranormal experiences.

If we view the collective unconscious as a closed, self-contained system, then we can see that it may limit the possibilities of human experiences. But if we have an open system, then experiences such as paranormal ones have a much larger context to exist in and can be examined and experienced on their own merits. Dr. Jeffrey Raff, a Jungian analyst, has studied the area beyond the collective unconscious for many years and has suggested that the first explorers of this realm beyond were the shamans.

The following will be a presentation of three clients: Mary, Bob, and Kelly. Mary's and Bob's journeys will be used to illustrate soul retrieval and healing through dream analysis, and Kelly's will illustrate soul retrieval and healing through a shamanic journey.

The healing process within a Jungian context is commonly done by searching out and strengthening the ego through dialogue, dreams, dance, sandplay, body work, art, and active imagination. The primary intent of the therapist is based on heart, center, empathy, and compassion. The initial experience between a therapist and client is a transference/countertransference. For example, a woman may have a strong, positive mother transference onto a male or female therapist. The positive transference is what draws out a traumatic ego or traumatized fragments of an ego. Dreams serve as a medium for uncovering unconscious material, locating the ego within a conflicting context, and providing the necessary symbols for the healing of the psyche.

In our first session, Mary arrived in a manic condition. She was so bright, witty, intense, and beaming with life that it felt unrealistic and incredible. What had happened is that her soul, or ego, became possessed by the sky realm of the father. Instead of relating to the father values and subsequently integrating them to strengthen her personality, she identified with the father and lost her own identity. Her initial dream was as follows:

> She is on her hands and knees with two old wise women, digging into the sacred earth of the Garden of the Gods. The three of them uncover two large boulders in the form of dolphins.

The dream is compensatory in that it pulled her down from the sky realm, grounding and stabilizing her in her body and the earth. The image of the Garden of the Gods, juxtaposed with earth, symbolizes unity and wholeness. The two old wise women represent wisdom and the feminine. The dolphin is a symbol of connection. It is able to move between the two worlds (sky and earth, seen and unseen, and ego and collective unconscious), and, through that movement Mary was able to experience her ego. As she traversed the two worlds via the dolphin, her heart was touched at each encounter, and a heart connection was created that was the beginning of the healing. Dreams were used in this manner to retrieve her soul, or ego, from the father complex (sky realm) and to bring her back to her identity and center her in relation to the sky and earth.

One and a half years later Mary was back into the swings from mania to depression and brought me this dream:

> *She is in a huge storm at sea. The waves are twenty feet high. She finds herself standing at the middle of a gigantic battleship but does not feel afraid.*

Both of us realized at that moment that she had become very strong and that she could survive any future attacks of manic-depression. We talked extensively about the value of stillness and peace which is also the heart connection. We talked as well about how the heart connection is the relationship of her life to the life of the greater mystery of the Self.

Another example is Bob, who was depressed and caught in the family complex. His dream was as follows:

> *He is in his childhood home, but it is set in the plains. On the front porch his schizophrenic sister attacks him for being involved in Jungian analysis. He is really hurt and depressed, but then he feels something behind him. As he turns around he sees a huge star suspended above and in front of him. The star comforts him and affirms his path, and his feeling is to follow the star.*

The star is the Self or God image, and to follow it is to follow his individual path and not the path of the family.

The soul or ego possession is the tremendous weight of the family complex (an unhealthy conformity) laced with the insanity of the feminine. The retrieval is the restoration of his energy within his individual path via the power of the star. Of course, the function of the therapist is to carry the image of the star as it is being projected onto the therapist. The danger is if the therapist identifies with it and therefore falls into an inflation. The boon is if the therapist carries, protects, and honors the projection of the Self (star) until the client can integrate it.

Kelly, a twenty-four-year-old, was brought to my office by her mother. She was extremely withdrawn, and when spoken to would either whisper into her mother's ear or remain quiet. Her mother would speak for her.

As the story unfolded, I learned that when Kelly was fourteen she smoked some hashish and was running around on a parking lot that her mother thinks was once an Indian burial ground. Kelly said that something picked her up and threw her into a tree about ten to fifteen feet away. It then picked her up and dropped her on the ground away from the tree, and it began to throw her upper body back and forth as she sat on the ground. Then for the next ten years it would occasionally make her run around in circles until she was exhausted. Once she collapsed, it would pick her up and march her to the liquor store because it wanted a drink. It would ply her with alcohol until she was drunk.

Kelly was in and out of mental institutions and alcohol treatment centers for a number of years, growing worse. In the meantime, she had married, given birth to a child, separated from her husband, and given her son up to her in-laws. Her situation looked very bad, and I did not feel competent enough to take on such a challenge. But I had a series of dreams that made me look at the case again and convinced me to give it a try. I spent four days and nights on a shamanic journey to learn drumming, chanting, and connecting with my ally spirits in preparation for the soul retrieval. The process took six months on a weekly basis to heal Kelly. Four journeys into Kelly's psyche will be given to illustrate the process.

As I enter into the lower world during the drumming, I see blackness, and only a few outlines can be discerned. The smell, the stench, is almost unbearable. I begin to call her name, but there is no answer. A thick, sticky tar pulls at my feet as I slowly make my way into the darkness. After a time I notice a bumpy object covered with tar. A flat metal scraper appears in my hand, and I kneel down to clear away the tar from the bumpy object. Slowly human flesh appears and I move quickly to remove the rest of the tar. It is Kelly. She is half dead, and I am not sure if she is breathing. My drumming increases, and energy begins to move into her.

In the meantime the tiger ally has come across a huge tear in her psyche. The tear is twenty feet high and separates two distinct universes. The membrane is waving in the cosmic wind. The tiger comes closer to inspect it. Suddenly an evil black demon lurches out of the darkness and lands on the tiger's back. Once I see this, my drumming seems to automatically increase in intensity. My chanting changes from a monotone into a tone of deep concern, fear, focus, and power. The increase in intensity puts a great strain on my body. A gigantic battle unfolds with the tiger roaring, swatting, and clawing while the demon continues to suck at the neck of the tiger. The demon finally retreats from exhaustion. The tiger goes immediately to the tear and begins to bind the wound using its strong jaws and teeth.

Kelly begins to awaken as the last bit of tar is scraped away. I notice a concrete slab under her, and I increase my chanting and drumming. A faint light appears in the distance southwest of us. The ground begins to shake, and two walls come out of the ground to form a wedge around her. The walls rise fifty feet into the air, and a blue mandala window forms on the top of the southwest wall. In the middle of the mandala is a translucent orb. Light begins to build in the center of the orb. The power slowly builds and when it reaches its peak intensity, it shoots into Kelly and the concrete slab. The slab rises up into a table. Kelly is suspended a foot off the table, and her heart is pulled out of her chest and suspended a few inches away. Golden light begins to permeate and expand her heart while the cathedral structure and Kelly are bathed in a soft hue of red-gold light.

In the outer world, Kelly was more relaxed, and she said that although she did not understand what was happening, she felt better.

Returning to the site, I find the same setting, with the light continuing to feed Kelly's heart and body. As I look around I see another figure in the tar. What I uncovered is a falcon with broken wings. It is scarcely alive and barely moving. I take the falcon and kneel before the concrete table, offering it up to the light. Light begins to touch its tortured body, and slowly it begins to move. In the meantime, the tiger ally continues to do battle with the demon. The battles are relentless, and at times I fear the tiger may lose, but I continue drumming and chanting, hoping the energy and love is enough to sustain him.

The above scenario continued for the next four sessions with slight variations and increased healing of the falcon's wings. What Kelly began to notice when she and her mother drove into town to see me was that birds would appear. She would watch them from the car as they soared toward the vehicle and then away. One flew right at the car window, suspending itself momentarily in the air in front of the window before it flew off. During a trip out of town to visit her five-year-old-son, birds continued to appear. After she had spent a few days with her son, he turned to her and asked her to send him feathers once she returned home.

An eagle appears in this session. He is a new ally for Kelly, which is something totally unexpected and welcome. He is twice the size of the falcon and immediately begins to fight the demon with tremendous ferocity. Kelly is off the concrete table and is moving through the jungle, exercising her muscles and gaining strength.

Outwardly Kelly is stronger and the running in circles has stopped, although the drinking continues, albeit with less frequency.

The final session shows four figures facing north. First is Kelly's little boy; second, Kelly; third, the falcon; and fourth, the eagle with its wings outstretched and enclosing the three. A beam of golden light shoots through the four hearts, and there is a red golden glow setting off the aura of love that encompasses the four of them. The exorcism of the demon is complete, and the love in Kelly's heart for herself, her son, the falcon and the eagle is intact.

Kelly continued the sessions after this point, but she began to bring dreams that dealt with more mundane issues. The continuation of her healing using dreams will help her find her path in life.

The most important issue regarding an integrated process of Jungian psychology and shamanism is knowing the levels one is in and dealing with them appropriately, especially if the difference is between a soul possession within the psyche (that is, complex) or a soul possession outside of the transpsychic (that is, pure evil). In Kelly's case, the eagle and the falcon are the positive manifestations of the reality beyond the transpsychic realm, and they serve to heal and to bring a new reality into human experience.

REFERENCES

Jaffe, A. 1984 [1968]. *Jung's Last Years*. Dallas: Spring Publications.

Jung, C. G. 1969 [1948]. The Psychological Foundations of Belief in Spirits. In *The Structure and Dynamics of the Psyche*. Bollingen Series XX: The Collected Works of C. G. Jung, vol. 8. Princeton: Princeton University Press.

Chapter 7

Shamanic States in Our Lives

Patricia Damery

Patricia Damery, a Jungian therapist practicing in northern California, tells about the importance of altered states of consciousness—that is shamanic or ecstatic states—in her life and work. Entering into such a state enabled her to transcend the tormenting pains of childbirth and, in another example, to break through to a deeper caring and understanding with a difficult patient. She has gradually learned to use these altered states for both her own benefit and that of her patients.

One of my earliest memories is of standing on the porch with my mother as she pointed out wild geese flying overhead, presumably in a V formation. I remember pressing my cheek against the warm curve of her hip as I strained to see. But all I could perceive were large, clear spheres floating down to earth. Since I knew what a bird looked like, I was aware in that moment that my mother and I were having different experiences, but because this thought was threatening, I remained confused. Were these spheres the wild geese?

This realization of differing perceptions, particularly during what I have since learned to identify as altered and often ecstatic states of consciousness, was a compelling factor in my resolve to become a psychotherapist. The paradox it embodies—rational versus irrational—is one I have had to struggle with in both my personal life and my professional work. The etymology of the word *ecstasy* can be traced back to its Indo-European roots of *exo* "out" and *stā* "the place that is standing," hence "out of the place that is standing," a place or state outside where we most often stand, out of the confinement of ego reality.

So much of our training as psychotherapists is within the place we most often stand, relying on reason. The awareness and use of ecstatic states during the analytical hour are rarely addressed. We find other ways to focus on these experiences, ways that better fit our rational beliefs. We talk about transference and countertransference, about projective identification, and maybe even about the imaginal field. But much gets lost in the intellectualizing, namely the quality of the ecstatic state itself. And as Eliade says of shamanic healing, the ecstatic experience is what changes the religious status of the initiate, not the theoretical or practical training (Eliade 1964, 33).

I was raised in a farm community where perceptions outside of ordinary ego consciousness were common. Mrs. Jostes, a distant relative and a close friend of my grandmother, had seen angels when she was young and in later years could spit on warts and have them disappear. She had done away with a wart on my father's index finger in just this way before he married my mother. Both Mrs. Jostes's grandson Bill and my father did water witching, a practice accepted to be as normal and useful as driving a tractor. My grandmother herself never planted her garden on or after the full moon, and if her nose itched, she knew company would be arriving soon. But these were the old ways, scoffed at by my mother, who was not raised on a farm.

When I entered puberty I became very ill during my periods, having intense cramping and vomiting very much like that of the transition stage of labor. Each month I would try a new drug, a new attitude, but to no avail; each month I would be bedridden for two days, trying to find that place in myself that was impervious to the pain. In time I found that spot by submitting to the pain itself. Then I would be transported into a deep sleep state in which there were sometimes images, sometimes presences, but always rest.

Later, in my first labor, seventeen hours of intense contractions left me exhausted and very cognizant that without medical help my baby and I would die. I felt a presence three feet to my left that I associated with my death. I felt as though I were being pulled apart, and I had the peculiar experience of being present in it. I felt my skin stretch and tear. I marveled at how much pain I could tolerate. I knew, for the presence had told me, that there was a lot I could tolerate that I thought I couldn't. A light went on in this other realm during the moments before my son's birth, and I was fully aware of the reality of that realm. I could not have been more awake.

A knowing happened in me, a knowing that I had not had as much confidence in before. In this other realm existed presences and resources that I was not aware of in my everyday waking state.

As I have read and listened to accounts of people's initiatory experiences into shamanism, I have been reminded of my labors and menstrual cramps and other times of extreme duress when presences have appeared and I have felt deep peace. These times are sacred to me and I've seldom spoken of them, yet each time they have changed my life, leaving me more open to the dimensions in which these experiences happen. When we are in pain or fear, it seems we are more likely to be open.

Health professionals have for a number of years overmedicated birthing women to stop the experience of pain. In our culture we are phobic of pain. We have no larger context in which to put physically or emotionally painful experiences. So when and if an altered awareness occurs, it may well not be remembered or spoken of, or it may be attributed to the drug; the state itself is not valued. These days we honor the mother-child bonding that happens in those early moments following a birth, and we pay attention to the mother's and baby's health and to the cost of this care. But we pay little attention to providing women with an environment that supports the tremendous psychic event of having one's body immersed in the overwhelming instinctual process of childbirth.

I am going to take this a bit further because I think it is pertinent to psychotherapy. What helped me in labor and delivery—and during the comparable pain of my menstrual cramps— was the support I received allowing me to be in myself and to tolerate the pain—support conducive to ecstatic states. When I was a child, my rational mother paradoxically supported these states by letting me rest quietly away from my loud and noisy family and attending to me only when I needed her. In labor my husband supported me, breathed with me, and intervened with medical personnel so that I would have to interact with practical matters as little as possible. Afterward I had a quiet room with a window where I could watch a rainstorm and listen to myself without the distraction of a TV or visitors. These conditions supported communion with other dimensions, other presences, other aspects of the self.

As psychotherapists, we can also allow for access to this state. Nathan Schwartz-Salant describes this state:

> Jung's approach to alchemical symbolism can be focused upon the interactional field. This fertile area, invisible except to the eye of the imagination, is constellated in the transference-countertransference process. . . . A crucial issue is the locus of these elusive energy fields; the inability to locate them within our normal space-time perception leads to the recovery of the ancient

concept of the subtle body. This concept is a mainstay of alchemical thinking and refers to experiences that can be called neither physical nor mental but partake of both realms. Moreover, the subtle body concept is inseparably linked to the alchemical notion of the imagination (in Latin, *imaginatio*), which was viewed as having both a psychic and material nature. . . . The subtle body is a realm through which projections pass and transform; while its processes can be perceived by the imagination, they are not usually available for discovery by the rational mode. (Schwartz-Salant 1989, 6–7)

Too often I have accessed these other, less rational dimensions in secret, embarrassed to describe my real experience, so much like the dilemma of my early childhood years. What do I do with these other perceptions that so often give direct access to the unconscious? And how do I let them have their own rightful place along with the more rational modes?

I now want to describe a clinical experience that shows how I have integrated my own perceptions of these other realms into my work (identifying information has been changed). This work was with a young woman, the second and last child of parents who had conceived her after the death of a toddler son. She spent her first six weeks of life in the hospital nursery due to digestive problems and was colicky much of her first year. She was told that she did not like to be held or touched.

She suffered her parents' disappointment in almost everything she did. A learning disability made school difficult and brought more criticism and rejection from her parents. In her late teens she became pregnant and married the father of the child. She self-medicated with a variety of prescription drugs during the course of their ten-year marriage. Because she was unable to function the father was given sole custody of their daughter at the time of their divorce. When she began treatment with me, she had been off drugs for two years. She was seeking help because she was unable to have healthy relationships.

In sessions she was wary of me, often silent and withholding. When she did talk, she would focus at length on her illnesses and body pains.

Almost from the start, I found myself overcome with sleepiness. Often I would imagine myself to be the tree outside the window, going down deep into the roots in a desperate attempt just to stay awake. I could barely keep my eyes open. We discussed what she called her thorniness, her attempt to keep me away. We discussed the implicit anger in her withdrawal. But I continued to feel as if I had been drugged from almost the moment she entered the room.

After two years she came in one day and after her usual greeting (which consisted of telling me how hard it was to get to the session) she sat, arms folded across her chest. I felt the overwhelming sleepiness. We had talked of the recalcitrance she often felt with me, and this day I felt it particularly strongly. For some reason (it is not my usual mode) I suggested she let her body move to express itself. She immediately responded by curling up on the floor in a ball. I allowed myself to relax into a trance. I felt such relief at not trying to stay awake. It was like slipping into a cool pool of water.

It was not sleep, however. I felt my body relax, and at once something inside me became very alert. I was sitting in another room in a rocking chair, rocking an infant who was crying inconsolably. For forty minutes I rocked, holding this infant. I felt the pain of the infant. I felt the frustration and pain of the mother. Occasionally I would open my eyes, but in the other dimension the rocking continued.

I waited until she stirred. When she sat up, she made some report about her body experiences. I honestly do not remember what she said. I never did discuss with her my own experience of the hour. I'm not sure why. Another time, under other circumstances, I might have. Had she said, "I felt like a crying baby," had her experience been more similar to my own, I might have then. But as it was, to say something felt too much as though it would be infringing on her experience, touching the crying infant who just needed to be held and suffered with.

Something changed in that session. I was never again sleepy with her. Instead, I felt alert and present. I think my own resistance to the feeling in the room diminished when I honored the pull into the unconscious. In that trance I was able to be with the deep psyche in a way I was not capable of in a more waking state. I was able to be with the suffering pair: the infant who could not be comforted and the mother who could not comfort. Each could only be with the other: the helpless infant, who is not comfortable in her own body and who is screaming for someone to do something, and the mother, who is helpless to do anything except witness and be with her raging infant.

According to John Perry, every complex is bipolar. Emotions are the result of the interaction of the poles (Perry 1970, 1–12). In this case, the intensity that we were not able to tolerate (manifested in me by my sleepiness and in her by her overinvolvement with body processes and withdrawal) was the intensity of that complex. We were both affected by this mother and child. When I was able to tolerate the feeling and she synchronistically in her rolled-up state on the floor was able to tolerate the feeling, then we could both get better. Until then we had been polarized: I the mother trying to console, she the crying infant; or she the mother trying to comfort me into thinking I could help her, and I the crying infant unable to tolerate the intolerable. I suspect this was also the energy enacted in her life in the unhealthy relationships with men.

When I look at my notes before and after this session, I find they are full of regressive work around abandonment and rage. I followed the unconscious commentary in these sessions, hoping to shed light onto what was going on in the room between her and me. We explored her past, her relationship with her mother and father, and the patterning that was formed there and carried into present relationships. We spent a good deal of time with what went on between us. But for my own healing in the context of that work with her, this session was most important. It revealed to me, in a way no other method could, the energy in the room, the unconscious field that was operating between us. That is what shamanic states offer: an immersion in the unconscious that is unavailable in waking states and which allows a deep consultation and interaction with the psyche.

I often think of healing the psyche as a homeopathic process. In homeopathy, a patient's symptoms are supported by a remedy because the symptoms are seen as the organism's attempt to heal itself. The remedy is not the crude substance but the essence of the substance. The dilution is so great that not one molecule of the original substance remains. Only the pattern of energy, or what I think of as the archetype of the substance, remains. This is what heals.

In healing the psyche, the deepest work is also with essences. In the case of my patient the crude substance may be a literal reenactment of this mother-child bond with me (and others) in its positive and negative aspects. The real healing comes from a felt awareness of the complex, and more remotely the archetype, operating.

As Schwartz-Salant says, the space in which this can happen has both a material nature and a psychic one. We are used to giving validity to the material realm and considering all the rest illusion, or something only in our mind. So to become sensitized to this other realm requires practice. In this particular work it was facilitated by my sleepiness (the pull into the unconscious) and by the forty-minute period during which there was no talking. Then I could forget unconscious commentaries and interpretations and how I felt about her withdrawal. My inner eye could open, unimpeded.

A personal healing has come as I have learned to honor the experience of the third realm. I am no longer at odds with something very basic and instinctual, something I knew quite well as a child but learned to override in favor of a more rational mode. Our task is to hold both modes in our work. Then we are immersed in the third realm, where energies can truly be transformed. V. Walter Odajnyk expresses this beautifully:

> With full immersion (*in the unconscious*), one stops talking so much. Words and images aren't that important any more. They have their place, but are not overvalued and examined with such consuming interest. The impact of psychic reality becomes so strong, the soul is reduced to silence—the silence where no images reign. (Odajnyk 1984, 48)

REFERENCES

Eliade, M. 1964. *Shamanism: Archaic Techniques of Ecstasy.* Translated by W. Trask. Bollingen Series LXXVI. Princeton: Princeton University Press.

Odajnyk, V. W. 1984. The Psychology of an Artist: The Imaginal World of James Hillman. *Quadrant: Journal of the C. G. Jung Foundation for Analytical Psychology,* 17, 48.

Perry, J. 1970. Emotions and Object Relations. *Journal of Analytical Psychology* 15, 1–12.

Schwartz-Salant, N. 1989. *The Borderline Personality, Vision, and Healing.* Wilmette, Ill.: Chiron.

Chapter 8

The Felt Vision

Jeffrey A. Raff

In this article Jeffrey Raff has brought together the wisdom of the mystics who are close to being shamans, and the modern experience of analytical psychology to describe and differentiate the "felt" vision as it appears to each of them. While one usually thinks of a vision as an image that is inwardly seen, there are other powerful visionary experiences that are mainly felt. These can be strong and transformative visions with an immediate effect on one's being and one's fate.

My introduction to inner work came through the study of general mysticism. The mystics were, therefore, my first real teachers, and I have always felt a great debt of gratitude to them. Over the years I have become aware that many of the writings of the mystics have lost relevance and a sense of immediacy for the modern individual. The context in which they were written no longer applies in our modern world. Yet there is much in these writings that can be used to help understand the exploration of the visionary world, for their authors were true explorers of this realm. Of great interest to students of visions is the mystic's notion of the felt vision.

One of the great modern students of mysticism was Evelyn Underhill, who wrote in the early twentieth century. Though unconsciously biased toward Christian mysticism, she presents the major ideas of the mystics in a clear and concise way that has never been equaled. She writes of the felt vision:

> Vision, then, is recognized by the true contemplative as at best an imperfect, oblique, and untrustworthy method of apprehension: it is ungovernable, capricious, liable to deception, and the greater its accompanying hallucination the more suspicious it becomes. All, however, distinguish different classes of visionary experience; and differentiate sharply between the value of the vision which is "felt" rather than seen, and the true optical hallucination which is perceived, exterior to the subject, by the physical sight. (Underhill 1990, 281)

The natural suspicion that the mystic has for visionary experience is clearly presented in this quote, but the important point is that for the mystic, even with this great distrust of visionary states, the felt vision is acceptable. The felt vision may be trusted, for it is a visionary experience that does not merely partake of one of the five senses; rather, it includes a different mode of perception. There is to my knowledge no word in the English language for this mode of perception, so I am forced, as Underhill was, to use the word *felt*.

As used in the expression *felt vision*, feeling does not refer to emotion nor to a psychological function. Rather, it refers to a kind of sixth sense, which perceives with such a profound sense of reality and intensity that no doubt can remain in the visionary that his experience was real. There are many different kinds of felt vision.

The first type of felt vision is the one most accessible to the ordinary individual. In fact, almost everyone can experience this type of feeling with just a little practice. Most simply put, the first level of felt vision is to follow one's feeling in every moment. This is all very easy but almost never practiced. Many of us have heard the Zen saying "Eat when hungry, sleep when tired." This phrase neatly sums up the first level of felt vision. By consulting one's feeling's in a given moment, one becomes conscious of the state of one's own self, as well as of the environment around one. For example, I was once engaged in trying to sell my car to a Swiss businessman. Unknown to me, he was rather a shark and was hoping to cheat me out of quite a bit of money. Being naive about such things, I assumed he was as honest as I was. As we progressed in our deal, I got angrier and angrier, without knowing why. Finally I could stand it no longer and told him I was furious with him. He thought me quite mad and beat a hasty retreat. Talking later with a wiser friend, I discovered the swindle I had almost allowed. My own deeper sense knew I was being cheated even though consciously I was not so smart.

Picking up the feelings of a moment can be tricky, even for feeling types. Very often the feelings we might be aware of are unacceptable or confusing or so quiet we cannot make them conscious. But with a little attention our feelings can sometimes very quickly become known to us. It is then necessary to express them in some way. I would like to relate a wonderful Sufi story told by Idries Shah that illustrates this level of the felt experience beautifully. It is called "The Man Who Always got Angry."

The story tells of a man who all his life was very easily angered. He got into many difficulties because of this. He learned of a very wise dervish, and he hastened to ask his advice. The dervish bid him to go stand under a tree and offer water to all travelers. The man did this, and he became renowned as a man of charity and self-control.

One day a man in a great hurry passed by and would not even turn his head or say thanks when the water was offered. The man offering the water said, "Come, return my salutation. Have some water." The man paid no attention, and the charitable man became so angry he took his gun and shot the traveler in the head. As the man died the withered tree beside the one who offered water broke into bloom.

You see, the man hurrying off was about to commit a most heinous crime, the worst in his career. (Shaeh, 1969, 79–80)

Like all Sufi teaching stories, this story may be interpreted in a number of different ways. From the point of view of the felt vision, however, the story presents the paradoxical idea that the worst feeling at the right moment is right. Rather than suppressing his anger or denying it, the man gets angry at the right person at the right time, and as a result even the act of murder turns into a blessing. Of course, the angry man had been angry all his life, and previously his anger had done him no good. What changed? He visited a Sufi master and was placed in the right spot, where his anger was appropriate. The feeling that arises must be related to the wisdom of the personality in order to find its right place. For example, if I feel angry at a friend and do not know why, it is best to work with my anger first—to reflect on it and, if possible, understand its origins. If this is not possible, the next step is to find an appropriate way to express my anger. Instead of going to my friend and punching him or yelling at him, I might tell him I was angry. I could tell him the reasons or even explain that I did not understand why. In communication, the meaning might well turn up.

Feeling must therefore be followed with consciousness and with expression that is appropriate both to the feeling and to the moment in which it is expressed. This takes great wisdom indeed, and since most of us are not Sufi masters it takes trial and error. But even a mistake made in the service of the felt moment is better than denial or repression. The examples so far have to do with emotion, but the feeling can be almost anything. I can feel uneasy; I can feel another person's fear or uncertainty; I can feel the rightness of a decision or the sense of joy an idea gives me. As Obi-Won Kenobi (from *Star Wars*) explains to Luke Skywalker, one must reach out with one's feelings to encounter the force. The more one does so, the stronger one's felt sense grows.

Closely related to this type of felt experience is living with one's impulses. Impulses are ideas or images that spontaneously come to one and which usually need expression of some kind. I can have the impulse to get a candy bar, to go home from work early, or to call a loved one unexpectedly. I can get an impulse to change jobs or start dating. In short, I can have an impulse about almost anything. Impulses are felt, but they are not feelings. Wanting spontaneously to get an ice cream cone is something I can feel in the sense of knowing irrationally. It is important to remember that having *feeling* simply means an unusual way of knowing or perceiving. Feeling the need to act in some way is following an impulse. Whereas consulting one's feelings, consists of being aware of the felt perception of a situation or a person, the impulse is an irrational bid for action, a push to do that comes from a source unknown to the conscious mind. What are these impulses?

The psychologist and philosopher C. G. Jung spent most of his long life studying the nature of the human psyche. Among the topics that fascinated him was the nature of such impulses. He concluded that impulses arise from the very center of the psyche, via instinct and archetype. He further felt that psychic health requires cooperation with impulses and that, coming as they do from the center of the psyche, impulses could be regarded as the "will of God":

> So when I say that the impulses which we find in ourselves should be understood as the "will of God," I wish to emphasize that they ought not to be regarded as an arbitrary wishing and willing, but as absolutes which one must learn how to handle correctly. The will can control them only in part. . . . I should also like the term "God" in the phrase "the will of God" to be understood not so much in the Christian sense as in the sense intended by Diotima, when she said: "Eros, dear Socrates, is a mighty daemon." The Greek words *daimon* and *daimonion* express a determining power which comes upon man from outside, like providence, or fate, though the ethical decision is left to man. He must know, however, what he is deciding about and what he is doing. Then, if he obeys he is following not just his own opinion, and if he rejects he is destroying not just his own invention. (Jung 1970a, 27)

This is quite a remarkable statement, and one that must be applied to all levels of the felt experience. The impulses, like the visions to be discussed later, arise not from the conscious mind but from the deepest part of the psyche. They are not arbitrary and do not serve the wish fulfillment of the ego, but rather represent the will of the inner god or daimon. To follow one's impulses is therefore to be in harmony with the inner divinity.

Jung himself not only wrote about impulses but lived with them as well. There is a story that Jung would often follow the inner promptings of his daimon. Despairing of ever being able to visit Rome, Jung struck on the idea of bicycling over the Alps to the city. He invited two well-known authors to accompany him. They accepted rather reluctantly, and off they went to Rome. After a day on the road they camped for the night in the mountains. In the middle of the night Jung awoke with the impulse to return to Zurich. Undaunted, he simply abandoned his companions and biked back the way they had come. The two authors, needless to say, were not pleased when they awoke to find Jung gone!

This is similar to the Chinese story about a learned scholar who, in the middle of a blizzard, had the impulse to visit a friend miles away. Off went the scholar with many of his retinue. On reaching the hut in the woods of his friend, the scholar simply turned around and went home. When challenged by his tired and frustrated retinue, the scholar replied that he had had the impulse to visit his friend but on arriving found the impulse gone, so he simply returned home! In Chinese philosophy, this is known as having no deliberate mind of one's own (Chan 1973).

These stories illustrate the irrational nature of impulses and the apparently bizarre behavior of those who follow them. However, living with one's impulses creates a freedom in one's life that is hard to imagine if one has not lived that way. Moreover, commitment to such a way of life unites one's conscious mind with the center of the soul. Following an impulse creates a way of acting, but at the same time it also creates a way of being. Every time one follows an impulse, one is creating a deeper connection with the self. Acting and being are therefore brought together by paying attention to the felt impulse.

There are many mysteries about living with one's impulses that I cannot address here. However, I must point out that underneath the apparently bizarre and random character of impulse lies a much deeper order based on meaning and on self-identity. At the moment that one has an impulse, it may be impossible to understand its meaning. However, it is possible to review a number of impulses that have arisen over time and see a pattern behind them. The meaning of the impulses then may be understood as the expression of an aspect of one's deeper self previously unrecognized.

A profound problem now arises, however. It is one thing to view impulses as arising from the Self and therefore being the will of God. But what if these impulses arise from the dark area of the psyche known as the shadow? The shadow by its very nature is not to be trusted, for it contains the parts of one's personality least socially adapted. It may include feelings and ideas that are questionable at best, evil at worst. For example, the shadow of an individual may contain bigotry. This bigotry could give rise to an impulse to harm a member of a different race. This impulse might be followed under the justification of expressing the Self. I have seen cases in which an individual will justify shadowy behavior by reference to the self, and I have even been attacked by an individual who rationalized his behavior by declaring that the Self told him to do it.

In order to honestly follow one's impulses and live in harmony with the Self, without fear of trickery, the sixth sense I am calling feeling must be developed; that is the one sure safeguard against trickery by the shadow. If one can feel into an impulse and its consequences, one can decide how best to follow that impulse. I once had a patient who attacked me in a very devious fashion. I might have been able to handle the case much differently if that client had been able to feel the source of the impulse, or his relationship to me, or the implication of his action. Short of this, one can only make an educated guess about the impulse and how best to follow it. An educated guess is better than slavish following, but cultivation of the felt sense is the best way yet. Hence I have learned to educate people in feeling before I talk to them about impulse; I do not talk about it at all to those individuals who are incapable of feeling. Needless to say, any form of freedom and relationship to Self is dangerous, and the best protection against such dangers is the conscious development of feeling. There are individuals who should never be taught this mode of acting, such as those with a strong psychopathic shadow. Fortunately, such people are in a minority. Most people who strive to follow the promptings of the inner center do so with a sense of responsibility and ethical commitment.

Like following one's impulses, opening up to visionary experiences has dangers. There is no question that visions can have deleterious effects, such as inflation, or that they can lead to misunderstanding and misinterpretation. As I have mentioned, the mystics were suspicious of visions and with good reason. However, the same cultivation of feeling that protects one from false impulses can protect one from the dangers of visions as well. Even the mystics, with all their suspicions, recognized the value and relative safety of the felt vision.

Every genuine vision is a felt vision. The feeling sense and the feeling interaction that accompany the vision are the guarantors of the reality and depth of the experience. For example, the mystics distinguish between hearing the voice of one's own imagination and hearing a genuine locution. As Underhill explains:

Genuine locutions may however be distinguished from those "words" which result merely from voluntary activity of the imagination as much by the sense of certitude, peace and interior joy which they produce, as by the fact that they force themselves upon the attention in spite of its resistance, and bring with them knowledge which was not previously within the field of consciousness. (Underhill 1990, 274)

Genuine locutions have feeling impact. While they most often convey a sense of certitude, peace, and joy, as Underhill notes, it is also true that auditory experience may bring one a feeling of discomfort, fear, or awe and still be genuine. The criterion is that the experience consists not of just words but of words accompanied by some feeling reaction. Most often the words spoken in a felt experience of this kind have a direct effect on the one hearing them. They may produce emotions or may actually create physical and psychological change. I was once very ill, suffering all the horrid effects of severe flu. At some point as I lay in bed, I felt my ally appear and heard it say, "Watch what I can do!" As I heard the words I also experienced a complete healing and was able to get up immediately without a trace of symptoms, then or later. The words of the ally actually had power connected to them, and the act of hearing them was transformative for me. Felt visions have power, and the power is experienced during the course of the experience itself. If I had imagined my ally saying to me that it would heal me and then I remained sick, the experience, while having its own reality, would not have been a felt vision.

The felt vision, then, contains power and has a transformative effect. There is a spontaneity and forcefulness that accompanies the locution and conveys the feeling that one is not "imagining" the words but actually hearing them. Finally, the experience often conveys something previously unknown to the individual and is not the mere repetition of something known.

This is true, of course, not only of locutions but also of all visionary experience. In some cases the felt vision consists of no images, no sensations or sensory input at all, but only of feeling. For example, one can feel the presence of some being or entity without seeing or talking with it. One has only the felt awareness. Much information can also be gained in this way. For example, the visionary may suddenly possess information previously unknown and not have any awareness of how that information was gained. One minute of such experience often contains enough information to think about for weeks.

In the typical felt vision, however, the experience consists of an encounter with another reality that is seen, heard, and felt. These types of experiences can range from the shamanic ecstatic movement into another world to the mystic's direct encounter with the divine. I would like to present an example from Jewish mysticism that illustrates a powerful felt vision. In this type of mysticism the practitioner engages in the combination of Hebrew letters, considered to be the sacred alphabet, in an attempt to form the names of God. If one is successful in this attempt, one not only sees the letters coming together in the mind's eye but also actually experiences the name of God so formed. Here is how one Jewish mystic describes his successful effort to combine letters into the highest name of God:

> I set out to take up the Great Name of God, consisting of seventy-two names, permuting and combining it. But when I had done this for a little while, behold, the letters took on in my eyes the shape of great mountains, strong trembling seized me and I could summon no strength, my hair stood on end, and it was as if I were not in this world. At once I fell down. . . . And behold, something resembling speech emerged from my heart and came to my lips and forced them to move. I thought—perhaps this was, God forbid, a spirit of madness that has entered into me? But behold, I saw it uttering wisdom. (Scholem 1974, 150–151)

One is seized by this type of felt vision, and all unfolds effortlessly and without conscious control. This is another hallmark of the felt vision, for in this kind of experience the conscious mind is not in control. Rather, the individual finds herself in the presence of a force that is powerful and autonomous. One can interact with this force, but one cannot control it. In one of my own experiences, which always seem to happen in the middle of the night when I would much prefer to be sleeping, I awoke to find my bedroom filled with golden stars. Fascinated, I watched them and noticed that they were beginning to pulsate. They all pulsated in a certain rhythm, and I found that somehow I was breathing in the exact same rhythm. Soon I felt that I and the stars were deeply connected. Suddenly, and quite spontaneously, a star entered into me. I cannot quite explain this, but I knew the star had entered and become one with me. In amazement I experienced one star after another enter and become one with me. Finally, though there were still stars in the room, I felt like a balloon about to pop and could absorb no more. I quietly entered an ecstatic state as the stars that remained disappeared. Like many of us gripped by the power of the unconscious, this mystic is first worried that he is possessed or insane. He is only reassured when he realizes that the words coming out of his mouth are wise and reflective of the mystery of the Great Name of God. In other words, the content of the experience itself and the way that it feels are the necessary reassurances that all is well. In recognizing the wisdom of the messages both in content and in feeling the mystic is bolstered in his belief that he is in touch with the true mystery of God's name.

This experience took me many years to comprehend. At the time I could not understand it at all, though I also could never for a minute doubt its reality. After the stars had entered my center, I was never the same again. My center was, in the space of an hour, transformed into something much greater and more powerful than I could have imagined. It was as if my own center had eaten these stars and become transformed in the process. Moreover, the stars themselves were transformed. They were now part of my center and different than they had been before the experience.

Quantum physics has established that the very act of observing energy particles has an effect on them. The observer cannot be separated any longer from the observed, for the simple act of perception is transformative. The same is even more true in felt visionary states. The visionary, by the act of perception, alters forever the entity, realm, or force that is perceived. My experience altered me, but it altered the stars as well. The felt vision is a shared and mutually transformative experience. In fact, a felt vision must be felt not only by the conscious perceiver but by the perceived as well. At the deepest level, while the visionary is having the experience, the seen is having it as well.

The mutual effect of the interaction between a conscious seer and the seen was noted by Jung in his study of the effect of attention. When the conscious mind pays attention to some content of the unconscious, such as an archetype, both are strongly effected. Jung describes this effect as follows:

> The attention given to the unconscious has the effect of incubation, a brooding over the slow fire needed in the initial stages of the work. . . . It is really as if attention warmed the unconscious and activated it, thereby breaking down the barriers that separate it from consciousness. (Jung 1970b, 152).

In short, the attention of the ego empowers the unconscious image attended to. For example, a perceived archetype has more energy and is able to be seen more clearly by the ego. In addition, it can influence consciousness more easily. If the ego follows up its initial attention with direct engagement with the archetype, the latter can be transformed. It can move from a negative position in the psyche to a more positive one and can be integrated into the psychic center far more easily. Or, if the ego attends to an ally, the relationship between the two can become deeper and deeper, and the ally itself seems to embark upon its own psychic transformation. All through this transformative process, the ally depends on the ego's attention and perception.

In this and in other ways, the act of perception impacts the entity that is so perceived. From the creation of a relationship to integration and to transformation, the felt vision produces effects that impact seer and seen equally.

In both the simple act of knowing what one is feeling and to the deepest visionary experience, the key is the capacity to access one's feeling. But what allows such visionary experience to occur at all? Modern psychology gives us very little help in understanding the deeper states of altered perception. To gain a theoretical construct capable of explaining such phenomena, we must turn once more to mysticism. This time it is the Sufi mystics that offer us the best explanation.

Ibn ꜸArabi, a Sufi mystic of the thirteenth century, was not only a highly developed mystic but a theoretician of the first order. His writings greatly impacted the whole development of Sufism and may contribute greatly to the modern search for understanding of the visionary experience. Among the many ideas Ibn ꜸArabi developed was a concept of imagination that provides us with the possibility of understanding the felt vision.

According to Ibn ꜸArabi, imagination is a type of perception that allows one to experience an intermediate reality, the imaginary realm, which is also the realm of spirits and divine manifestations. Moreover, he believed that the act of imaginative perception was also a creative act, much like the creative act of God. Henri Corbin, the leading expert on the thought of Ibn ꜸArabi, writes:

> The initial idea of Ibn Arabi's mystic theosophy . . . is that the Creation is essentially a theophany. As such, creation is an act of the divine imaginative power: this divine creative imagination is essentially a theophanic Imagination. The Active Imagination in the gnostic is likewise a theophanic Imagination; the beings it creates subsist with an independent existence *sui generis* in the intermediate world which pertains to this mode of existence. The God whom it "creates," far from being an unreal product of our fantasy, is also a theophany, for man's Active Imagination is merely the organ of the absolute theophanic Imagination. (Corbin 1969, 182–3)

This amazing quote needs a little explanation. God creates the universe through an "imaginative theophany." Incredibly, however, the gnostic, or mystic, also possesses the same power. Hence, whatever the gnostic imagines comes into being. The first task of the gnostic, according to Ibn ꜸArabi, is to imagine his personal god, with whom he can live a life of love and union. But the god that he imagines comes into being through the act of imagination! What gets imagined by the gnostic comes into existence in the world of imagination, which is a world more real than the outer world of daily life. In that world, the deity or spirit exists in its own right and with its own autonomy.

Of course, by imagining we must not suppose Ibn ꜸArabi means having a daydream or some such thing. He means, in fact, what I am calling the felt vision. The capacity to feel, or imagine, such visions belongs to almost everyone, but very few develop it to the depths that Ibn ꞋArabi did.

Through the felt vision, one can not only develop a relationship with God but also create an individual and unique God, which I have called the ally. Through additional such experiences a relationship and union with the ally can be developed. Through this incredibly powerful imaginative capacity one can experience healing, transformation and all manner of remarkable experiences. One can explore one's own unconscious world to gain self-knowledge, interact with the ally and so learn the mysteries of the infinite, work with the past and the future, and explore all the dimensions of imagined reality. It is a gift beyond measure but one that lies mostly unused in the human psyche. For those who risk its development, however; rewards are immense.

After all is said and done, the felt vision is about creation and transformation. The act of creation is not confined to the imaginative realm; rather, it affects ordinary reality in a variety of ways. For example, by tuning into one's feelings about people or events unfolding in the world, one gains insight and perspective about how one is in relationship to them. By being open to impulses and acting in harmony with them, one comes to live in the outer world in full union with one's inner center. Moreover, one is living creatively with few predetermined notions of behavior. Living with one's impulse guarantees an element of spontaneity to the day and shapes the flow of daily events in such a way as to guarantee that one's inner self is being expressed.

In the deeper visionary experiences one is actually creating the experience being perceived as one has it. And not only is the fleeting experience created; with effort a living ally or other entity can be created whose advice, relationship, and impact can shape one's inner and outer world and indeed one's own consciousness. The very nature of the world that one lives in is altered forever, as is one's own experience of self.

The hallmark of the felt vision is creation and transformation. Knowing this permits one to evaluate one's own experience as well as another's to determine if indeed it is a felt vision. Is the experience transformative? Has one changed as a result of it? No matter how small a felt vision may seem, if it is genuine, one has changed. The greater the experience, the more profound this change. As one gains experience, one can also ask whether the other has changed as well. Has my ally changed in some way? Is the archetypal figure I have encountered different? In the felt vision the seer is transformed while transforming the seen.

The felt vision is, then, a nonordinary mode of perception that sees, transforms, and creates all at once. The potential that this power of perception has not only for the transformation of the human psyche but for the divine realm as well is now clear. It is essential for the legitimate and healing use of this power that more study be done of the felt vision and of the realms that it opens to the human mind. At this time we are like children wandering in a new and unexplored forest with very few guideposts and signs along the way. To help us orient ourselves and continue our exploration, the study of the past with all of its wonderful traditions is invaluable. The study of the mystics opens up one such tradition, which has still a great deal to teach us. Combining modern experience with ancient thought, the Western world may yet come to understand the extraordinary wealth lying in the imaginary realms.

REFERENCES

Chen, Wing-Sit 1973. *A Source Book in Chinese Philosophy*. Princeton: Princeton University Press.

Corbin, H. 1969. *Creative Imagination in the Sufism of Ibn Arabi*. Princeton: Princeton University Press.

Jung, C. G. 1970a [1951]. The Self. In *Aion*. Bollingen Series XX: The Collected Works of C. G. Jung, vol. 9, part 2. Princeton: Princeton University Press.

———. 1970b [1955, 1956] The Personification of the Opposites.In *Mysterium Coniunctionis*. Bollingen Series XX: The Collected Works of C. G. Jung, vol. 14. Princeton: Princeton University Press.

Scholem, G. G. 1974. *Major Trends in Jewish Mysticism*. New York: Schocken.

Shah I. 1969. *Tales of the Dervishes*. New York: E. P. Dutton.

Underhill, E. 1990. *Mysticism*. New York: Image.

Chapter 9

The Clinical Use of Animals in Dreams

June Kounin

In this essay, June Kounin, a Santa Fe analyst, shows us how vividly real and powerful dream animals can be. They represent a part of the Self that is not human and not attuned to living in civilized ways. These imaginal animals can be very helpful and, on occasion, very dangerous. They must be treated, as she insists, with great reverence.

Nearly thirty-five years ago I was working with two women who did not know each other and who came to analysis on different days. One brought in a dream in which a seal appeared at a crucial point. The other woman brought in a dream involving the appearance of a walrus. Both animals were healthy. When asked for associations, both women said that the animals involved were endangered mammals, and lived primarily in Arctic seas, all of which is true. But why does a seal appear in one dream and a walrus in the other? I didn't know any more about each creature than my analysands did. I suggested that each woman find out about the particular animal in her dream by getting information through research and active imagination. I wanted to avoid intellectualization since I feel strongly that intellectualizing the "animal" in the concept "instinct" and making such an interpretation simply destroys the vitality and direct affective experience of instinct as archetype.

Factually, the seal woman found out that the seal has a short infancy of from fifteen days to two months (depending on species). The baby seal is fed a very rich milk in order to put on a thick layer of fat for protection against the abrupt departure of the mother, who has already mated again. The baby seal has usually not yet learned to swim or hunt before the mother leaves. A week or so later the baby seal will enter the water on its own. It must swim, evade predators, and learn to hunt without help from its parents. The baby seals generally stay with their peers from one to three years before they join an adult group. As adults, both male and female seals seem to be more aggressive with each other than other social sea mammals are. I was shocked by the short infancy period and the apparently scanty mothering for this species. By some unconscious standard, I had carried the asumption that all mammals in general were somehow "better parents" than other kinds of creatures.

The walrus has about a two year period of babyhood. It is born underwater and lifted to the surface by the mother so it can breathe and then be nursed by her. After the nursing period it is fed by the parents and other members of the pod. Shellfish, primarily clams, are scooped up from the sea bottom with the long curved tusks of the adult and macerated, and the bits of shell are blown out so that the remaining meat can be fed to the baby walrus. Before it is taught to swim and dive, the baby is carried on the flippers of the adults. Until the walrus becomes almost adult size and has grown serviceable tusks, it is protected by the entire group, which will place the young in the middle of the circle if danger threatens. If a baby walrus is taken by a hunter in the water, the adult walruses will charge the boat, often overturning it.

The woman who dreamed of a seal had an alcoholic mother who apparently gave very little consistent care to the infant daughter. She remembered that as a very young child she dragged a chair to the sink and climbed up on the chair to reach the counter, and from there she got dry cornflakes from the cupboard to eat. There was a sister three years older who helped this woman survive, but both children were on their own from early infancy. As an adult this woman had chosen to work with a variety of body therapies but had not gained very much psychological understanding. I suspect that her choice of therapies and her choice of career as a masseuse was based on the early absence of touch. She was married, had two sons, was a very good athlete, and came into analysis because she was angry and confused by her relationships with her family members.

The other woman was born to very wealthy parents who turned her over to nursemaids and nannyies, with the result that everything was done for, and to, the child. Until she was eight years old, she had not attempted to tie her own shoes. She had little contact with her own parents, usually being dressed to go see them for a short period in the early evening. Unlike many children raised by a series of employed caretakers, she had no recollection of being mistreated or seduced. As an adult, she had been married four times, had borne three children by different fathers, and had tried, more or less, to become a painter. The family money was still her main source of support. The relationship with her current husband was in serious difficulty, hence her coming into analysis.

Needless to say, the kinds of babyhoods described earlier are appropriate for walruses and seals but are not in the best interests of human babies. So both women had dreams of endangered species in the coldness of the Arctic seas. The reasons for both women being endangered as humans were quite different. One woman believed she could do nothing by herself and felt helpless and dependent, while the other woman felt she had to do everything by herself and expected to do so. Neither of these extremes makes for satisfactory human relationships. The effect these dreams had on both women was profound. That there was a source of wisdom, of knowledge, within their psyche that could choose the exact image that conveyed their condition with such parsimony was overwhelming. A recognition of this wisdom helped them to shift their narcissistic focus on the ego to confidence in the psyche as a whole. Why animals? Seals and walruses are instinctive mammals and do become competent members of their species. These women had access to the instinctive factors within them, although the work of becoming a "human animal" still had to be done. These animals appeared only once to each woman. They were not in the generally accepted categories of "animal animals," "medicine animals," or totem animals."

Another woman, a successful CPA, dreamed that she had vomited up a grayish, passive, thick, slimy snake, which lay supine in her lap. She was disgusted, revolted, and frightened and wanted to fling it away. She told me the dream and immediately asked me what the snake was. I told her that I didn't know. I asked if she could just hold it on her lap and see what it was. It evidently wanted to be seen, to become conscious. She objected violently, and a burst of affect followed: disgust and the desire to smash it. I listened and only commented that the snake didn't seem to be threatening her.

What emerged from her violence was a contempt for all the "juices" of life, the products of all the autonomic functions, such as sweat, blood, urine, feces, tears, semen, and saliva. At the end of the hour I asked if she could just keep the snake in a safe place at home and check every so often to see how it was doing. She told me later that this was the most difficult task she'd ever done. What emerged in the ensuing analysis was the analysand's experience of a cold mother who herself was disgusted with body products and with touching. As a child she was often told how her mother gagged over her daughter's diapers, her spitting up, and so on. The mother bragged about how she had controlled the baby's bowel movements by holding its feet up to its abdomen. As the baby strained to push her feet out, she would evacuate her bowels. Consequently there were no unplanned bowel movements, nor did the baby apparently experience any pleasurable sensations of having produced a product of her own.

Before seeing me, this woman had been studying with a fanatical Christian Science teacher (not one of the ordained practitioners of the established church). This teacher taught my analysand that she was supposed to transcend all her physical symptoms. However, my analysand had a strong solar aspect that could not countenance any earth, matter, or body aspect at all. This is a very serious problem not only because it results in one-sidedness but also because it results in a refusal to recognize the generative function of all those juices. This causes her to want to get in there and clean up all that mess, to make it antiseptic, and consequently to stop all further potential generation. It can also result in a variety of health problems, including spastic colon, bladder infections, painful menses, and sexual dysfunction. Despite her disgust and contempt for it, her body was demanding constant attention.

There are so many symbolic meanings to the snake that one could explore them for years without coming to any real comprehension of the image. In this instance I stayed strictly with her affect toward autonomic functions, toward her mother, and toward control and denial as psychological constructs. It seemed to me essential to keep the snake alive—not to interpret, not to conceptualize, not to abstract, not to amplify, and not to handle it. She did keep the symbolic snake in her house and could occasionally feed it, although she wanted to feed it vegetation rather than meat! She could not watch the snake eat live meat. The snake did gradually get healthier and regained its patterned coat and some activity. I would like to be able to say that she was eventually able to integrate her snake, but that was not so. It remained something she began to appreciate, but it always required her conscious attention, and she was not truly comfortable with it. Her physical symptoms gradually disappeared but would reappear if she did not think consciously of what she had to do. In most women with a healthy relationship with their bodies, the voice of the body uses the term "you". "You need rest." "You are hungry." "You can't eat that 'particular' item now." It doesn't use the pronoun "I," although that is what is spoken verbally and accepted as an ego function in this culture. My analysand remained, psychologically, at this point.

In the late sixties I worked with a man who was married and had two small children, was facing bankruptcy, had a bleeding ulcer, and sought therapy because he was unable to be faithful to his wife. He said he'd been with a lover the morning of the day he married, and that he became so anxious when having a sexual relationship with his wife only that he was compelled to seek another woman or he could not stay married. He claimed he loved his wife and children very much. After two months he brought in a dream involving the blackened struts of a building sticking up at all angles from stagnant water. On the struts were sitting cats, and all were alive but badly mangled. Some were disemboweled, while others had mouths and jaws mangled, and still others had limbs torn off. He did not seem distressed by this dream, but I was shocked. I had the sensation of going down in an elevator very fast: I was slightly dizzy and my stomach was churning. His associations were minimal. He didn't recognize the destroyed building, but sometimes he went for hikes in the country where there was brush and stagnant water. When I asked him about the cats, he said he'd never paid much attention to cats. He neither liked nor disliked them, and he had not had cats around while growing up. When I asked him about the devastation in the dream and if there were any events in his life he felt were devastating, he replied that the death of his father when my analysand was eight years old had been the most devastating event he could remember. The rage and grief had been suppressed through the years. He had attached himself to his mother to the extent that his relationship with his wife was essentially incestuous, hence the compulsive necessity for other sexual partners. From what he said, his mother had tried to get him to become more independent of her. He described her as a mature woman who ran her own business and had never remarried.

I was alarmed by this dream and told him that he must be very careful to pay attention to where he was and what he was doing and not to undertake impulsive actions. The "cats" in him could not land on their feet when falling or jumping from heights, and their proverbial nine lives were not functioning in him. Psychologically, he couldn't depend on autonomic or instinctual responses to get him out of trouble. A couple of weeks later he came in to tell me he had taken one of his impulsive wilderness excursions and had attempted to cross over fine shale, which began to slide. He fell on his back (which probably saved him) and slid to the bottom of a canyon. He was miles from his car but eventually got out and made it home. It was both disturbing and revealing to me that he was not particularly frightened, upset, or pleased by his narrow escape.

His work with me was terminated shortly after this incident due to circumstances beyond the control of either of us. I felt he was courting death and might indeed die without frequent and prolonged work, most probably with a male analyst. I don't know what happened to him, but he is included here to illustrate the extreme damage and failure of instinct that can occur. It does not seem to me that the damage to instinct is directly related to his incestuous relationship with his wife for the simple reason that sometimes animals do mate successfully with members of the family (sons with mothers, and daughters with fathers) in some species. This situation would not have caused the mangling, wounding, and inability of the cats to survive.

Another woman analysand was identified with a lion. She had even taken the nickname of Lyon. She was a tall, beautiful blonde, large and voluptuous, who often modeled for artists and was herself a painter. She brought in many dreams of lions, both male and female, along with imagery that was Egyptian in both content and as style; flat images appeared, although the people were moving and speaking. The lions in her dreams were healthy and generally did lion things, except for hunting. Her attitude toward lions was one of appreciating what she called the "noble beast." She discovered Shekmet, the Egyptian lioness-headed goddess, who later was absorbed into the Semitic concept of the Lion as the solar, male Lion of Judah. The goddess Shekmet is the female solar principle of both the killing aspect of the desert sun and its life-generating warmth; her healing aspect is Bastet the Cat. This woman's attitude toward lions was idealized and queenly but did not recognize the compulsive and destructive aspect, that of the hunter-killer; nor did she see the sun as unremitting, blazing, parching everything and drawing all moisture into itself. (As far as the goddess Shekmet is concerned, I believe that the Egyptians had the female in this position because they knew lions well. They knew the female lions are the hunters who work strategy, hunt together, nurse each other's young, and do not necessarily mate with the resident male lion. His life is generally a short one, because the alpha male is able to keep his position for only two to three years before some younger and stronger male takes the alpha position and the older lion is driven from the pack. It is my belief that the Semites changed the sex of this powerful deity because it simply gave too much power to the female principle.)

This woman was not animus-driven, but she was one-sided because she identified with the active principle of the female. She had a good mind, a talent for organization, and a talent for painting and sculpture. If working within a group, she often found herself in charge because she was intelligent, gifted, and capable in many areas. I want to emphasize that these positions of authority were not sought by her; rather, she would take a job to support her own artistic work and then get drafted to manage the enterprise. This was in fact one of the reasons she came into analysis.

The other reason she had for coming into analysis was her marriage. She was married to a gentle, tender man who was devoted to her and who, according to her, had treated her much better than had any other man she had known. She loved him but would often find herself in a rage against him. He was a tender lover to whom she responded with orgasm, but she would be swept with passionate sexual impulses that she found impossible to resist. She would literally "go on the prowl" and pick up a man for the night. She didn't want a relationship with any of these men, and there was no impulse toward kinky or sadomasochistic sex; all she wanted was a night of impersonal fucking. However, she found it difficult at times to just drop these men, who wanted to pursue her. Her husband was more like a gazelle, while the other men she slept with were predators, as was she. As a Catholic-reared girl, really loving her husband, she found these forays into lust and impersonality very troubling.

From a very early age she was the recipient of threats about the consequences of masturbation, predictions that she would become a whore, and so on. She responded to this by getting pregnant at sixteen, and she was sent away for the birth and was expected to give the baby up for adoption. Since she was from a "good" Catholic family, her guilt over this was profound, as it was over her own compulsive sexual activities. Before marrying she had chosen and been chosen by men who had similar strong sexual drives, so it was easy to hold them responsible for her own sexual requirements. She had been convinced that men used her without regard for her feelings and attitudes.

I found it difficult not to be entranced by the beauty, splendor, and innocence of the lioness in fusion with this troubled woman. I spoke to the woman, however, and seldom to the lioness in her. I made many amplifications and many interpretations of the connections between the numinosity of the lioness, its symbolic function, and her personal experience, conflicts, and history. I also emphasized that it was dangerous to have a lion in the streets unconfined, either literally or intrapsychically. I told her I was worried because she did not seem to realize that the lion is a predator on the savanna (which is its place in nature), while she was a woman living in urban conditions.

My own experiences are relevant to this analysand's case. Fifty years ago, when I was in analysis with Hilde Kirsch, a beautiful tiger appeared in my dreams. To this divine energy I had a similar powerful attachment. I dreamed I was lying in bed with the tiger lying next to me. It was so beautiful, and I was stroking the gold and ebony of its satin fur. I awoke and felt as if I could actually live with a tiger. When I told Hilde the dream, she warned that I was enchanted with its beauty and that I could not live that intimately with such a powerful, creative instinct. She said that I must find a way to give it form. At the time, I was married to a man who had a similar pattern of instinctual sexual energy, so my sexual instincts were well satisfied. He was not a gazelle, as was the husband of this woman. When my husband was drafted into the service during World War II, I had no way of dealing with my creative and sexual energy in his absence, so I entered analysis with Hilde.

I didn't understand Hilde at all. Why couldn't I live with the tiger? It wasn't hurting me, and I thought it was domesticated. After many more dreams of the tiger, one night I dreamed I was in a small forest hut and a ferocious tiger was leaping at the door, clawing to get in, growling and grunting. I was crouching in the corner of the hut, terrified, not certain the door would hold. I was convinced that if it got in, I would be devoured like so much meat. The affect of the dream was so great that there was no longer any doubt at all that I could not live with a wild tiger. I realized there was no such thing as a tame tiger. I had to learn the hard way about the power of such terrible beauty, to which the fragile ego is only too willing to surrender itself.

My analysand did believe me when I told her that an unconfined lion was dangerous, but the danger simply wasn't real to her. In one particular hour she told me she must find out about this side of the lioness soon. I had the sensation of being hit very hard in the stomach and not being able to get my breath. I believed that this side of the lioness meant death. I said this was dangerous and she must be very careful in asking for this without also specifying how she would find this out. She said she could think about this aspect but couldn't know it that way. I told her I would send my eagle to watch over her.

That evening she and her husband visited friends, taking their beloved small dog with them. The dog belonging to the friends was a large dog, but the two dogs had often played together with no problems. As the four people talked together, the large dog made a sudden leap, snapping the neck of the smaller dog and killing it instantly. There was no warning, and none of the people had time to move. The large dog nudged the small dog with its nose, looked up, and wagged its tail. Later my analysand told me that as the large dog leaped, she "saw" a huge eagle hovering; from its wings shot golden-tipped arrows in a circle around the lioness, making a cage. At that point my analysand turned her attention to her dead dog. Later, as she held her pet in her arms, she imagined herself going into the cage and cutting off the lioness's front paws.

Both of us were stunned by the suddenness with which her request for realizing the overwhelming impact of the destructive aspect of instinct had been granted. I don't know how to tell of the devastating grief and guilt she felt for having exposed her beloved and trusting dog. I was shocked and empathic but grateful that she had not been killed instead. Both the image of the lioness with its paws cut off and that of the eagle shooting golden arrows from its wings are from alchemical studies, although at the time neither of us was familiar with these images. In Jung's *Aurora Consurgens* the eagle is interpreted as successful "Sublimation" with the arrows as "Fixation." Jung has more than two columns of references to the lion, but they are references to the male Lion of Judah and not Shekmet; besides which, I could not find the reference to the cut-off paws.

Returning to my own case, I had given my tiger a very large stockade where it could prowl and hunt its food. The containment was so large it could live freely, but the tiger was protected and not at large on the city streets. The tiger is the energy that powers the tapestries I make; I make illustrations not of tigers but rather of what the tiger wants me to make, and because the tapestries are not ego-determined I do not sign them. I had not been called upon to injure my tiger, as my analysand had done with her lioness. This may be because the lion is a social creature while the tiger is solitary. My analysand was an extrovert, and I am an introvert of the first water. My psyche had provided the necessary experience of terror at the power of instinct in a dream, while my analysand had to face this reality in the external world. Either way, the necessary experience was provided.

It would be a nice, neat presentation to say that this woman stopped her episodic sexual excursions, but this was not so. She did become more selective in the men she chose and made it clear to each that this was not to be a permanent relationship. She became much more conscious of the role her parents had in setting her up as the sexually obsessed child. I don't believe she was any more sexually obsessed as a child than any other child. She was a golden child, as many of us have seen. This is a child who has the *élan vital,* who draws people to her by radiating an amazing magnetic quality. Such a child is "born with *mana,*" making it difficult for others to attend to anything but the child, even if it is asleep. This is more than the beauty that parents find in their own children. It is not a quality to be envied. It is a difficult fate. Much of what this woman carried could have been seen and interpreted and analyzed as animus, which would have been a fatal error. As a matter of fact, she needed animus energy to help structure, comprehend, and channel the instinct—not to kill it like the Mithraic bull, not to dishonor it, not to be possessed or compelled by it, but to live it as a difficult fate as well as is possible. When she began to understand that she actually did have this instinctual power and probably had it at birth, the actions of her parents became explicable—not wise or helpful, but explicable.

She became fascinated with Gnostic scriptures and used the imagery in her paintings for a while. Then she shifted to painting masked Mexican wrestlers on very large canvases, seven by ten feet, that were barely able to pass through a gallery door. These paintings were so powerful that they were uncomfortable to be with for very long. They radiated physical power at its peak, strained, pushing, struggling. The canvases were painted with such precision that the masked faces became like the masked gods of preliterate cultures, shocking the viewer into realizing that this is a power still present and not to be denied.

In conclusion, the first dreams of the seal and walrus had the effect of wakening both women to the existence of the objective psyche and also served a necessary curb to narcissism. The animals made only one appearance, but the message had been received. The man with the damaged cats was in a similar situation but, as far as I could tell, did not get the message. The woman with the lioness dreams was experienceing a totem animal in that it indicates the aesthetic of a culture. In her instance, it was Egyptian. My tiger has the same totemic quality. In my case, it is Chinese or Siberian.

These totem animals often appear in dreams or in literal experience. They are not medicine animals, as they do not have anything to do with healing, nor are they necessarily shamanic in character, although they may be. In my experience, they seem to be related to creating form in aesthetic productions, whether it be dance, music, the visual arts, writing, or another form. I feel they are too powerful to be used in therapeutic work because of their demand for the creation of form. The medicine animals have different qualitites and make their demands in the area of service. If there are strong medicine animals within the psyche and fate of a person, then that person must use the gifts given or they will become sick. A totem animal must aid in the creation of form, or the individual will become sick in some way. It is very dangerous, I feel, to use a totem animal in therapeutic work because the creative aspect will do its work on another human being. This would be a violation to the person who is seeking help in becoming herself.

In analysis the analyst's objective is to assist the client in developing an appropriate relationship between the ego and the Self. The ego becomes the necessary observer and servant of the Self in the present consensual reality of the culture, regardless of how illusory that consensus may be either spiritually or philosophically.

Chapter 10

Serpent Fire Arousal: Its Clinical Relevance

Louis Vuksinick

In this essay Lou Vuksinick explores the relationship between Kundalini energy, shamanism, and analytical psychology not only theoretically but in his own mental and bodily experiences. He does not just speculate about these experiences; he has personally felt them, and he has gradually learned to use them in his work with patients. He brings great insight to his analysis of the workings of these inner energies.

As Jung has stated, the wisdom of nature intervenes at times to bring about a needed balance in our lives.

In pursuit of a profession in psychiatry, I immersed myself in Western scientific thinking and became well versed in Freudian theory. I began Freudian analysis in 1966. At that time, I had no interest in Eastern religions or philosophies, despite the resurgence of interest in Eastern thinking during those volatile years. In 1968 I was involved in a serious automobile accident. Soon after, I had the first of what I now regard as a shamanic dismemberment dream:

> *I see two bands of Indians moving along the plains, one behind the other. Suddenly a rifle is accidentally discharged from the second band, killing a mother and child in the first group. I am then led to an opening in the ground. The passageway leading downward is covered with dismembered body parts. At the deepest level underground I enter a*

labyrinth and am taken to a chamber where a huge monster with blazing red eyes holds captives, many of them children.

After recovering from my accident, I began to have telepathic dreams about my analyst's personal life. These dreams seemed to unnerve him. Although he found rational ways to interpret them, I knew that something quite extraordinary was happening. I simply did not know what it was. In my fifth year of this four-times-a-week analysis, a major dream occurred on three consecutive nights.

I look up at the huge mountain that dominates the front view of my childhood home. A bright, mystical light is glowing about three quarters of the way up the center of the mountain. It marks the confluence of two great rivers, the Snake and the Siskiyou. Behind the confluence is a cave with a treasure. The scene then becomes a photograph with the date 1932 boldly displayed.

My Freudian analyst repeatedly interpreted this dream in a reductive manner.

On the fourth night, I dreamed that Carl Jung gave me a book on dreams. This marked the beginning of my study of Jungian thought, which led in turn to my Jungian analysis in 1970 and ultimately, to my understanding of this dream as foretelling my encounter with Kundalini. That understanding, however, did not occur until several years later, and the meaning of 1932 would not become clear to me for nearly a decade.

As I explored Jung further, I discovered the transpersonal aspects of the psyche and then watched my psychological life blossom and my neglected religious feelings surface and deepen.

Early on in my Jungian analysis, I embarked on a course in body awareness. I was engaged in deep somatic relaxation exercises and proceeded to have rather remarkable body sensations. My body would suddenly go into paroxysms of convulsive movement, first in the face, then in the feet, and then slowly coursing through my entire body. As each new area became involved, it felt extremely hot and painful. I would then experience a number of sensations: loud popping sounds in my head, particles and brightly colored lights dancing about in my visual field, and buzzing and high-pitched sounds rattling my eardrums. I was left with headaches that required my taking strong analgesics. The headaches went on for months, and at times I was fearful of losing my sanity because of them. Sharp pains would shoot along nerve pathways throughout my entire body, causing involuntary jerks and intense pain. My abdomen at one point became boiling hot, so much so that my partner could not sleep next to me. From time to time I would see a physician; despite the severity of my symptoms, medical examination revealed no illness.

This constellation of symptoms went on for a long time before I was able to exert some degree of mental control over them. Accompanying these somatic experiences were dreams fully identifiable as Tantric Kundalini images. Some eighteen years later, a Jungian consultant helped me see that my early dismemberment dream and automobile accident were typical of the shaman's initiatory process and, in fact, my whole Kundalini experience seemed to link to shamanism. Jung has equated kundalini experiences with his concept of the anima. When fully developed, the anima leads to the real-ization of the Self; Kundalini, he believes, represents the instinct of individ-uation. Jung stated that individuation will not begin to manifest itself, even in a minor way, until total purification of the subtle body chakras takes place and Kundalini pierces and activates the heart chakra.

In Buddhist tradition, the "subtle body" is portrayed as having seven cen-ters of energy. They are called chakras and are depicted as wheels that ascend up the middle of the body from the pelvis to the crown of the head. Kundalini, symbolized as a snake and representing female energy, is the force that, when awakened, activates these chakras from below, moving energy from one chakra to the next toward higher consciousness.

The following is illustrative of the dreams I was having during this phase of my shamanic journey:

A wicker basket is placed over my head and strongly shaken until I am quite dizzy and perhaps in another state of consciousness. I then am a priest with vestments on the upper part of my body but waistdeep in a pool of water, perhaps a baptismal font. Two fierce Chinese guards usher in a woman carrying a crescent-shaped jeweled dagger, which con-tains a piece of the moon, also crescent-shaped.

This dream took place during the time when I was experiencing severe headaches and fears about my mental stability. What I see in its symbols is an archetypal feminine energy penetrating my Christian spiritual con-sciousness and perhaps pointing to the integration of the body (the Christian shadow). This interpretation is also consistent with a later dream I had in 1976:

An Asian woman and I discuss the vulnerability of the snake to other animals during daytime hours. At night, the snake can freely roam in secret. The woman relates that she developed from a snake, and she points to a crab in a stream of water. It is without anten-nae, but they will soon develop, she maintains. She makes a connection to its develop-ment and to mine. In the stream I find an ancient Indian artifact in the shape of a femur. There are several tiny passageways connecting two bulbous ends. This artifact represents an image of my future development. I am told to keep this secret for a long time before I tell others of the process.

From this dream, I knew clearly that my experience of this feminine snake energy needed protection. I was encouraged that my development through the snake (Kundalini) and its connection to the ancient wisdom of India might help shape my future. The femur symbolized my chakra system from head to pelvis, and the tiny passageways connecting the two ends symbolized the channels in the spinal pathway through which Kundalini energy rises.

A final dream that occured during this early phase of body awareness work was equally rich in symbolic elements:

> *I go through a beautiful garden in the Sheraton Palace Hotel in order to get a ticket to see the statue of one of three black female Buddha figures in the world. In the lobby a statue containing only the image of the Buddha's head is seen, but behind a beaded screen one can find the way to the full statue. I am to pour Clorox on the floor—I believe as a purification rite—before I am allowed to see the sacred object. In the antechamber one is first to view a vast cache of precious gems. Finally I am allowed to see the awe-inspiring goddess statue. She sits proudly and beautifully on a golden pedestal whose two legs are snakes. There is a third snake image on the floor. Suddenly an electric charge animates the statue and the snakes. They come alive and begin to move gracefully until suddenly the black goddess transforms into a winged being. A transparent curtain is then pulled aside and a lovely woman disrobes as two men approach in preparation for ritual intercourse with her. One of the men wears a circle of white beads around his neck—like a rosary or a noose.*

I awakened from this dream with electrical energy coursing throughout my entire body. This dream speaks to me of the myth of the goddess Kundalini, who is described as a sleeping snake lying at the base of the spine with its mouth sealing off the central pathway up the spinal cord. When she is awakened, the pathway opens up and she starts her ascent through the chakras until, in the region of the head, she unites with her male god counterpart. This merger, when it occurs in an individual, is thought to bring about deep, intuitive insight.

This dream provided new insight into the meaning of the first dream. I felt I now had a system for understanding the somatic disturbances I had been experiencing. In prior dreams, I was trying to awaken a sleeping lady, but to no avail. This dream shows finally the awakening of this feminine energy. The original black goddess, when she becomes winged, demonstrates a movement of that energy from the purely instinctual to the spiritual realm. The image of her coupling with her male counterpart held the promise, for me, of a full unfolding of the Kundalini process.

The first four years of this journey continued to bring pain and chaos as far as the bodily disruptions were concerned. Gradually, however, I found myself entering periods of ecstatic bliss, states of mind I learned to control to some extent by consciously moving my energy and breath into each chakra. If I overdid these sessions, I would again experience depression and bodily pain. Over the last ten years, this energy has shifted from being harsh, erratic, and localized to being increasingly refined and intense; it now totally permeates my body.

About two years after this process began, while leading a group therapy session I began internally moving the energy in my body from one chakra to another. After the session, a young man from the group approached me. He looked quite pale. He described movements he was feeling in his body; they corresponded exactly to the pattern of energy movement I had been experimenting with during the session. How that exchange translated into clinical uses is elaborated below.

CLINICAL USES OF KUNDALINI

One of the first patients I worked with in this newfound mode was a man I will call John. John, nineteen years old at that time, came from a rigid family setting. During his adolescence he had taken LSD, which resulted in a bad trip that left him with gross visual distortions, severe headaches, feelings of depersonalization, hallucinations, time distortions, mental confusion, and panic attacks. Not surprisingly, he suffered from depression associated with fears of psychosis and brain damage.

We had been working in an analytic mode for several years, particularly on his serious negative-mother complex. Although we had some success, his physical symptoms persisted. During one session, John said he was experiencing "wonderful vibrations" in his heart that seemed to occur only when he was with me. This gave me the idea of working with his energy system. I had already formulated the theory that his LSD experience had disrupted his ego defenses, causing him to live closer to his unconscious and thus leaving him at the mercy of primitive energy that streamed into his head chakras.

I suggested that we could use my energy as a way to pull his energy from his head and ground it in his abdomen. He agreed, and we sat with eyes closed while I worked to pull my energy downward. Gradually he felt his energy descending. We continued this practice over a number of sessions. John became increasingly skillful at it until he was able to do it on his own without my intervention. The result was a dramatic reduction of his symptoms. Soon after he had gained this physiological control, he reported the following dream:

> I was searching for my sister in a large department store near the university. I saw her several stories below, near an escalator. I searched for her but in vain. I descended level

after level until I reached the basement. This area looked like a museum of anthropology or natural history. It was multileveled and three-dimensional—set up like a cyclorama. It evoked an aura of the antediluvian age. Figures were half animal and half human, and there were cavemen in different postures, all huge and beautiful. In the center of the exhibit was a rotunda beneath which was a collection of crystals and minerals. Emanating from the crystals was a warm, bright, rosy red-orange glow. ["A pleasing atmosphere, like your office, Doc," he said.] A cold blue-green glow emanated from the area where the primitive creatures predominated. Embedded in the exhibit were impressions of the Egyptian gods. The blue-green color seemed to extend up and back forever and it exerted a powerful force on me. I felt afraid and helpless. But when I moved toward the red-orange colors at the center, I felt warm and comfortable and experienced enjoyable heart vibrations. The center seemed to pull me away from the darkness and toward the light.

I saw this as a healing dream in which his search for his sister (anima) led him into the primitive depths of his psyche, where a struggle ensued between his falling into deep regression and his finding his center. In the months following, he succeeded in connecting with the central energy of the Self, which brought about the reversal of his major symptoms, both physiological and psychological.

I was interested that the colors of the lowest two chakras were red and orange, for these colors correspond in Eastern thinking to the *hara*, the energy center located one inch below the navel, just anterior to the vertebral column. Months later, John began to experience pleasurable vibrations in his gut and learned to differentiate what was healthy and what was toxic for him by paying attention to these gut feelings.

Another vignette from my clinical practice also illustrates the way my body sensitivity, wrought by Kundalini energy, has served me. I was in a session with a middle-aged man when I spilled a cup of hot coffee on my left foot. In that split second I realized that frequently, when I saw this man, I had pain in my left foot. Immediately I asked what had happened to his left foot. He revealed an incident he had kept secret from everyone. He had once put a gun to his head to kill himself and, at the last second, took the gun from his head and shot himself in the foot instead.

Since then, I have been able to hone in on some hidden aspects of patients, through either my dreams, my intuition, or my bodily sensations. These experiences are not always present but when they are, I know they are Kundalini experiences that are informing me. Nathan Schwartz-Salant (1986) and Donald Sandner (1986), both noted Jungian analysts, have written about such phenomena as aspects of somatic empathy. In his seminar on the psychological analysis of Nietzsche's *Zarathrustra,* Jung mentions this form of empathy as residing in the somatic unconscious (Jung 1934–39).

A final clinical example deals with an occurrence that more closely parallels a typical shamanic healing. My patient was a middle-aged academic who had spent many years living with a group of tribal people. Years prior to my seeing him, he had a breakdown living in that environment, and a relative living with him died traumatically. When the patient began analysis with me, his problems were rather mild—mainly centering around family relationship issues. At the same time, when we were in session and sometimes for minutes afterward, I would often feel intense anxiety, but to a degree I had never before experienced. Naturally, I asked my patient whether he experienced anxiety in our sessions or at any other times. He always seemed surprised at the question and disavowed having such feelings.

About sixteen months into the analysis, he did report intense anxiety; at the same time, all feelings of anxiety I had experienced in his presence disappeared simultaneously. At this juncture he reported the following dream:

> In a very primitive setting an extremely wild man was captured by two moderately wild men. He was held down and his left hip opened with a crude knife. Into the wound the blood of a wolf and wild boar was inserted.

As we proceeded to discuss this dream, again I was overtaken by intolerable anxiety. After the patient left the office, I began to eat my lunch, using my hands in a most primitive manner. My appetite the rest of the day seemed insatiable. A day or so later, my left hip and lower abdomen became more and more painful. A trip to the emergency room a week later revealed no evidence of infection or other pathology. Only then did it occur to me that these symptoms related to my patient's dream. For several weeks I continued to live with pain and apprehension. As for my patient, his anxiety vanished with the telling of the dream. Now, several years later, neither of us has been visited again by that primal fear.

Having felt the patient's deep, unconscious anxiety (energy) first in my body, then returning to his body, followed by its final somatic embodiment in mine, corresponds for me to the dream figure's primitive hip incision. This experience furthered my awareness of how powerful nonrational healing processes can be. That such a deep psychological illness on the part of the patient can be taken into the body of the analyst and then released struck me as what a shaman attempts to accomplish. I look back in wonder at this occurrence and once again conclude that Kundalini was and is working, totally unbidden, through me.

SHAMANIC DREAMS

As dramatic as my body experiences have been, my dreams have revealed more typical shamanic themes, and they have helped me connect

Kundalini development with shamanic healing. Three shamanic themes that have appeared clearly in my dreams are magical flight, cleaning and sacrificial images, and animal power. The following dream represents the magical flight that recurs as an integral part of all shamans' stories.

> *A former female patient tells me I have helped her greatly. I attempt to give the credit back to her but she insists we share it. Next I am on a flying mattress, feeling very insecure. I look behind to see I have a male companion flying with me. Suddenly I direct him to globules of light racing higher up in the sky from every direction toward a central point. They collide in a huge explosion of light and sound. Looking down, I see the whole of South America. Each country is illuminated from deep within with bright, neonlike light, and each has a distinctive color. I am in an ecstatic state.*

The woman in the dream speaks to my relationship with my anima. Having worked on her woundedness leaves us with mutual respect. It is from her activity that I have regained my body and my connection to nature, considered vital to shamanic experiences.

The next dream represents the theme of cleaning and sacrifice:

> *At first my alarm clock, then later my wristwatch, needs to be cleaned. The person who chooses to clean them is identified as a shaman. He is aware that putting them into a solution would cause an explosion and his death. He chooses to sacrifice himself. Following the explosion, a coral snake emerges and identifies herself as Kundalini.*

Many similar dreams involved such mythical figures as Osiris, Dionysus, Shiva, and Orpheus, all of whom experienced death and dismemberment as a prelude to bringing new life, hope, and sustenance to the world. Again, the concept that the old body must die in order that the radiant body can emerge is archetypal.

The third dream involves animals, which, along with plants and the elements, are regarded as the shaman's sources of power. The lower five chakras all carry animal symbolism, each indicating a different aspect of wisdom. Animal wisdom is seen as more valid than that of humans. Animals tend to stay true to their natures and are not thrown off by the intellect. The dream that follows has special meaning: it is filled with a wide variety of animals, most of which had appeared frequently in prior dreams.

> *I am holding a new baby. Suddenly I see a large number of animals moving toward some central destination. Horses, bears, deer, giraffes, goats, and elephants are all clearly identifiable among the huge group. Two powerful tigers (white, yellow, and black) come on the scene. I am fearful for the other animals, but they seem to be in harmony. A Chinese*

woman then appears and informs me that I must learn ten characters from her. Somehow this relates to the harmony of the animals.

From this dream, I interpret that the Chinese lady (Kundalini) has come to teach me and my baby (my new consciousness) something very important about harmony in nature. Her ten characters I know will be different from the ten commandments I have been taught. My current conscious hope is that I will learn her teachings quickly and be able to pass them on in some manner in my work.

CONCLUSION

Telling of this unexpected journey I embarked on some twenty-seven years ago, and sharing the ways I have since incorporated these Kundalini experiences into my clinical practice, have cleared up the final mystery I hinted at earlier: the appearance of the number 1932 in the second dream. This number perplexed me, and its meaning eluded me for years. The number predated the year of my birth and had no apparent connection to anyone or anything in my family history. The answer came unexpectedly in 1988.

I was in the process of compiling my first paper on Kundalini, and in my research I learned that a lecture on Kundalini was first given in Zurich at the C. G. Jung Institute in 1932 (Jung 1975–76). Jung offered a psychological commentary on philosophical material presented by J. W. Hauer. When I came across this piece of information, I was stunned. Joseph Henderson, a well-known Jungian authority, speculated that the lecture, revolutionary for Western culture at that time, had imprinted itself into the cultural collective unconscious. My dream, he suggested, tapped into it because it had relevance to my process of individuation.

This awareness has been extremely meaningful, sustaining me through difficult times and providing the courage to write publicly about my experiences. I now fully believe that these Kundalini eruptions, which seem to be on the rise in Western culture, are part of a universal evolutionary pattern. If Jung's theory that the wisdom of nature will intervene, when needed, to bring about balance, it may well be that feminine energy is coming to us at this time as an antidote for our extreme disregard of the environment and our increasing reliance on technology.

The wisdom the unconscious holds has long been of great interest to me, and the myriad ways in which it reveals itself continue to astonish me. It is my hope that this sharing of my process will encourage others to do the same so that the transformative power of Kundalini will be more easily recognized and valued. For me, the integration of my Kundalini experiences, the shaman's journey, and Jung's psychological insights have enriched my life and work immensely.

REFERENCES

Jung, C. G. 1934–39. The Psychological Analysis of Nietzsche's Zarathustra. Unpublished seminar notes.

————. 1975–76. Psychological Commentary on Kundalini Yoga. *Spring*.

Sandner, D. (1986). The Subjective Body in Clinical Practice. In Stein, M. and Schwartz-Salant, N., eds. *The Body in Analysis*. Wilmette, IL: Chiron Publications, 1–17.

Schwartz-Salant,N. 1986. On the Subtle Body Concept in Clinical Practice. In Stein, M. and Schwartz-Salant, N., eds. *The Body in Analysis*. Wilmette, IL: Chiron Publications, 19–58.

Chapter 11

The Ally

Jeffrey A. Raff

Jeffrey Raff, in this masterly paper, presents us with the full meaning and experience of the encounter with one's ally. At once teacher, guide, healer, and lover, the ally, he says, "enters the life of the modern individual with the promise of ecstasy, love, and knowledge and with the gift of the power of the imagination." Nowhere else in shamanic literature will you find the ally described in words so alive with gratitude and love.

In my junior year in college, when I was all of twenty years old, I was in the habit of taking a shower every night in a little shower cubicle in our dorm. One night as I was showering I found myself confronted with an experience unlike anything I had ever had before. I felt that the shower cubicle was filling up with the presence of a being whom I could not see but felt very distinctly. This being was outside my range of experience and seemed very alien to me. Instead of being frightened, however, I was filled with ecstasy and love and felt as if I was being seen and known for the first time in my life. So great was my ecstasy that I began to cry with joy. In a very incoherent and uncontrolled way I spoke to this being, and it spoke to me, though in a fashion I could not understand. Instead of speaking with words, we felt each other's thoughts and moods. In a flash I knew my life would never be the same, and I was glad.

This being visited me every night for six months and became part of my shower ritual. Once the initial shock of the repeated experience wore off, I grew curious as to what this being was and what my experience could possibly mean. I began to study books about all the major religious traditions, hoping to find an explanation of what I was encountering. I didn't know anyone I could trust with this, so I had to rely on books. In mysticism I thought I had found my answers at first, but it wasn't until the force of the experiences led me to enter Jungian analysis that I felt at last I was on the right track. My study of Jung and my own analysis led me to Zurich, where I soon discovered the writings of Carlos Castaneda and the wider literature of shamanism. Combining my inner work with my studies, I came to the realization that I had won an ally, who wished to bestow on me both knowledge and power.

Shamanism is perhaps the oldest spiritual tradition known to mankind. It incorporates within itself many elements that are still of great value today, and it can be studied with great success by anyone interested in the human psyche. There are many elements and clusters of ideas to be found under the name of shamanism, but perhaps the two most interesting are ecstatic travel and the ally.

Mircea Eliade, in his fascinating book *Shamanism: Archaic Techniques of Ecstasy* (1974) characterizes shamanism as the art of the ecstatic. Eliade, perhaps more than any other writer, is responsible for reintroducing shamanism and its symbolism to the modern world. While studying shamanism as it appears across many cultures, he was able to isolate and outline some of its major features. In the shamanic art of the ecstatic, the shaman enters an altered state of consciousness in which he is able to commune with spirits and travel to other worlds. Among the spirits that he is able to contact is the ally, or the familiar spirit.

The encounters between the shaman and the ally that Eliade reports are remarkably similar in many diverse cultures. Here are two meetings between shamans and allies from two cultures that clearly have much in common. The Priest is Grom, male Siberian (Goldi) shaman:

> Once I was asleep on my sick-bed, when a spirit approached me. It was a very beautiful woman. . . . She said: "I am the 'ayami' of your ancestors, the Shamans. I taught them shamaning. Now I am going to teach you. . . . You are to become a shaman."
>
> Next she said: "I love you . . . you will be my husband." . . . I felt dismayed and tried to resist. Then she said: "If you will not obey me . . . I shall kill you."
>
> She has been coming to me ever since, and I sleep with her as with my own wife. . . . Sometimes she comes as a winged tiger. I mount it and she takes me to show me different countries. (Eliade 1974, 72)

The second is from the Savara, an aboriginal tribe in India:

> The dream which forces a girl into her profession . . . takes the form of visits of a suitor from the Under World who proposes marriage. . . . In nearly every case, the girl at first refuses, for the profession of shamanin is both arduous and beset with dangers. The result is that she begins to be plagued with nightmares. . . . After the marriage, the shamanin's spirit-husband visits her regularly and lies with her till dawn. . . . The important thing is that the tutelary husband should inspire and instruct his young wife in her dreams, and when she goes to perform her sacred duties he sits by her and tells her what to do. (Eliade 1974, 423)

There are several important themes in these two quotations that relate to all ally experiences, ancient and modern. First is the theme of love and marriage: The ally comes not simply as a guide but as a lover. Second, the ally comes to impart wisdom and teaching. Third, the young man or woman chosen by the ally usually resists until threatened with death. Not every ally experience includes all three of these elements, but all will include at least one.

With the appearance of the ally, one has entered into a magical realm. It is a realm of healing and possession, of demons and helping spirits, but most of all it is a world of adventure and terror. The chosen individual resists out of fear, and the fear is very often justified. The crossing over into the world of spirits is a journey of great danger for even the most powerful of shamans; consequently it is not surprising that an apprentice would be terrified. On the other hand, the ally offers great magic and power. He is one of the principal means by which the shaman enters the ecstatic state that permits her to cross the boundary of normal reality and enter the psychoidal world of spirit. Moreover, the ally provides teachings that allow such adventures to be carried out successfully, and he provides protection from demonic forces that might attack the shaman. The ally is thus friend, lover, protector, husband or wife, and teacher. In addition, the ally can be the steed upon which the shaman mounts to fly into the over world.

Clearly, then, in shamanic cultures the ally was a valuable but dangerous acquisition. Though many in a tribe or clan could acquire a helping spirit, only the shaman procured an ally, and only the shaman was a master of the ecstatic. In the Middle Ages in Europe, as Western civilization began a series of momentous changes, shamanism was forced underground by the Catholic Church. It seems to be at least possible that witchcraft is an altered branch of shamanism. Though our records of witchcraft were created by its enemies in the Church, the similarities with shamanism are there to be found. The witch's familiar, for example, may be the ally, and some of the sexual contact between witch and familiar that so shocked the church fathers is reminiscent of the ally lover. The deadly hostility of the Church, however, guaranteed that any form of shamanism would either disappear or go into hiding.

Modern Western civilization had for centuries very little use for such "primitive" religions as shamanism, and had anyone been foolish enough to claim to have an ally or familiar, they would have met with skepticism at best. By the turn of the twentieth century, however, momentous rediscoveries were being made. Sigmund Freud opened the world of the dream for the modern psychologist and made the study of such inner experiences at least tolerable, if not respectable. To Freud is owed a great debt for his rediscovery of the power of the dream and of the inner world of the unconscious.

A contemporary of Freud was C. G. Jung. He also studied in depth the inner world of the unconscious. At first a disciple of Freud, Jung was driven by the force of his own creativity to break from Freud and establish his own psychological theories. Many of these theories are now well-known, and the impact of Jung's profound insights on religious and psychological thought is growing all the time. What is perhaps less well-known is how many of those insights Jung owes to a wisdom figure named Philemon. Soon after his break with Freud, Jung began an inner exploration using a technique he called active imagination. This procedure involves entering a state of consciousness that allows one to have a type of waking dream. During this waking dream one is able to engage with figures of the unconscious in a variety of ways: drawing, dancing, and dialogue. Jung dialogued with Philemon at great length about the nature of psychic life and the mysteries of the inner world. Philemon acted as an ally to Jung by being a teacher, just like the allies of the earlier shamans.

Jung describes his encounter with Philemon as follows:

> Philemon was a pagan and brought with him an Egypto-Hellenistic atmosphere with a Gnostic coloration. His figure first appeared to me in the following dream.
>
> There was a blue sky, like the sea, covered not by clouds but by flat brown clods of earth. It looked as if the clods were breaking apart and the blue water of the sea were becoming visible between them. But the water was the blue sky. Suddenly there appeared from the right a winged being sailing across the sky. I saw that it was an old man with the horns of a bull. He held a bunch of four keys, one of which he clutched as if he were about to open a lock. He had the wings of the kingfisher with its characteristic colors. (Jung 1963, 183)

Though Philemon appeared to Jung first in a dream, much as did the ally of the young woman from the Savara tribe in Inddia mentioned above,

Jung was soon holding long dialogues with him. Philemon, Jung says, became "a mysterious figure to me. At times he seemed to me quite real, as if he were a living personality. I went walking up and down the garden with him, and to me he was what the Indians call a guru" (Jung 1963, 183).

The ally appears quite clearly as a teacher, but the dream tells us even more about it. A dream such as this one could be interpreted in many different ways, but I would like to point out the characteristics of the ally as it appears in this and many other shamanic dreams. In the first place, like the winged tiger mentioned earlier, this ally has wings and can fly. Wings generally symbolize the spirit realm and the ability to fly in a natural way and points to a connection to the spirit. There are also obvious comparisons between the winged ally and the angels of Judaism, Islam, and Christianity. Ally images in visions and dreams are very often animals, sometimes mythological animals. Philemon has the horns of a bull, indicating a connection to this powerful, masculine animal. He holds the keys, meaning he is the key to wisdom and power. As his horns relate him to the bull, the wings relate him to the kingfisher. So Philemon is a spiritual being capable of flight and is the embodiment of power (the bull) and wisdom (the keys). All of these attributes belong to allies in general. They are spirits capable of bestowing power and wisdom on those they visit.

Finally, Jung comments that Philemon "represented a force which was not myself. . . . It was he who taught me psychic objectivity, the reality of the psyche" (Jung 1963, 183). It is this insight that is crucial to understanding the ally and the ally experience. The ally is a force other than the human personality and is autonomous and objective. It has a reality all its own, with a particular consciousness and personality. Rather than being some disembodied fantasy, it is a living reality by which one can be touched. Allies are not simply seen but are felt in the deepest part of the soul. As I discovered in the shower, such deep and intimate communication occurs with the ally that it is impossible to deny the reality of the encounter.

One characteristic feature lacking in Jung's description of his ally experience is ecstasy. Jung does not tell us of the feelings created by his contact with Philemon, only the thoughts. Consequently it is impossible to know how much of the ecstatic entered his experience. However, Jung did experience ecstatic states later in his life following a near fatal heart-attack. He experienced then the "ecstasy of a non-temporal state." (1963, 294) Jung's writings are often so intellectual and theoretical that it is important to remember that, like the shamans before, he spent many hours in the ecstatic and in a "state of purest bliss" (Jung 1963, 294).

With the writings of Jung the modern world was reintroduced to the wonders of the inner world of allies and dreams. For many years, though, Jung's writings were known to only a relatively few. But within a decade of

Jung's death there appeared a poet gifted with the talent for bringing the worlds of the non-ordinary to life in a vivid and tremendously exciting way. That poet is Carlos Castaneda, whose works electrified me and many others in the early 1970s and popularized the notion of the ally and shamanism. Castaneda reached an audience far greater than anyone writing on such topics had reached previously. I have studied these books and taught classes on them, and I have come to the conclusion that they cannot be taken as objectively real or as works of non-fiction. But neither do they seem totally fictional to me. The closest analogy I can make for them is that they are poetry that gives voice to the needs, desires, fears, and hopes of an entire generation of seekers. Castaneda has many faults and distortions in his writings, but, unlike any other writer I have ever encountered, he brings the worlds of magic to life and gives the reader the feeling not only that magical events are possible but that the reader himself might come to experience them.

As I mentioned earlier, I first learned of the word *ally* in the books of Castaneda. When I was a student in Zurich, I, my friends, and my analyst would all wait excitedly for the next book about Don Juan to emerge. We would devour it in short order and then discuss its images and techniques at great length. Of all the ideas presented in these works, the one I could most easily identify with was the ally. Here at last, I felt, was a description of a magical entity like the one I was encountering. I will always be in debt to Castaneda for providing me with imagery and framework for first coming to grips with the experience that has most defined my life.

Having said that, I must also say that much of Castaneda's work seems forced and far-fetched and some of it seems distorted by Castaneda's own psychology. Moreover, there are such discrepancies in the descriptions and explanations of the ally from the first book to the last that it becomes impossible to reconcile them. I will confine myself to mentioning some of the encounters with allies Castaneda sketches in his earlier books.

In Castaneda's first book, Don Juan tries to explain to Carlos the nature of power. He talks about a variety of power objects a sorcerer might use:

"There are limitations on those types of powers," he went on, "but such a point is, I am sure, incomprehensible to you. It has taken me nearly a lifetime to understand that, by itself, an ally can reveal all the secrets of these lesser powers, rendering them rather childish. (Castaneda 1968, 22)

Later on, Don Juan explains:

An "ally," he said, is a power a man can bring into his life to help him, advise him, and give him the strength necessary to perform acts, whether big or small, right or wrong. This ally is necessary to enhance a man's life, guide his acts, and further his knowledge. . . . An ally will make you see and understand things about which no human being could possibly enlighten you. (Castaneda 1968, 52–53)

According to Don Juan, the ally is a bestower of power and knowledge. Having an ally enables a person to accomplish tasks that would be impossible without an ally. In addition, the ally bestows knowledge unobtainable in any other way and serves as a guide for its human partner. Power, guidance, and knowledge are the gifts an ally bestows upon the human with whom it has united.

In Don Juan's teachings, the ally must be won by the fearless courage of a warrior:

When a man is facing the ally, the giver of secrets, he has to muster up all his courage and grab it before it grabs him, or chase it before it chases him. The chase must be relentless and then comes the struggle. The man must wrestle the spirit to the ground and keep it there until it gives him power. (Castaneda 1991, 234)

Finally, Don Juan explains that the appearance an ally assumes depends on the individual to whom it comes:

"All in all then, we can say that for you the ally is a moth. But I cannot say that it is really a moth, the way we know moths. Calling the ally a moth is again only a way of talking, a way of making that immensity out there understandable."

"Is the ally a moth for you too?" I asked.

"No. The way one understands the ally is a personal matter," he said (Castaneda 1974, 89).

According to Don Juan, the ally is a spirit that must be wrestled with and forced to yield its power and knowledge to the sorcerer. This spirit will enable the sorcerer to perform great tasks and acquire knowledge beyond the normal human ken, and will appear to each individual in a unique way. It is quite obvious by now that having an ally is a tremendous boon to an individual, and even though the acquisition of an ally can be dangerous and taxing, the benefits outweigh the risks. So far, however, it is unclear what the ally gains by its encounter with a human. In some of his later books, Castaneda hints that the ally is hungry for human awareness, but his presentation of this idea is inadequate and hard to separate from his later notion that allies are not worth having. As I mentioned earlier, some of Castaneda's writings about the ally are inconsistent and confusing. To clarify the question of the ally's motives, we must look elsewhere.

Fortunately, William Reed, in a rare psychological study of the ally, has tackled this problem. He reviews in his article the nature of the ally in shamanism and reaches the conclusion, as we have already, that the ally is power and the bestower of power on the shaman. He writes that "whatever its counterpart in our own conceptions of the psyche, the helping spirit has a psychoid character and needs the ego's cooperation in its destiny" (Reed 1978, 44).

Further, he argues, "initiatory upheaval is neither a response to mal-adaptation nor to a stage of life; instead it represents a particular spirit's need for actualization through a human partner" (Reed 1978, 47). In this work Reed adds a valuable dimension to our understanding of the ally-human relationship. The ally is in fact as desirous of establishing such a relationship as the human partner, perhaps even more so. The ally is a spir-it that wishes transformation and requires human consciousness to effect this transformation. In exchange for this transformation, it is willing to give love, knowledge, power, and guidance to its partner. As a psychoidal entity capable of its own individuation, the ally enters the human world to expe-rience love and transformation.

How in fact can the ally be understood? To call it a psychoidal being or a spirit is fine, but what exactly do these terms mean? The theories of Jung provide information that may help us answer these questions. In the first place, the nature of the psychoid must be examined. Aniela Jaffe, Jung's longtime secretary, collaborator, and friend, has written a great deal on the concept of the psychoid. According to Jaffe, Jung was much influenced by the writings of early alchemists, who speculated that the psychoid realm was a place of subtle bodies, whose nature included the physical as well as the psychic. Moreover, the alchemists, like the Sufis of the same period, believed that imagination allowed one to experience this world of subtle bodies. As Jaffe writes:

> Astonishingly enough, the alchemist conceived his *imaginationes* as something quasi-corporeal, a sort of "subtle body" that was half spiritual. They were, therefore, of a psychoid nature, forming an intermediate realm belonging to both matter and spirit. On account of the mysterious and manifold implica-tions of the *imaginatio*, Jung called it "perhaps the most important key to an understanding of the *opus*." (Jaffe 1984, 72)

In other words, the psychoid realm is a world beyond the ordinary physical world and yet is also other than the inner psychic realm. It is a world that seems to be intermediate between the inner and the outer worlds, a place where imagination reigns. It is crucial to understand that imagination, as meant by both the alchemists and Jung, does not refer to daydreaming or fantasy but to the perception of this intermediate realm. Imagination is the means by which one experiences the psychoid world.

The ally as a psychoidal entity lives in the world of imagination. It is neither physical nor spiritual, but rather a subtle being with its own consciousness and will. The ally can be experienced only through imagination, such as in the dialogue that Jung carried with Philemon. In the same way, the other experiences described earlier in this essay are all imaginal experiences in which the shaman was able to contact the universe of subtle bodies. However, once more Jung neglects the ecstatic part of the ally experience. It is necessary to modify our formulation by stating that the ally experience is an ecstatic imaginal encounter with an entity from the intermediate world of the psychoid.

The ally, then, has its own reality and its own existence. It is not dependent on the human mind for its life or creation. However, the human capacity to imagine, understood as a nonordinary mode of perception, allows the ally to enter the realm of human life, where it may experience its own transformation. Moreover, the power, wisdom, and guidance of the ally allow the human partner to explore the imaginal realm in ways he could never do on his own. The vast, perhaps infinite, scope of imaginal life provides a richness and sense of adventure to life that is astounding.

I have studied the psychoid world for almost as long as I have had an ally, which is to say thirty years. In addition, I have analyzed dozens of people who were engaged in psychoidal and ally experiences, and I have taught many workshops on ally meditation. It is clear to me that the experience of the ally is as relevant today as it was at any other time in history. Yet the experience of the ally seems also to be evolving in some ways. People who encounter the ally in the modern world bring to the experience a different set of expectations and a different consciousness than earlier shamans would have. The ally seems to be less often seen today as the bestower of healing power and more as a divine partner on the road to transformation and individuation. As Donald Sandner, a Jungian analyst and an expert on Navajo shamanism, has written, the nature of healing has changed as the patient has taken more and more active responsibility for her own healing processes than in the past (Sandner 1979).

Yet for the modern individual as for the shaman, the ally brings ecstasy, love, and an exquisite sense of fulfillment, as a few examples might show. Many years ago, while lying awake in bed, I found myself transported to a mountaintop. This mountain was in the psychoidal realm, and I was totally aware of being on the mountain while at the same time I was lying in bed. The mountain was so steep that my normal fear of heights reasserted itself, and I clung in terror to the ground. Suddenly I became aware of a figure in a robe and hood walking toward me. He said, "Why are you afraid? I am here on this mountain as I am everywhere with you. Stand up." I did so, and this being who was my ally touched me in the chest, at which point I was transported into a state of wild ecstasy and bliss. I found myself at home in bed and remained in ecstasy throughout the night.

My "imaginary" experience was more profoundly real than any other experience I had ever had, in any world. Imagination of this kind is quite simply another reality, where the most marvelous and transformative events can occur. Clients have reported similar experiences with their allies. Some have reported waking up in the middle of the night to find the ally present. In one such case the individual hid under the covers for as long as possible, but when he finally emerged the ally taught him secrets of nature and of life he never forgot. In another case, the client reported repeated experiences as a child of what she thought was an angel. She felt warmth and love and total acceptance from this "angel" until she told a priest of her experience. Sternly scolded, she did not see her "angel" for many years. It came to her later in her life and taught her that it was her ally. They have not been separated since.

Some clients have reported traveling back in time in their imagination and totally participating in another historical period. Others were lifted physically into the air by their allies, while still others told of being healed instantly by their allies. Such experiences clearly teach us that the ally experience, while occurring in the imaginal, can have a profound impact on the physical realm as well as the psychic realms.

The ally does not just transport one to the imaginal realm. It also acts as a companion and guide in our everyday life. One client, faced with a serious and life-threatening disease, was ill for more than ten years. She reported that at the onset of her illness she was made aware of the presence of an imaginal being, who filled her with love and reassurance. It did not heal her, but it comforted her every day and acted as a companion through the pain of the treatment she had to undergo. Upon making a full recovery, the client discovered that the ally had gone. Years later, after much work on herself, she was delighted when the ally finally returned. Another client fell asleep at the wheel of her car and was awakened by her ally yelling at her just in time to avoid going over a cliff. A man thinking of getting a divorce was urged by his ally to hang tough in his marriage, which was transformed in a few years to a deep and meaningful relationship. Spirit or not, the ally has great wisdom about the most ordinary and mundane events and is a guide and advisor in all the worlds.

The experiences of the ally discussed in this article are very real. Though they may appear strange and uncanny even to the sympathetic, such experiences occur with greater and greater frequency as the modern individual opens doors long shut. These doors lead to realms of imagination where the ally is supreme. Perhaps it is time for those of us who engage in the work of healing souls to put aside our concern with reason and appearance and admit that the human soul has the capacity to experience infinite worlds of wonder. Moreover, it is time to acknowledge the existence of beings of a non-physical nature, who occupy some of those wondrous worlds. The ally enters the life of the modern individual with the promise of ecstasy, love, and knowledge and with the gift of the power of imagination, whereby the human being can transcend the ordinary and embrace the miraculous. At the same time, the human being offers the ally the chance to be known and loved and the opportunity to transform. When human and ally wed, the ordinary and the miraculous are discovered to be two sides of the same coin. Imagination, which opens the door to the psychoid and allows the union with the ally, can also transform the so-called ordinary world into the place of magic that it should be.

REFERENCES

Castaneda, C. 1968. *The Teachings of Don Juan: A Yaqui Way of Knowledge.* Middlesex: Penguin.

———. 1974. *Tales of Power.* New York: Simon and Schuster.

———. 1991. *A Separate Reality.* New York: Washington Square Press.

Eliade, M. 1974 [1951]. *Shamanism: Archaic Techniques of Ecstasy.* Princeton: Princeton University Press.

Jaffe, A. 1984 [1971]. *Jung's Last Years and Other Essays.* Dallas: Spring Publications.

Jung, C. G. 1963. *Memories, Dreams, and Reflections.* New York: Vintage.

Reed, W. 1978. Shamanistic Principles of Initiation and Power. in *The Shaman from Elko.* San Francisco: C. G. Jung Institute.

Sandner, D. 1979. *Navajo Symbols of Healing.* New York: Harcourt, Brace and Jovanovich.

Part III

DARK ENCOUNTERS:
PERSONAL TRANSFORMATIONS

Chapter 12

Pain and Surgery: The Shamanic Experience

Arthur D. Colman

In this paper, Arthur Colman brings us a chilling view into the world of pain, surgery, and healing. Through various means of active imagination—and finally its apotheosis in a full-scale shamanic journey that was all too close to physical death on the surgical table instead of ego death in the psyche—Arthur brought the healing power of shamanism into the antiseptic rooms of a modern hospital.

For seven years of my adult life, I lived with continuous and severe back pain. The trouble first began in adolescence. I had bouts of pain that incapacitated me for three to six months at a time, but the big pain came without warning one morning when I was forty-six. I got out of bed, and as I stood I felt a jolt of searing fire down my right back and leg. The agony crescendoed until the pain filled me so completely that I fell to the floor unconscious. I vaguely remember the ambulance, a Demerol shot, a painful hospital stay, and a very slow return to chronic pain and limited function. Seven years in the world of pain—acute pain powerful enough to jolt me from ordinary consciousness, chronic pain powerful enough to change my "ordinary" work and social realities—initiated me into the study of shamanism, both experientially and as a healing art.

Shamanism and pain are intimately related. Shamanism, alone of the healing traditions, overtly depends on both the healer and healed achieving an altered state of consciousness for the healing process to occur. Pain is the key that unlocks the door to these states of consciousness and the "other world." While the body and mind's ultimate defense against pain is total loss of consciousness, pain gradually teaches all its sufferers to stay conscious and enter other states of consciousness—other worlds—where pain can be dealt with differently. Shamans and shamanic initiations take advantage of this and deliberately use a variety of painful conditions—extreme cold and heat; sensory, food, and water deprivation; prolonged immobility; burning, piercing, and cutting of the flesh—to learn how to make their other-world journeys for the purpose of healing themselves and others.

Even though initiates present themselves in many different ways, pain is at the center of all shamanic initiations. So it is that shaman acolytes are placed in ultimate survival situations: huddling in a tiny igloo with only a threadbare blanket and little food on the frozen Siberian tundra for six months; hanging from a tree by two hooks anchored in their chest in the middle of the Dakota plains at a ritual Sun Dance; covered with bloody wounds from scarification, piercing, and tattoos in an Indonesian jungle. The initiatory circumstances vary from culture to culture and tradition to tradition, but using the context of pain to learn the way of crossing into the other world is fairly constant. Not everybody successfully emerges from the initiation experience. Some initiates are permanently maimed, while others return broken, humiliated, or just a bit wiser about their need to find another path in their lives. Furthermore, as Montero and I discuss in another essay in this volume ("Beyond Tourism: Travel with Shamanic Intent"), the human sacrifice implicit in these ordeals may actually have a healing purpose, unrelated to the individual's fate, for the larger community. But those who successfully survive the experience return as shamans fully *authorized* by their community to begin their healing work. Whatever their initial motivation—personal test, penitence, or duty—these initiatory experiences are so transcendent that those who pass through them have crossed into the collective realm of wounded healers.

This authorization by a community of a specified training and initiation is a critical matter in our own culture, in which shamanic techniques are often used but rarely sanctioned. All communities need to trust their healers. In today's western societies, we initiate and authorize our healers by sending our brightest college graduates to a training school that teaches them the science of medicine and sanctions their placing their hands on and in the body in the most intimate of ways. Our culture trusts information, technology, and pragmatic experience and therefore sees these schools, and the abstract and practical work that they entail, as a proper training for and initiation into the healing profession. And yet this kind of medicine, anchored as it is in science, technology, and the pragmatic, does not altogether fulfill the spiritual and healing requirements of the ill and suffering among us. For almost all of us who have pain and illness, the medical center is only one of the stops in the healing odyssey. The physician who takes a medical history of a suffering patient is only sometimes told about the many other healers that are visited: the acupuncturists, massage therapists, psychotherapists, chiropractors, psychics, herbalists, and "urban shamans" on whom we spend vast amounts of money and time—almost as much as on traditional doctors and hospitals. In the present context of care, finding a perspective that integrates these two separated healing realms is left to the individual.

My own experience with severe chronic pain eventually led me to many kinds of healers, in both traditional and nontraditional realms. Along the way I experienced many techniques that purported to deal with pain and suffering, as well as many techniques for entering that other world. Some of what I learned was useful and helped me through my hardest times (and also helped some of my patients). Some were not helpful. But beyond efficacy, each new drug, herb, and meditation, each body massage and exercise and manipulation, brought hope and dashed hope. Each disturbed a hard-won acceptance of the status quo. And so, after seven years of initiation into the world of pain, I gradually learned what every pain patient must learn— to live in the tension of opposites between hope and acceptance. I emerged wiser (though far less happy). I was also essentially unrelieved of continuous incapacitating pain and, more ominously, of the likelihood of permanent nerve damage and muscle weakness as the condition continued.

Back surgery had always been a possibility, but because of the nature and placement of my particular anatomical lesion, it held a high risk of complications and a poor probability of success. However, as the pain increased to new and more debilitating levels and the weakness in my leg became increasingly disabling, I decided on yet another consultation with a surgeon, my third. This one was an eminent and skilled neurosurgeon who was also my colleague at the medical center. On a continuum of hope and acceptance, surgeons usually stand for that ultimate hope, the hope of cure. In many ways surgeons are the modern physician most closely related to the shamanic tradition. Like shamans, surgeons do not overly honor passivity or the Tao. They are magicians, not gurus. Like shamans, the extremity of their training and initiation supports a belief in the transformative potential of their own grand and decisive action. Like shaman's too, the surgeon's healing method is a mysterious journey into an other world, a world—where hands and knives are placed *inside* another's body, beneath skin and membranes; a world where the living unconscious body is transformed for the purpose of healing; a difficult yet ecstatic world which they must leave to return to this world and bring back information and healing images and report these to the patient and his community.

The shaman-surgeon I consulted was considered very handy with the scalpel and had a reputation of being eager to use it. After reviewing my records and examining me, he was silent. Then he turned his gray eyes directly on me and held me in his gaze. "Arthur," he said, "the level of pain, spine and disk pathology, and nerve damage is great. But surgery is very risky. There is a reasonable possibility of impaired bowel, bladder, and sexual function, and the possibility of recurrent pain, even if the operation is anatomically successful. Frankly, I would not do it if I were you. I don't think I can help you except to seriously suggest that you addict yourself to narcotics. That may sound severe, but I do not believe you can continue to suffer as you have and remain functional much longer."

When I now tell friends about this last comment, they usually shudder and question this man's ethics and humanity. They are wrong. Like all healers of the shamanic sort, he cut ruthlessly to the core by speaking the truth. His invitation to "addict" myself to narcotics was devastating to me not because of ethics or coarseness but because he was correctly mirroring the magnitude of the pain and the devastation it had already exacted on my life. Narcotic addiction was indeed the sensible option, yet I also remembered with horror the time I had used codeine for several weeks to diminish the pain. I had been lying on my back on the floor in the living room, stoned, a pillow under my knees. My daughter, who was beginning college and leaving home for the first time, had come to say good-bye. She had been in tears, but I had felt nothing. That experience upset me so much that I stopped the codeine that day and turned to strong rock music—a less potent and less dehumanizing soporific. Despite its risks, surgery was a better alternative than the nonrelational haze of the poppy.

So against his advice, I sought and found a surgeon, Michael, who felt he could help me and whose skills I trusted. The operation he suggested was relatively new: my back would be approached through my abdomen. Two surgeons would be required for this paradoxical strategy: a vascular surgeon to peel back the huge vital vessels—the inferior vena cava and the abdominal aorta—that lie anterior to the spine, and an orthopedic surgeon to remove the disk(s), scrape the nerves if needed, and transplant a small piece of bone from the femur of a dead man into the vacant space opened. Shamanic indeed. What he was describing was dismemberment on a scale that would make even a Siberian shaman proud. Of course, Michael did not define his work in this way. Perhaps if I had questioned him in depth he might have described trance induction as he dressed and scrubbed, and an altered reality as he put scalpel to flesh.

Michael outlined the same risks as the previous surgeon but also emphasized the significant possibility of a successful outcome. As I listened to his proposal and weighed it against the last seven years, a future of painkillers, and nontraditional and managed-care remedies, I felt a strong sense of rightness about trying the extreme solution. With that feeling came a surge of adrenaline along with the image of embarking on a great and dangerous adventure, a breakout from the siege I had been under for so long. The adventure required using this surgeon's skill and tradition, but if I was going to be successful I was sure it would also need a larger perspective, and that, for me, could only be the shamanic one. This would be the big journey, the culmination of all my prior journeys and work, for it would incorporate mind-altering drugs, out-of-body consciousness, altered realities, dismemberment, retrieval of body parts from another world, and a new body—literally somebody else's bone inside of mine—and all this would take place in a strange archetypal realm of death and rebirth. My seven-year initiation into the shamanic perspective was to become absolute reality.

It will be obvious to the reader that from the moment the first surgeon presented his alternatives—and particularly in my response to Michael's proposal, I had already crossed into an altered state. From a clinical perspective, the rush of adrenaline and the vainglorious conceptualization of surgery as some great shamanic journey was filled with denial and inflation. Understandably so, for the first surgeon had presented a paradoxical alternative that had brought me to the threshold of an entirely nonrational course of action, while Michael had described an utterly unreal scenario, a world of miracles and a world of horror that had propelled me directly into that other world. I had to be in an other world to go ahead with a journey of such risk, and so I found a frame that made that other world meaningful, a very large spiritual perspective that fit my experience. In Jungian terms, I wanted to find a way to work at the level of the second stage of the *coniunctio*, the conjoining of the *unio mentalis* (the unity of spirit and soul) with the body (Jung 1963). In my case, I wanted to conjoin the great Western tradition of surgery with the ancient tradition of shamanic healing. In concert with the surgeon and all the other medical personnel who would be involved in my repair, I needed to authorize myself as the shaman healer. Inflated or inspired, all of it felt critical to my survival and potential healing.

Writing now, it is easy to recapture the moment of decision, that exalted sense of crossing into the other world in which ordinary reality dims and becomes background for the gathering of the spirits and archetypes, that ecstatic realm where survival is the issue and all thought and action is entrained to its purpose. I was leaving my long incubation in a sacred space of pain; I was entering a most dangerous transitional world in which, by joining forces with Michael the archangel with burning sword in hand, I would become my own shaman enacting a long and difficult journey into the land of death, rebirth, and recovery.

I had two months to prepare and one procedure to undergo before the actual surgery. In that procedure, called a discogram, a long needle was placed directly into the diseased disk and a dye injected to increase the pressure and reproduce the *in vivo* conditions in which the pain occurred. If the pain was not reproducible, the surgery had less chance of succeeding. Of course, no anesthesia could be used, since I had to be able to feel the pain. I can only describe what happened as akin to medieval torture. I lay almost naked on a cold slab of steel. A nurse stood by with a fixed smile on her lips. The radiologist inserted his long needle deep into my innards and injected the burning dye into the place of pain. Each bit of injected fluid increased the pressure, and pain surged through me until I raised a finger signaling I could no longer bear it. Then he would reposition the needle and begin again. It took every meditative technique I had ever used not to physically move, which I was assured would create further damage, or to disassociate, which would have decreased the information available to my surgeon. At one point the nurse held out her hand and gripped mine and that moment was sweeter than morphine. Later, when I asked the nurse what had motivated her to do that, she said that it had been suggested in her procedure manual as a help in such procedures. (That day I blessed manuals for the first time in my life.) While I lay recuperating on the day ward, my woman friend braved hospital convention by creeping into my narrow bed and holding me. This was another huge balm, this one even better for its enactment from a personally compassionate and loving frame. Both actions got me through a procedure deemed successful for the pain it produced and the kind of back lesion visualized with the spreading dye. The synergistic balance between inner control and interpersonal connections was very important throughout the process. Human connection and love is part of any healing endeavor. But love comforted me best, in concert with an intense, isolating inner work that reduced all human connection. This paradox is well known to shamans; I think it is part of the sacrifice that healers and those who will be healed must accept.

With the surgery rapidly approaching I took several hours most evenings to meditate, drum, and in general allow visionary material to emerge as it would. What I did was not substantively different from what I had done in meditation previously except that now I had a different, very specific intent: that of facilitating the surgical healing. No shaman lacks this intent in a journey; intent, I believe, is what separates this tradition from other kinds of altered consciousness. I conjured up my intent whenever I went into a trance, focusing sometimes on the surgical procedure, sometimes on the tangibles and intangibles of healing. Occasionally I actively imagined the surgery, even anxiously "forcing" a successful completion and outcome. I found such visualizations extremely seductive, in the way that magic is seductive, but also far less meaningful than allowing mental space for the unimagined and unanticipated. In this latter mode, one image kept emerging quite spontaneously, first in just a flicker of feeling and then over the next few weeks in a series of images of ever increasing clarity and detail. What I saw was Michael and I dancing in the ecstatic Hasidic manner in front of the Wailing Wall in Jerusalem. (In the Hasidic dance tradition two men often dance together sometimes holding hands, sometimes holding a handkerchief between their hands.) In our dance our hands were outstretched toward each other, and we were holding something strange and sinister between our fingers as we dipped and whirled together. Night after night I saw this dance and never could quite get what it was we were holding. And then three nights before the surgery I saw that it was the gelatinous, amorphous sticky, blotchy, diseased disk that had been removed from my back. And with that realization came another image: Our dance had become a surgical ballet, a joyous operation in which both of us first placed a glistening white bone deep in my back and then threw back our heads and danced in utter abandon.

Hasidism was not unfamiliar to me. When I was a little boy I would spend every other Friday night at the house of my great-uncle, Rabbi Jacob Minkin, in what I thought was a traditional Friday evening Sabbath dinner. I say "thought" because I had no way of knowing that it was unusual for a rabbi to get up suddenly from the table in the middle of dinner and dance, slowly at first and then faster and faster, while singing and chanting in an unfamiliar language. Minkin had introduced Hasidism into America in a book called *The Romance of Hasidism* (1935). He apparently had his own version of this discipline—an ecstatic Hasidism that made traditional Jewish worship feel dry and stodgy to me, then and now. I remember watching him dancing, singing, and praying on those magical nights, seeing the light around him shimmer and glow like emanations from a burning candle. Later, as a young man, I spent two years in Jerusalem searching for more experiential communion with his mysterious practices, finding something like them for myself in the weekly celebrations at the Wailing Wall on Friday night. At that time I thought hard about staying in the sacred bubble of Jerusalem but eventually decided to leave with the hope of bringing something of Jerusalem into myself rather than relying on its awesome vicarious power. Jerusalem—not just the real and sacred city but also Jerusalem as metaphor for the Self—remains a central image in my spiritual life. So when these presurgical visions occurred at the holiest place in my sacred city, I knew that I was in very special hands. I took the dance image with me into surgery, a moving mandala that permeated and colored and largely contained the preoperative world.

When I came to the hospital the morning of the operation, I felt part of two worlds: the steel-and-glass world of the surgical suite, and the other world of this and other visions. I held the latter world myself; there was no one among the medical personnel whom I could trust to understand it; there was certainly no way to ask for one who might. I stayed in the dance at the Wailing Wall as the anesthetist asked me to count backward from ten slowly.

I woke up in both worlds. There was a total euphoric thought that whirled in my brain, something like, "My God, I did it. I really did it. I've had back surgery. It's happened." The feeling was exuberance, amazement, and exultation. I knew that I was drugged and that the morphine must be part of the euphoria, but that knowledge was irrelevant. From the moment I awoke I was aware of an absence; something was missing that had been part of me for seven years. The pain was gone; the pain that I had thought would be my fate as long as I lived was totally gone. In amazement and joy I moved slightly, and a different kind of pain, unbelievable in its own right, flooded in. This was the surgical pain, the pain of the body that has been disrupted on the most fundamental level: organ bruises, spinal dismemberment, bone transplantation, cutting, sutures, catheters, stomach tubes. That pain also contained a closeness to death and the possibility of a new life after a very long journey up from the lowest reaches of vulnerability to healing and health.

With that pain and vulnerability also came a light, an emanation that entered through the other world, a door of perception very different from my thought of the operation and its effects. The light was not the blinding brilliance described in spiritual epiphanies or near-death experiences. It was very small but very bright, and it seemed to dance just in front of my chest, defining a path that I could and should move along. This light was a strong positive force, and the light was also me, the vitality of me, as I existed in that other world. Lying euphoric in the recovery room, I watched that light intently even as part of my mind was taking in the fact that I was alive and there was no more back pain, just the pain of surgery and healing. During the next several months, but especially in the first few postsurgical weeks, I learned to work with this light, and that work was synonymous with healing. Pragmatically, the light was my guide through the agonies of the postsurgical period; in spiritual terms, it was the closest experience I have yet known of a very personal life force, a kernel of energy that was neither Self nor self but a connecting link between the two.

The work I did with that light was the hardest physical and spiritual work that I had ever attempted. This was particularly true as my ego emerged from the shock, pain, and haze of postoperative drugs. Ego consciousness was antithetical to this healing work. My connection to the light needed to be absolute and there were many ego parts of me that would have none of it. Whenever ego consciousness dominated, the light flickered and dimmed, the healing stopped, and my tolerance for the formidable post-operative pain decreased. At these times the long effort to recover function seemed overwhelming. But as long as that light danced and made its path mine, I knew there was no danger of dying, no danger of not recovering. When the light dimmed, though, I knew failure and even death were too close. I knew with certainty at these moments that this was the light that would go out when death called my name.

I can best describe the process of this work with the light by analogizing it to extreme forms of mind-body meditations and other profound and difficult body-mind adventures in which everything depends on the discipline of letting go and the sense of a journey. As every shaman must know, one of the critical aspects of these journeys is the creation of a supportive and sacred ambiance that contains the journeyer. Fasting, drumming, smudging, community praying, the creation of altars, and cleansing rituals are all needed to protect the journeyer from the considerable dangers of the other world as the healing mission is pursued. Unfortunately, the hospital room and the medical environment and personnel afforded little protection for my spirit, for medical personnel are almost exclusively concerned with the body. Friends and family were of some use in this, but I felt the lack of a sympathetic hospital "spirit" very keenly. It would have made my own work much easier, because creating and protecting my own sacred environment was often antithetical to my extreme dependence and vulnerability as well as to the state of consciousness I needed to hold.

There were far too many disruptions from inertia-driven hospital routines. When meaningless activities were forced on me, my concentration lapsed, the pain would increase and the light would flicker and dim, and I had to work even harder to refine a deep connection to my light-guide and return to the healing task. Drugs were another potentially powerful intrusion. I had a self-administered morphine drip at my side. When I let my ego take over, no matter how slightly, the level of pain increased; I could decrease it by pressing the plunger. But then the light became distorted and hazy, and I had to wait for the drug to wear off until I could get back to the business of healing.

But it was not only the hospital activities that were difficult and disruptive. Almost anything that was unrelated to non-ego-intentional state was intrusive. Even the beautiful view of the hills of Sausalito from my window, ordinarily one of my greatest delights, was an intrusion. People who visited me oohed and aahed about what I could see from my bed, but I was in a different dimension of experience, connected to a vision whose meaning transcended any outside beauty. Even the most powerful force in my room besides the light—the love of the people around me—could deter my concentration. Time and time again I learned from the way that the light flickered, the way the pain increased, and the way healing seemed to ebb that I had to withdraw from family or friends and their loving world in order to stay self-aligned.

Sometimes the disruptions were unexpected and functioned as both a trial and a seduction. During my third postoperative night I was awakened by a nurse who told me that there was a psychiatric emergency going on. She explained that a postoperative patient who had undergone throat surgery was psychotic and pulling at his stitches. She said he had bipolar disorder and had been taken off lithium for his surgery, and she asked if I could advise them. The surgical resident on duty knew nothing of psychiatric drugs and the psychiatric consultant was nowhere to be found. "I hear that you're a famous psychiatrist," the nurse added, "and I read your book on pregnancy when I had my first child." And, she whispered confidentially, "I know that you're the shrink for one of the heads of department here." My ego rose like a phallus. "I" wanted to help and "I" knew how. The light flickered and bounced. I disregarded it and began to get a history, then caught myself as the light dimmed further and the pain increased. This wasn't my job; the light was. I stopped talking and closed my eyes, watching the flickering change to a steady glow. With relief I heard the nurse sigh and leave the room.

I count the discovery of this light of mine as one of the best, if eccentric, outcomes of my surgery. It stayed in the foreground all the while I was in the hospital and only gradually receded over the next six months. It is a variant of the light that is described in so many spiritual experiences. It is certainly similar to the kind of guiding light described in many shamanic initiations and healings. For those familiar with the literature of shamanism, a light such as I experienced is sometimes described as a companion or helper similar to more-usual helpers such as animals, gods, or humans. Perhaps the actual body dismemberment was so great that something as primal as light emerged and was never embodied in any other way. I'm sure that for some people this power comes as a tone and that for others it is a particular kind of body feeling or more formed image, such as a totem animal. Having the light so central and so important for so long was and is a great gift. I believe it to be an embodiment of my vital energy focused as a healing force, the vital energy that must be harnessed for any kind of healing to occur. It is not surprising that the oldest healing tradition, shamanism, operating without today's technical miracles (of which I was a major recipient), would seek out this force in other-world journeys; it is sad that modern surgery, with so much of the miraculous at its disposal, would ignore it.

I have taken many other spiritual journeys, some consciously invoking hardship and pain, some also adding powerful drugs such as Ipegan and psychedelics; most important, of course, was the journey of seven years of pain and its effects on my body and soul. But the trial of surgery and my recuperation and healing brought me to a different dimension of difficulty and, ultimately, meaning. I wonder whether others who experience surgery feel it as a remarkable journey into body and psyche? Can it ever be just something to get through? I imagine it is possible to dull the whole experience with drugs, television, and all the rest of the secular environment that a hospital provides. I imagine, too, that many more would engage with the profound crossing that is an element in such a potent dismemberment, or death-rebirth experience if instead of an aseptic and mechanistic setting and perspective, there was a context for another kind of experience. The surgical environment could do much more to help provide this context for those who want it, and maybe it will as patients demand more from medicine. After all, only thirty years ago birth in the hospital was partly a surgical procedure that excluded husband, family, and spiritual and initiatory context. Birthing centers and other humanized in-hospital environments are now the rule, and they work because women and their families want the larger purview and alternatives of experience they offer (Colman and Colman 1991). It would have taken very little to alter my pre- and postsurgical environment, and I would have changed hospitals—but not surgeons—to be in one.

There is a great deal more that could be said about the many connections between the surgery experience and the shaman's healing journey, but I want to end by briefly describing one eccentric and unexpected connection. I said earlier that when Michael described the surgery I was struck by a sense of a great adventure about to happen. The journey I have described above felt like pure adventure in the very highest sense of the term, despite a context in which the surgeon was the hero and the patient was the victim. Just before surgery Don Sandner, one of the editors of this volume, gave me a book to read that he thought would be interesting for my recuperation. The book was Gary Jenning's's *Raptor* (1990), which describes the journey of survival and self discovery of a foundling left at a monastery in Italy in the sixth century. His travels took him through the declining Roman Empire of southern and eastern Europe. The physical aspects of his journey were extreme enough for me to feel a bond between his adventure and my own recovery from the pain and surgery. But the most intriguing part of the journey was the hero's coming to terms with being a true hermaphrodite, for he was born with both a penis and a vagina, both pleasurably functional, and felt a matching male and female soul within. When I read at all postoperatively, I found myself turning again and again to this book; in fact, it was the only external stimulus besides carefully selected music that didn't destroy the kind of ego concentration that was so necessary to my recovery.

I began to understand my fascination with *Raptor* when, on the fourth day after the surgery, Michael entered my room, took off my bandages, and inspected the gaping abdominal wound that lay below. I felt like a woman lying undressed on an examination table, my vagina open and exposed. What I experienced was not so much sexual as organic, as if my body had added a new sexual organ and my psyche had formed a corresponding structure deep within me that matched. The physical reality of my surgery was that I *had* added a new inner pathway and a new structure. The incision had begun deep in my lower abdomen, almost at my pubic bone, and the cut had gone straight through to my spine. Michael had used that channel to insert his instruments and leave a piece of bone and several steel screws deep between my lumbar vertebrae. Lying in the bed as he inspected that wound, I could feel his penetration from front to back. The feelings I experienced as he inspected the wound, the new channel, were the sensitive stirrings of newborn flesh. Undoubtedly my transference to the healing surgeon was part of this response, but what I felt and still feel evolving in me went beyond that psychological reaction. It was if I had gained a new sex and a new sexual identity, and that too was a necessary part of my healing.

I now understand why so many shamanic journeys include sex change and why so many experienced shamans refuse to be coerced into the dress or role of either a male or a female. To heal at the deepest level is to accept dismemberment and ego dissolution. The change in the ego is the last and most dangerous part of the transformation, just as the last two hours of a psychedelic drug trip are the most dangerous and most important, the time when the archetypal wonders no longer hold sway and change must be incorporated into the very small consciousness of personal identity or split off as some strange presence in the psyche. As Freud correctly pointed out, the earliest and strongest part of ego identity is sexual identity, so that too has to become fluid and change for the ego feeling to change.

For healing to occur, a sacrifice is required. The sacrifice of a persistent and accepted sexual reality may be the strongest offering possible. As I lay in my bed feeling that strange new twinning—the aching new channel and its connection to my catheterized penis—I glimpsed an incipient, perverse, but potentially viable wholeness that might just make the light spinning in front of my chest glow a little more brightly in the future.

REFERENCES

Colman, L., and A. Colman, 1991. *Pregnancy: The Psychological Experience.* New York.
Jennings, G. R. 1990. *Raptor.* New York: Bantam.

Jung, C. G. 1970 [1955,1956]. The Conjunction. In *Mysterium Coniunctionis.* Bollingen Series XX: The Collected Works of C. G. Jung, vol. 14. Princeton: Princeton University Press.

Minkin, J. 1935. *The Romance of Hasidism.* New York: Macmillan.

Chapter 13

Cancer, New Age Guilt, and the Dark Feminine

Dyane Neilson Sherwood

Dyane Sherwood begins with the moment of her terrible realization that she has breast cancer and takes us step by step through suffering that rivals Job's. When the ego is faced with a power greater than its own, one that threatens pain and death, it is at first drastically wounded. But by stubbornly searching for a healing vision and a true meaning for such an experience, a meaning beyond too facile psychological explanations and too sweet spiritual truisms, Dyane gives us a deeper insight into the transpersonal psyche and the way it works.

I had been walking in the heat for hours, walking on the dry earth, past piñon and cactus, when I saw a grove of cottonwoods and felt the presence of an underground spring. I stretched out on my back in the shade. Against a background of deep silence I could hear the distinct staccato buzzing of a fly near my face and the harmonies of the round yellow bees drinking nectar from the cactus blossoms. After some time I became aware of the guttural sound of a man's voice accompanying his drumming as he danced. He was twenty or thirty feet away, in his own private world, unaware of me. I rested on the earth, savoring my solitude in the presence of the drummer. An intense knot of agitation in my chest became distinct within the calm of my body, like the sounds of the insects in the larger stillness. I tried to make it go away or to detach from it, but the agitation in my chest did not move or change in any way. When I finally ceased making any effort, five or six Native American women appeared and sat down around me. I didn't want them near me. I really just wanted to be alone with my pain, resting my body on the earth and lis-

tening to the man dancing and singing. But they had come, so calm and without words. I felt each woman put her right hand on my chest. Despite their benevolent intentions, I could not let them in, could not let their healing energy flow into my body. I struggled, wanting the healing and yet unable to open the barrier over my heart. The women remained calm and present. They knew what they were about. Each kept her right hand on my chest, and their outstretched arms formed the spokes of a wheel. A very old, deeply wrinkled woman said, "This is the Wheel of the Sun."

I BECOME A CANCER PATIENT

Within two weeks after I attended the drumming ceremony at which I had this vision, my doctor found a very tiny lump in my breast. She told me that its characteristics were not consistent with a malignancy. Unworried, I took my time getting a mammogram, and then I was told that I should have a biopsy even though the lump was probably a cyst or a benign tumor. I remained unconcerned up to the very moment the surgeon drew her scalpel through the soft skin of my breast into the flesh below. I saw her drop two pieces of tissue, pink flesh filled with tiny fat globules, into a saline-filled jar, ready for the pathology lab. A surge of anxiety filled my body and then settled in: What about the chance that the lump was not benign? I counted the days until I would know for certain, one way or the other.

On Wednesday morning, five long days after the biopsy, the surgeon called and asked me to come to her office to discuss the results. I knew immediately that there must be bad news, but what?

I had waited only a few moments in the consultation room when the surgeon, Dr. Mahoney, came in and sat down. She is a somewhat stocky woman with simply cut reddish brown hair. Her presence feels rooted to the ground like a large oak, and yet she likes tiny, flowered prints and dainty things. Her mother sews soft cotton gowns for her patients to wear in place of the typical throwaway paper gowns. That day her blue eyes looked tired and kind. She spoke to me thoughtfully, in a low, almost hoarse voice. She was unhurried, as if she had all the time in the world to spend with me. She was gentle without being overly sympathetic. She told me that I had breast cancer. She then outlined the alternatives for treatment: a modified radical mastectomy, or a lumpectomy followed by radiation treatment. In either case, the lymph nodes under my arm would have to be removed in order to determine whether the cancer had spread into the lymph and beyond my breast. If it had, then another course of treatment, including chemotherapy, would be indicated. She recommended that I see an oncologist and get a second opinion. As she talked, she wrote down what she was saying, in a neat and organized fashion, on a sheet of white quadrille paper. I was grateful: the paper, with its intersecting lines and hundreds of tiny, containing spaces, was a comfort when finding out that my cells were out of control, uncontained, genetically derailed in an aberration of nature.

I began to weep as I walked from Dr. Mahoney's office near Stanford University Hospital to my own office in Palo Alto. I passed a shopping center, a consumer paradise, where people stroll among trees and flowers as they purchase tastefully displayed supplies and especially luxuries for a continuing life. It looked like an apparition to me. I felt apart, as if I were walking through a parallel universe. Was my life nearly complete? Knowing that I had cancer, I felt so exposed and vulnerable, and I hoped no one would notice the tears on my cheeks. Cars whizzed by. I waited at a crosswalk while an exquisitely dressed woman in a sparkling BMW sedan, the color of pink champagne, turned into the Neiman Marcus parking lot. Two out-of-kilter men, scruffily dressed, their eyes darting in every direction, drove by in a rickety truck. I somehow kept walking, finally reaching the busy four-lane road bordered by stately palms that connects Stanford to Palo Alto. I felt as though I were walking a gauntlet.

I gathered myself together when I arrived in downtown Palo Alto by focusing on the comfort of telephoning my husband, Jacques. In the sanctuary of my office, I pushed the buttons of the telephone. As soon as I heard Jacques' voice, I knew I was not alone. Even on the telephone, I could feel him close to me as we shared the shock. Amazingly, I worked the rest of the afternoon, aware of a calmness deep within myself, not knowing whether or for how long I would be able to continue to be a therapist. I believe I worked well: there is nothing like living with death to place you in intimate association with the archetypes.

I had cancer. I tried to absorb the reality of it. I wondered what it meant—not symbolically at that point, but concretely. Was I going to die from the cancer? Was I going to die after submitting to debilitating medical treatments? Would I spend what was left of my life in doctors' offices and hospitals, weak and bald from chemotherapy, depleted from radiation, my body being attacked by medications and consumed by the cancerous cells it was growing? I felt too vulnerable even to consider what it might mean at some deeper level, why cells in my right breast had gone out of control, whether it might be some signal from within my body that my soul or my life was seriously out of order.

For the next few weeks I woke up in the night to find my face wet with tears: I even cried in my sleep. I wanted to experience my illness fully. I did not want to deny or avoid anything, whether concrete or symbolic. Jacques and I began telling our friends and family. I had, without realizing it, expected them to back away, to recoil from the cancer. But they didn't. No one tried to cheer us up. They shared our sadness and shock. I accepted their offers of help gratefully, and our tiny cabin was quickly filled with beautiful flowers and our freezer with homemade meals.

At a concrete level, I wanted to know what the cancer looked like and how it behaved. Dr. Stebbins, an oncologist recommended by Dr. Mahoney, generously met with us on a Saturday morning for more than two hours. He copied sections of recent medical textbooks and up-to-date research articles for us. He even arranged for me to examine the slides of my breast tissue, which were at the Pathology Department at Stanford University Hospital. He explained that I had a rare form of cancer, called tubular, because the cells tend to form tubes as they grow. It is the type of cancer cell that is closest in form to normal cells, and it is only rarely fatal. I had a visual image of the tumor and an intellectual understanding of the prognosis. The unknown was a little bit smaller, and I felt some relief.

For a second opinion, Jacques and I drove some distance to a highly recommended breast cancer specialist located in Marin County. She was seductively attired in a low-cut blouse with intriguing gold necklaces that drew attention to her breasts. Her jacket was somewhat conservative but her short skirt had slits up the sides, revealing nearly all of her legs. She had asked me to remove my clothes prior to the interview, and the three of us met in her cold examining room for an hour while I shivered in a paper jacket. She nearly forgot to examine me, but then she unapologetically prodded and squeezed my breasts, compressing the tissue between her fingers so painfully that I was in tears. Had she forgotten that I was not under general anesthesia? Yet I didn't complain because I wondered if her exam would turn up an additional finding. Her recommendation was the same as the others: a lumpectomy to be followed by radiation therapy. I wouldn't know whether the cancer had spread until the surgery was over, after the lymph nodes were studied.

PREPARING FOR MUTILATION

During the weeks prior to surgery, I tried to prepare myself for the loss of my right breast, or at least my breast as I had known it. A large portion of my breast would be removed, including the cancerous tumor and a margin of healthy tissue around the cancer. Later I would be tattooed to aid in the alignment of the radiation machines. Radiation treatments would permanently change the texture of the remaining tissue: it would be firmer and grainier, and the skin would be darkened into a permanent tan. I tried to picture what my mutilated breast would look like: a darkened, scarred part-breast hanging higher than the other one. My tears poured out in waves, flowing silently down my cheeks.

I was grateful that I could feel my grief. This kept me calm at a deeper level. When I felt really brave, I'd go a step further, from picturing what my breast would look like to imagining what it would feel like as a part of me. Images of my adolescence surfaced. I recalled the humiliation of being a flat-chested, skinny kid at fourteen, one of only two girls in my eighth-grade phys ed class who didn't wear a bra. I remembered my distress and a new form of humiliation, when my breasts grew so rapidly within one year that there were always boys staring at them. I had hunched my shoulders in an attempt to hide the heavy masses of my newly formed breasts, which bounced around when I walked unless contained by tortuous wire-frame brassieres. I had been shy and terribly self-conscious, and the stares and remarks from boys were agonizing.

In my adulthood, my breasts became smaller, and I felt they suited me. I really liked them. Now this harmony between my inner image of myself and my physical body was about to be wounded, and I felt I had no choice but to submit to disfigurement.

For a long while I avoided imagining the loss of sensuality in my breast. What would a caress feel like through a firmer, grainier part-breast? Would there be nerve damage? Would I feel anything? I contemplated that joy in the body that you can't put words to, as when a touch sends energy flowing in surprising and powerful ways. Then I attempted to reassure myself that the freshly experienced sensuality of my middle age was an intrinsic part of me now, that it would remain like a hologram even though a part was missing. But my breast was a treasured aspect of me as a woman, and a wound to it was more than a wound to a body part. I had chosen to sacrifice my breast in an attempt to protect my life. Yet as hard as I tried, I had to admit that I had no way to comprehend or anticipate the implications of this choice.

WONDERING WHY

From time to time during the weeks prior to my surgery, I sat quietly in my living room or walked through the woods near my house. At these times I would wonder whether there was some deeper meaning to my cancer, some communication from my body about the state of my psyche. I looked to my dreams, but they reserved comment. In fact, they went ahead with other issues as if I were not ill. Distressed at the lack of help from my unconscious and feeling a duty to face my illness and discover its meaning, I complained to my analyst. She fixed her gaze on me and said firmly, "It doesn't have to mean anything." I felt an initial shock at her attitude: after all, isn't Jungian analysis supposed to help you find meanings? I sat silently and began to feel as if I had just been rescued from quicksand. There didn't have to be meaning. It occurred to me that perhaps my analyst had understood that I could all too easily have been taken over by my strong analytical and self-critical side, an animus that just doesn't want to let go when there is something to figure out. It was so tempting to try to figure it out, because if I knew at a symbolic level the meaning, the reason, for having cancer, my world could make sense again.

One night after work I was lying on the living room sofa in the dark with my eyes closed. The Indian women of my drumming vision appeared around me and placed their hands on my chest. I no longer resisted their touch. They were my comfort, and they stayed with me. I wondered why they had come to me, so shortly before I discovered my breast cancer. The Wheel of the Sun made by their arms was a medicine wheel for my breast—and my heart.

My husband stayed very close to me, and our relationship deepened as we shared the stresses of my illness and possible death. My friends and colleagues moved closer. I had not let people in easily, and now they welcomed the opportunity to express to me the ways in which I was important to them. I really had not known how much people cared about me. My disease had become an opening, a healing opening.

Two years after my cancer diagnosis, my breast had healed remarkably—and so had my heart. But I still wondered whether the cancer was some kind of message from the unconscious. Did I get breast cancer because of a problem in my heart, to teach me to be more receptive? Or could it be that the meaning was what I made of it, a meaning that unfolded as my psyche responded to the illness? I began to do some reading about the relationship between the psyche and cancer. What follows is not a comprehensive survey but rather a sampling of what I found.

CANCER AS A SIGN OF SPIRITUAL FAILURE

Initially I turned to a work in my own spiritual practice: *The Tibetan Book of Living and Dying* by Sogyal Rinpoche. He writes:

> Tibetan Buddhists believe that illnesses like cancer can be a warning, to remind us that we have been neglecting deep aspects of our being, such as our spiritual needs. If we take this warning seriously and change fundamentally the direction of our lives, there is a very real hope for healing not only our bodies, but our whole being. (Sogyal 1992, 31)

As I reflected on this, I wondered: Is it possible that an illness such as cancer offers a spiritual opportunity because we are living with dying, because cancer is so hard to detect until it's very dangerous? You can never feel you've been "cured": once you've had it, you live the rest of your life know-ing that it could recur anywhere in your body. Could there be any more effective thrust into the awareness than that your physical body is in a lim-inal state, in the Bardo, that state of suspension between life and death?

The theory that difficulties in one's relationship to the unconscious or to the soul could be a cause of cancer is prevalent in our popular culture, too. The most common notion seems to be that cancer is caused by repressed emotions. The New Age message echoes Sogyal Rinpoche's sen-timents and goes a step further. As presented by gurus, physicians, and therapists alike, this view seems to promise that something out of our con-trol, cancer, can be controlled by the I, the ego. If we can turn to a spiritu-al path, or learn not to suppress our negative emotions, or turn away from negative emotions and imagine healing and light, then our bodies will be healed. The implication is that we can choose to be emotionally or spiritu-ally correct, and then we will be protected from physical suffering and dis-ease, even aging and death. An example of this is the best-seller *Ageless Body, Timeless Mind: The Quantum Alternative to Growing Old*, by Deepak Chopra, M.D., a fuzzy amalgam of Indian philosophy, new physics, nutri-tional advice, and Western medicine. I have been told that Chopra appears on the New Age lecture circuit with women who say they have cured them-selves of advanced stage breast cancer by discovering a spiritual message. I have met women who have heard this message and have decided to forgo medical treatment in the belief that they will be cured through spiritual activities alone.

The belief that cancer is caused by a spiritual failing, one we can put aright by devoting ourselves to a spiritual practice, puts blame on cancer patients. Furthermore, it is not a very big leap to the smug and reassuring belief that those (other people) who get cancer must have a spiritual prob-lem. In my opinion, this is a New Age version of the primitive belief, pre-sent in all of us, that illness is punishment for wrongdoing.

BREAST CANCER AS A SYMPTOM OF PSYCHOLOGICAL DYSFUNCTION

Prior to my surgery, a relative with good intentions sent me a self-help book by Bernie Siegel, M.D., seductively entitled *Love, Medicine, and Miracles*. As I scanned the book, it seemed to say that women, with a certain personali-ty type, who had trouble expressing anger, were likely cancer victims. I was furious. It was bad enough to be struggling with breast cancer without being told, in a well-meaning manner, that it was because there was some-thing wrong with my personality. I was so angry that I threw the book on the floor!

In a similar vein, an article by the surgeon Max Cutler, M.D, entitled, "The Nature of the Cancer Process in Relation to a Possible Psychosomatic Influence" (1954), describes his study of forty breast cancer patients who were interviewed by psychiatrists. He described a character pattern of the women breast cancer patients, which included a masochistic character structure; an inability to discharge or deal appropriately with anger, aggressiveness, or hostility, covered over by a facade of pleasantness; inhibited sexuality; inhibited motherhood; and an unresolved hostile conflict with their mothers, handled through denial and unrealistic sacrifice.

I believe that Cutler is to be commended for attempting to study the issue scientifically rather than anecdotally. Unfortunately, Cutler's work does not meet the most basic standards for objective, scientific research. There was no control group of women who did not have breast cancer. And there were no checks on interviewer bias, such as a double-blind design, in which the interviewer is unaware whether it is a cancer patient or a control subject being interviewed. These controls are essential, as has been shown by countless studies on experimenter bias in the field of social psychology. These studies demonstrate that experimenters can unconsciously and unintentionally influence the outcomes of their studies with human subjects to conform to their hypotheses.

We might ask how Cutler came up with his hypothesis about women cancer patients' relationships to their mothers. He doesn't say. It's not hard to imagine a possible chain of associations: breast→mother→bad breast→bad mother. I also wonder about the frequent choice of women cancer patients for study. Is this because women are thought to have a greater number of psychosomatically based illnesses than men? I wonder if prostate cancer in men has received a comparable number of studies looking at its psychosomatic basis, hypothesizing, for example, that men who get prostate cancer are sexually inhibited and have poor relationships with their fathers.

C. G. Jung, in his 1925 seminars, used cancer as a metaphor to characterize deeply buried complexes:

> It is thought that cancer may be due to the later and anarchical development of embryonic cells folded away in the mature and differentiated tissues. Strong evidence for this lies in the finding, for example, of a partially developed fetus in the thigh of an adult man, say, in those tumors known as teratomata. Perhaps a similar thing goes on in the mind, whose psychological makeup may be said to be a conglomerate. Perhaps certain traits belonging to the ancestors get buried away in the mind as complexes with a life of their own which has never been assimilated into the life of the individual, and then, for some unknown reason, become activated, step out of their obscurity in the folds of the unconscious, and begin to dominate the whole mind. (Jung 1989, 37)

Jung did not say that *cancer* is *caused* by buried complexes. Although things may appear analogous, they are not necessarily causally connected. The attribution of a causal connection to analogous processes is a psychologically more primitive formulation, which I call the *concretization of a metaphor* (if A is like B, then A causes B).

More than thirty years later, Jung hypothesized a psychological cause of cancer. In a letter to his cousin Rudolf Jung, he wrote,

> I have seen cases where the carcinoma broke out when a person comes to a halt at some essential point in his individuation or cannot get over an obstacle. . . . An inner process of growth must begin, and if this spontaneous creative activity is not performed by nature herself, the outcome can only be fatal. (Adler, 1973–4, 297).

It is my impression that Jung's attitude about cancer and an unconscious block to inner growth has continued to be influential in Jungian circles (Cahen 1979; Lockhart 1977). Russell Lockhart a Jungian analyst, has written a very thoughtful article, called "Cancer in Myth and Dream." From an examination of the etymology of cancer and its myth and folklore, he concludes that the language of cancer is the language of earth and plants. He writes,

> In my experience I have begun to feel that cancer in certain forms is connected with something of the substance of oneself denied, undernourished, or cut down; something of one's psychic and bodily earth not allowed to live, not allowed to grow. Cancer lives something of life unlived. (Lockhart 1977, 2)

He concluded that cancer was caused by a transgression of the patient against himself and against the gods:

> I have seen in the background of many cancer patients something corresponding to a powerful psychological growth cut down or cut off. It is as if something very alive in themselves was killed. The person severed some living connection to the self, in service of an ego that would assimilate the self. Instead, the wounded self begins an inevitable course of assimilating the ego, and whether it comes out in psychosis or in cancer, we see man reduced to eating himself, feeding on his own flesh, rather than on the fruits of the earth whose spirits he has violated in himself. (Lockhart 1977, 19)

From Lockhart's viewpoint, the symbolism evoked by the illness contains not only a psychological meaning, but *the* psychological meaning, the nature of the transgression, and therefore *the* cause of the illness:

> If the Gods wound, and if the Gods become diseases, as Jung used to say, then it is necessary to understand sickness—even cancer—as a wounding and to go in search of the God at work in it. Gods are angered and strike when they are denied, defiled, or devalued. What is needed is to go into the symptom, into the sickness, and to connect again with the God hidden there. (Lockhart 1977, 14)

Looking for the meaning of an illness by analyzing the unconscious communication expressed as metaphor by the symptom was not an idea original to Jungians. It was formulated brilliantly by Freud in his work with hysterics (Freud 1963). Freud treated women who had somatic symptoms that did not have a physical etiology, and he proposed that hysterical symptoms "must be subjected to the same analytic procedure as we use in dream-interpretation (Freud 1963, 172). It is a tremendous leap to move from hysterical symptoms to actual physical disease processes, an unfortunate tendency of some contemporary Jungians who interpret all bodily symptoms subjectively.

The dangers and fallacies of such interpretation are the theme of Susan Sontag's book *Illness and Metaphor*, in which she describes "the punitive and sentimental fantasies" (Sontag 1978, 3) about cancer and tuberculosis. She believes that "the most truthful way of regarding illness—and the healthiest way of being ill—is one most purified of, most resistant to, metaphoric thinking" (Sontag 1978, 3). She shows that in the last century tuberculosis was viewed as a romantic disease afflicting sensitive and creative people. As the medical causes became known, this view disappeared. Might we speculate that the same process will occur with cancer?

In the midst of the prevailing analytic attitude toward cancer, the work of Jungian analyst Selma Hyman (1977) is like a breath of fresh air. Her work with cancer patients has received little attention, and I suspect it is because she did not offer a psychological theory of why patients are afflicted with cancer. She approached her cancer patients with openness and compassion rather than causal hypotheses. She did not offer cures or remissions. She discovered in the dreams of cancer patients that very often death and new life were presented as inseparable. The success of the work was not judged by how long the patient lived or whether the cancer was cured (which flies in the face of current attempts to prove the worth of psychological interventions with cancer patients). She understood that the healing of the soul may go hand in hand with physical death.

I do not propose that the psyche is completely uninvolved in causing cancer, nor that meaning cannot be found in symptoms. However, I do strongly question whether the causal mechanism of the disease can be discovered in the meaning of the illness to the psyche. We really don't understand to what extent and under what circumstances the psyche is involved in the etiology of cancer. We are beginning to learn more about how emotions affect the immune system, which in turn affects the body's ability to control the growth of tumors (Sapolsky 1994). We are also learning more about genetic predispositions to cancers and about dietary and environmental risk factors. This is a complicated business. As therapists, we must examine our own fantasies, projections, and reactions to physical illness and avoid simplistic, reductionistic, or general interpretations.

THE ARCHETYPAL BASIS OF BELIEFS ABOUT CANCER

Across many cultures and disciplines, cancer is believed to be caused by spiritual or psychological growth that is blocked. Does this attest to a universal truth? Or could it be that there are archetypes at work here? I would like to suggest that there are two powerful archetypes associated with cancer.

Physical illness as punishment for wrongdoing. I believe we easily slide back into this primitive belief, particularly when we don't understand the physical mechanisms that lead to illness. In my clinical work, I invariably find that young children believe that if they are mistreated by a parent, they must have done something bad. This is based upon their belief in a just parent and their belief in a just world where the innocent do not suffer.

Believing that the punishment is in response to her behavior, a child tries to figure out what she has done wrong, in a futile attempt to avoid future abuse. However, at later developmental stages a child can begin to understand that she is not responsible for everything good and bad that happens to her. She begins to realize that a parent is not a perfect judge but a flawed human being and, by extension, that the world is not always just.

When faced with illness, many people, even intellectually sophisticated people, revert to the belief that in fact they are responsible for the bad things that happen to them. Why would they do this? A childlike helplessness arises in the face of life-threatening illness. Like the mistreated child, they are hoping that if they can only figure out what they've done wrong, then they will have control over their suffering.

The life-taking, destructive aspect of nature, the Terrible Mother. From an archetypal perspective, cancer is a manifestation of the archetype of the Terrible Mother, "the hungry earth, which devours its own children and fattens on their corpses . . . the tiger and the vulture, the vulture and the coffin, the flesh-eating sarcophagus voraciously licking up the blood seed of men and beasts and, once fecundated and sated, casting it out again in new birth, hurling it to death, and over and over again to death" (Neumann 1955, 149–50). This aspect of nature is represented in many cultures but She does not have a representative in Judeo-Christian iconography. (In the Christian religion, the Dark Feminine is relegated to the moral realm, equated with evil.) In India She is the goddess Kali, who demands blood sacrifice, cutting off lives before they can be realized in the conventional life pattern. In ancient Mexico She was Chicomecoatl, who, "clad in a mantle of snakes . . . holds the deadly flint knife and has the claws of a Jaguar" (Neumann 1955, 183). In ancient Greece She was Medusa. Lacking an archetypal representation of this aspect of nature, might we be personalizing and projecting this archetype onto individuals when we conclude that women cancer patients have a poor relationship to their own mothers, when we talk about cancer patients having severed a vital link to their innermost being, or when we say a cancer patient has violated the spirit of the earth?

I believe that my analyst helped protect me from overpersonalizing these archetypes. She opened the door to nonego when she said that my breast cancer did not have to mean anything. She did not interpret my illness in an intellectual or reductionistic way; rather, she created a container in which I could have my own direct experience of the unconscious.

ANSWER TO JOB: FINDING AUTHENTIC MEANING IN SUFFERING

As I lived with not knowing the meaning of my cancer, I found that Jung's "Answer to Job" spoke to me most profoundly. "Answer to Job" was published when Jung was seventy-seven years old, after he had suffered a heart attack and had undergone what we would now call a near-death experience (Jung 1973). After this, he became less concerned with trying to present his ideas in a way that would be acceptable to the psychiatric community, and he wrote in a more direct way about his own experience of the deep unconscious. Jung wrote, "The motive for my book was an increasingly urgent feeling of responsibility which in the end I could no longer withstand" (Adler, 1973–74, 39). Jung was reluctant to express his views about the ambivalence of God and God's need to find wholeness through man. However, Jung felt himself to be the instrument of a higher power and wrote in a letter to Aniela Jaffe, "If there is anything like the spirit seizing one by the scruff of the neck, it is the way this book came into being" (Adler 1973–74, 20).

In "Answer to Job," Jung interprets the story of Job in the Old Testament as a shift in human consciousness that goes beyond the acceptance of human suffering as punishment from God for wrongdoing. This leads man not simply to question his own nature but to ask about the nature of God. Despite losing all of his possessions, all of his family, and his physical health, Job maintained his faith in God. At the same time, he refused to sacrifice the authenticity of his own experience, which told him that he had not committed an offense against God that would warrant his suffering. This leads inevitably to questioning what kind of a God would inflict suffering on a just man. Perhaps it was God himself who was not just. In *Transformation of the God-Image*, Edward Edinger's commentary on "Answer to Job," Edinger formulates four stages of the Job archetype:

1) There is an encounter between the ego and the greater power.
2) A wound or suffering of the ego results from the encounter.
3) The ego perseveres in insisting upon scrutinizing the experience in search of its meaning. It will not give up in despair or cynicism but perseveres in the assumption that the experience is meaningful. . .
4) As a result . . . a divine revelation takes place by which the ego is rewarded with insight into the nature of the transpersonal psyche. (Edinger 1992, 29)

This full sequence can take place only if it isn't short-circuited by a personalistic or reductive interpretation at step three.

You see, if Job had submitted to the advice of his counselors that some way or other he had it coming, even though he can't understand why, and he should admit that he's getting his just deserts, a short-circuit would have taken place and there would be no divine revelation. (Edinger 1992, 29)

As a result of my personal experience, I would like to modify stage three, the search for meaning, to deemphasize the ego's scrutiny. I believe the crucial aspect is the ego's willingness to remain in the dilemma and to open to the unknown. One must be willing, as was Job, to maintain faith in the higher power and at the same time to bear the suffering it has inflicted. This opens the way to a solution that comes not only from the ego but also from the unconscious.

I have found that the search for meaning can last a very long time. Remaining in this open state has been very rich and active for me because the ego's stillness allowed the greater knowledge of the Self to manifest. In other words, if I had been intent on finding the meaning of my illness by reading self-help books, interpreting symbols in an intellectual way, or accepting the directions of a New Age guru, I wouldn't have remained open to receive the meanings of my vision, which have continued to unfold.

CANCER AND SHAMANIC INITIATION INTO THE DARK FEMININE

There are striking correspondences between Jung's interpretation of the story of Job and shamanic initiation, as was noted by Joseph Henderson in a work originally published more than thirty years ago (Henderson and Oakes 1990). The shaman's initiation may entail experiences of illness, dismemberment, and death (Eliade 1964), which from a psychological perspective represents a wounding of the body-ego by a greater power (Edinger's second stage of the Job archetype). The shaman remains aware through this suffering (third stage). He is healed or receives new organs to replace his dismembered body (fourth stage). As in the story of Job, the shaman's wounding is, paradoxically, the doorway to a new quality of experience. Job returns to a materially more prosperous life, which symbolizes the enriched experience of ordinary life, which may be the outcome of a profound encounter with the divine. However, the shaman's path goes further. He returns to his community as new person, endowed with special healing powers. He may now heal physical and spiritual illnesses and even enter the other world, where he can retrieve souls (Eliade 1964). Psychologically, the other world corresponds to the deep layers of the unconscious, where the shaman may discover a lost soul, or an essential aspect of being that has been lost or unavailable to the conscious ego.

As a cancer patient, I faced illness, dismemberment, and death. In an attempt to preserve my life, I had to submit to the loss and disfigurement of a precious part of my body, my breast. The inevitability of my death became part of my daily life. Yet I refused to accept personal blame or guilt for my illness. I could then recognize the presence of the destructive side of nature at an archetypal level, not a personal level. From this perspective, my cancer was not an aberration of nature but an intrinsic part of nature, a destructive, dark side of nature. My tumor was a manifestation within my body of the archetypal Terrible Mother, initiating me into the beauty and mystery of the Dark Feminine. The flesh of my breast is my offering to her. She has, in turn, blessed me with a new and ever-present awareness in my body, in my cells, that life and death coexist inextricably at every moment.

The place of wounding and darkness can become a source of light or greater consciousness. The vision that I described at the beginning of this paper referred to this potential. You will recall that old women sat around me and reached out to touch my chest. Their arms formed a medicine wheel, called the Wheel of the Sun. The vision suggests that light, or consciousness, came from my submitting to the women's touch and allowing the healing of the wound within my body.

The vision points to a consciousness that comes through the body, through the earth, through the feminine and not from the sky above (cf. Henderson and Oakes 1990). This is the consciousness that comes from the dark recesses of matter. It is the spirit that comes from the earth. In the present era, knowledge of this feminine spirit is surfacing in many places and forms, from archeological findings of ancient goddess religions

(Gimbutas 1982) and the discovery of the poetry of Inanna (Meador 1992; Perera 1981) to the deep devotion that many Catholic women feel for the Black Madonna. She appears in the dreams and visions of women throughout the world. Lacking a positive cultural context, recipients of these visions may be fearful or not know how to value them. Analysis is one context within which a woman may learn to honor and be transformed by her experience of the Dark Feminine (Leonard 1993; Meador 1992; Rutter 1993).

Many years ago, at the beginning of my own analysis, I had a dream that helped to correct my unconscious devaluation of the feminine and point the way toward transformation from within the body, through matter:

> *I am looking at a beautiful, numinous Byzantine painting of a madonna and child. The voice of God says, "The miracle of transsubstantiation is in the woman's breast."*

Within the Catholic tradition, the Virgin Mother was valued for giving birth to a male child, as a vehicle for the instantiation of spirit from above. She was not a spiritual being in her own right. However, the need for an archetypal representative of the feminine spirit could not be permanently suppressed, and during the Middle Ages the cult of the virgin became powerful. In many places and for many individuals, in practice, the Holy Mother plays a more central role than God the Father. In the official dogma of the Church, she was eventually given an honored place but not an equal status in relation to the male father and son gods. Like the Christian male gods, she is all good; darkness and matter are equated with evil. My dream suggests that the Holy Mother, as a representative of the archetypal feminine, carries within herself the capacity for the most profound transformation. At a concrete level, the dream refers to the ability of a woman's breast to transform ordinary food into milk, a substance that contains everything necessary to sustain and nourish life—a true transsubstantiation. Women contain in their bodies the mysterious capacity to make new life and to sustain it. If they are open to this experience, might it place them in deep communion, through their bodies, with the spiritual mystery of transsubstantiation? In the Christian religions, this mystery has been usurped by the masculine: the Eucharist, which celebrates transsubstantiation, is a central belief and ritual of Christianity. The Catholic Church now allows women to conduct most rituals with the notable exception of the Eucharist. Is it possible that the priesthood, perhaps without even realizing it, is fearful of the power of the long-suppressed natural connection of women to this mystery?

While knowledge of the consciousness arising from matter has been suppressed by our Judeo-Christian culture for more than two thousand years (cf. Pagels 1988), it has survived in esoteric mystical traditions such as alchemy (cf. Jung 1968) and in non-Western religions, including Hinduism (particularly in Kundalini yoga), Tibetan Buddhism, and Native American shamanic traditions. This knowledge cannot be conveyed intellectually but can be learned only through experience—what Tibetan Buddhists refer to as "secret" teachings because they cannot be transmitted by explanation.

During my analysis I had experienced transformation through a consciousness arising from within the body, as distinct from intellectual analysis or insight. However, I felt I needed something more: something communal, something culturally transmitted. The women of my vision were Native Americans, which suggested my path to this knowledge. I was searching to fill a core deficit in my cultural experience. What I felt I was missing was simply and beautifully described by Ishi, the last survivor of the Yana tribe, which once lived not so far from my own home:

> Ishi was not given to volunteering criticism of the white man's ways. But he was observant and analytic, and, when pressed, would pass a judgment somewhat as follows. He approved of the "conveniences" and variety of the white man's world. . . . He considered the white man to be fortunate, inventive, and very, very clever; but childlike and lacking in a desirable reserve, and in a true understanding of Nature—her mystic face; her terrible and benign power. (Kroeber 1969, 229)

I had no idea how I was going to find a way to the experience I was looking for. It didn't feel right to go out and find a shaman. I remained in my own process and stayed open to what might unfold. As with my vision, what I needed so profoundly had already started to develop before I even knew I was looking for it.

Just after I had finished my radiation treatments, I went on a trip to New Mexico with Donald Sandner and a group of other candidates from the C. G. Jung Institute in San Francisco. Don's friend and a student of shamanism, Steve Wong, came from Denver to join us. I vividly recall our meeting for brunch in a restaurant near Santa Fe, where Steve immediately told us about a Lakota Sun Dance that he had witnessed. I was feeling emotionally raw and physically depleted from my illness and the subsequent treatments. Steve enthusiastically described the details of the piercing of the dancer's chest, the tying of a thong through the flesh, and the thong being tied to a tree; in an ecstatic state brought on by intense suffering, the dancer breaks free, tearing the flesh. I felt ill, almost in shock, and unable to distance myself from the dancer's mutilation and suffering. I was relieved to leave the restaurant and get into the fresh air, where I could avoid Steve and turn my thoughts in other, more benign, directions. It was quite some time before I realized that my reaction was connected in part to the wounding of my own breast and to my vision of the Wheel of the Sun.

Several years later, in 1993, I sent an early draft of this essay to Steve, who invited me to present it at the Psychology and Shamanism Conference at Winter Park, Colorado. At the conference I heard Pansy Hawk Wing speak about Lakota sacred ritual, and I attended an Inipi, or sweat lodge ceremony, that she conducted for the group. Near the end of the conference, a good friend told me that Pansy would be willing to work with a small group of women and to prepare us for a traditional Lakota vision quest. I had such a strong feeling about Pansy, as well as confidence in my friend, that before the conference was over I had offered Pansy a pinch of tobacco, a sign of my commitment to the vision quest. She accepted the tobacco, her pledge to guide me in that process.

I am continuing on my journey, now walking a road opened to me by my illness. The Lakota call it the Red Road. I am a beginner in the Lakota Way, and it would be premature to write about my experience. What I can tell you is that I feel a special bond when, in the utter darkness of the sweat lodge, I join in the song for women returning from a Humbleciya ("crying for a vision"), one of the songs may be translated as follows:

> I have been to the spirit world and I have returned.
> I have been to the spirit world and I have returned.
> I have been to the place where the Great Mystery lives.
> I have been to the spirit world.

ACKNOWLEDGMENTS

My deepest appreciation goes to my husband for his loving support and his impartial editing. Sheryl Fullerton provided astute editorial commentary and stylistic advice. Dr. Joseph Henderson read an early draft and made valuable comments on the symbolism of the vision. I would also like to thank Donald Sandner and Steve Wong for their encouragement, for bringing together our group to explore the interface of analytical psychology and shamanism, and for making this book possible. Most of all, I want to thank my analyst.

REFERENCES

Adler, G. 1973 [1972]. Editorial Note. In C. G. Jung, *Answer to Job*. Princeton: Princeton University Press.
Adler G. (1973–4). C. G. Jung: Letters. Vol. 2 Princeton: Princeton University Press.

Cahen, R. 1979. Cancer and Depth Psychology: Reflections and Hypotheses. *Journal of Analytical Psychology* 24:343–46.

Chopra, D. 1993. *Ageless Body, Timeless Mind: The Quantum Alternative to Growing Old.* New York: Harmony.

Cutler, M. 1954. The Nature of the Cancer Process in Relation to a Possible Psychosomatic Influence. In J. Gengerelli and F. Kirkner, eds., *The Psychological Variables in Human Cancer: A Symposium.* Berkeley: University of California Press.

Edinger, E. 1992. *Transformation of the God-Image.* Toronto: Inner City.

Eliade, M. 1964. *Shamanism: Archaic Techniques of Ecstasy.* Bollingen Series LXXVI. New York: Pantheon.

Freud, S. 1963 [1909]. General Remarks on Hysterical Attacks. In *Dora: An Analysis of a Case of Hysteria.* New York: Collier.

Gimbutas, M. 1982. *The Goddesses and Gods of Old Europe.* Berkeley: University of California Press.

Henderson, L., and M. Oakes. 1990 [1963] *The Wisdom of the Serpent.* Princeton: Princeton University Press.

Hyman, S. (1977). Death-in-Life—Life-in-Death. *Spring Annual of Archatypol Psychology and Jungian Thought.* New York: Spring publication.

Jung. C. G. 1958. "Answer to Job." In *Psychology and Religion: West and East.* Bollingen Series XX: The Collected Works of C. G. Jung, vol. 11.

———. 1968 [1953]. *Psychology and Alchemy.* Bollingen Series XX: The Collected Works of C. G. Jung, vol. 12.

———. 1973 [1961]. *Memories, Dreams, Reflections.* Edited by A. Jaffe. New York: Random House.

———. 1989 [1925]. *Analytical Psychology. Notes of the Seminar Given in 1925 by C. G. Jung,* edited by W. McGuire. Princeton: Princeton University Press.

Kroeber, T. 1969. *Ishi in Two Worlds. A Biography of the Last Wild Indian in North America.* Berkeley: University of California Press.

Leonard, L. 1993. *Meeting the Madwoman.* New York: Bantam.

Lockhart, R. 1977. Cancer in Myth and Dreams. *Spring.* An Annual of Archetypal Psyche and Jungian Thought.

Meador, B. 1992. *Uncursing the Dark.* Willamette, Ill.: Chiron.

Neumann, E. 1955. *The Great Mother.* Bollingen Series XLVII. Princeton: Princeton University Press.

Pagels, E. 1988. *Adam, Eve, and the Serpent.* New York: Random House.

Perera, S. 1981. *Descent to the Goddess.* Toronto: Inner City.

Rutter, V. 1993. *Woman Changing Woman.* New York: HarperCollins.

Sapolsky, R. 1994. *Why Zebras Don't Get Ulcers.* New York: W. H. Freeman.

Siegel, B. 1986. *Love, Medicine, and Miracles.* New York: Harper and Row.

Sogyal Rinpoche. 1992. *The Tibetan Book of Living and Dying.* New York: HarperCollins.

Sontag, S. 1978. *Illness and Metaphor.* New York: Farrar, Straus and Giroux.

Chapter 14

Learning to Listen: A Snake Calls Me to a Shamanic Path

Carol McRae

In this chapter, Carol McRae describes her active imagination with a snake incongruously named Rosie. Rosie stayed with her and firmly directed her actions throughout her discovery of breast cancer and ensuing life tasks. Here active imagination as it is practiced in analytical psychology segues over into a more powerful encounter with a shamanic ally.

The night before my gynecologist informed me of my breast cancer, I had a dream:

> A long black snake was jumping at my heart. I put my hand up to deflect it, but it would not stop. Finally, not knowing what else to do, I grabbed it behind its head, where it couldn't bite me, and went to look for someone to help me. I seemed to be on a college campus and went into a small classroom building. Everyone was busy and classes were in session. I could not find anyone to help me. I sat down on a wooden bench by an exit and, for the first time, really looked at the snake in my hand. It was dead! In my fear, I had squeezed it so hard it had died. I felt a great terror at this realization.

I was afraid the dream meant I would die, and upon discovering I had breast cancer, that fear seemed confirmed. I moved as quickly as possible through the various stages of talking to surgeons, having a biopsy, and finally undergoing surgery. The sacrifice of part of my flesh was taken. The week of waiting for the pathology report seemed to last forever, but the results showed that there was no lymph involvement and no further treatment was needed. The dream was not to be understood literally.

As soon as I had completed this physical confrontation with death and could step back into life, I sat down and did an active imagination: I closed my eyes and went back into the dream, a technique I had already been using for over ten years when I wanted to be receptive to the energy of a dream.[1]

> *I took the dead snake to a tree-lined road that marked the entrance to my inner sacred space. Beyond the road was a broad open space and stone steps that led up to a cliff that peered down into a small deep pool at the bottom of a tall waterfall. I took off my clothes and jumped into the pool with the snake. At the bottom of the pool was an old woman sweeping, a former dream figure. She had often advised me before, so now I asked her what to do with the snake. She said to go to the top of the waterfall, bury the snake, and come back in three days. I did as she instructed.*

Three days later I did another active imagination:

> *The old woman wore a robe because of the importance of the occasion and went with me to the place where I had buried the snake. We sat on the ground, Japanese style, and bowed deeply and fully. We told the snake we were ready to meet with it. Up from the ground rose a huge snake, fifteen feet long, standing straight up on the tip of its tail. It came toward me and slowly wound itself around my naked body, ending with its head inches from my eyes. It could crush the life out of me if it chose to, but that was not why it came to me. It informed me that its name was Rosie, and since I would never have chosen this name myself, I realized that this snake was something much more than a figment of my imagination.*

Rosie taught me to chant and to do body work to release the blockages in my upper chest, where I held too much of my energy, not allowing it to flow freely throughout my body. She advised me to meditate at an ashram a good friend was going to at the time. She was very specific. She would say, "Do this five times." "Come back to see me in three days."

Sometimes her teaching was startling if I wasn't paying attention enough. About four months after I began my relationship with Rosie, I was driving along the coast above San Francisco, on my way to a weekend retreat at a friend's house by the ocean. As I rounded a curve my car slowly and gently turned onto the grass and up a small slope until, before I knew it, the car was on its side. I climbed out while someone driving behind went for help. In a half hour my car was righted and I was on my way again. The only damage was that the rearview mirror was out of alignment and had to be adjusted. But I was very shaken. When I got to the house I sat down and asked Rosie, "What is happening here?"

She said sternly, "You need to meditate, and you need to do it now. No more stalling. Go to that ashram for seven days and don't come back to see me till you do. This gives you an idea of what can happen if you don't stay focused on our work together!

For about a year I was actively taught by Rosie. Then I met someone and began a deep relationship. My contact with Rosie was sporadic during the next ten years, during which time I became a Jungian analyst and my partner and I added our two children to our family. It had been right to focus on my relationship at first but Rosie began telling me it was time to resume our work together. She had been patient long enough. I was frightened again by two surgeries, three months apart, each carrying the threat of possible death. I thanked Rosie for my good fortune as the death threats passed.

Less than a week after we moved to a house backed by five beautiful live-oak trees, I had a car accident that could have seriously injured or killed me. Instead I was unhurt but very shaken. A few weeks later I was in a fender-bender at a stoplight with my son in the car. Both accidents were caused by my diverted attention. I went to Rosie for help. She said I needed to come and see her every night. Initially out of fear for my children's safety as well as my own, I got up every night at about 3 A.M. and went out on the deck of our house to commune with Rosie and feel the energy of the trees.

For three years I got up each night. I was assisted in this by the calming, deepening energy of the trees. I have always loved trees and feel a deep bond with them. At age twelve I was given a rope ladder, which allowed me to climb for the first time an eighty foot spruce tree in my yard. I spent the next year and a half in this tree, calmed by it, communing with it, loving it. The live-oak trees were the reason we bought our house in Marin. and I feel a similar soul connection with these trees.

I also was called in the night by a sound that seemed to be a woodpecker singing and tapping. Every night I heard this song, loud and clear, calling me onto the deck. In 1980 I had gone on my first vision quest, and at that time a woodpecker had made a complete circle around my sacred space, starting in front of me, tapping, tapping. He had taken six hours to move in a complete circle until he reached the front again and flew away. I knew the woodpecker was an important shamanic guide for me but I hadn't known how we would work together. Now in 1990 he was singing to bring me out. If I had had any doubts about his being a part of this process with Rosie, they were overcome on Thanksgiving Day of that year when a woodpecker, flying in a straight line toward where I was sitting, hit the glass window of my bedroom and died on the deck. I went to Rosie and asked "why." She said he needed to get my attention. I was to stop doubting the power of my connection with the spirit world. The woodpecker, I found, helped me to open closed spaces—in myself and between this world and the spirit world. Once I was clearly committed to my nightly practice, the woodpecker came less often, sang more softlys and finally stopped. Now I hear the woodpecker song only occasionally. However, I hear the tapping of woodpeckers almost everywhere I go. My heart always lifts when I hear it, for it is the greeting of a dear old friend.

Other inner helpers have recently joined Rosie. A foot-tall fly perched on my left shoulder in a dream and began guiding me in my work with Rosie. I would become the fly and fly over whatever I was struggling with at the time. Because flies have eyes that can see in a very wide angle, the fly has helped me to broaden my vision. I have also learned to shift my vision from ordinary reality to a mild trance state.

A bear in a dream lived in a cave and offered physical healing. Visiting her became a regular part of my practice, a time when I released body tension, realigned my body, and performed self-healing.

A coyote came to me on a ski slope, standing quietly and making eye contact. Close behind me was my son, who never saw him. Coyote now helps me develop the trickster aspect of myself: to take things more lightly, to laugh at the ironies of life, to twist a little and play with what could otherwise be very heavy and draining.

Finally, during my second vision quest, the dancing rhythms of the wind spirit taught me the communion of everyday life and the spirit world. The wind seems to help me find the connection between this world and the spirit world, to feel a communion with both worlds, largely through the immediacy of air all about me moving in dancing rhythms.

Rosie is different from the other animal helpers. In the shamanic tradition, the bear, the woodpecker, the fly, and the coyote are my helping animals, and Rosie is my ally spirit. Jeff Raff, a Jungian analyst, would call Rosie not only an ally but a separate reality from the psychoid realm (see his essay in this book on the ally).

Rosie came to the deepest part of me, my heart, at a time of great danger, when I was suffering from cancer. She needs my focus to express herself in this world, and I need her to grow in my calling as a healer.

From the work I've done with Rosie and my helping animals, I've come to notice occasional pulsating, tingling sensations. They have grown stronger, and each has its own special location in my body. The strongest and most frequent energies are the pulsing in my upper back, which is Rosie, and the energy moving through and out the top of my head, which is the bear. Increasingly I call on their help in my work as a Jungian analyst. In most sessions with my analysands I simply feel these animal's energy, which helps me to go deeper in relation to my analysands.

I have used active imagination with analysands to help them extend powerful dreams, especially nightmares, whose energy and usually incomplete action seem to be a call from the unconscious for attention to some new, emerging aspect. Many things can happen, since this active imagination process is deeply individual. I have noticed that gradually more people working with me are discovering animal guides—snakes, wolves, owls, even ants. There have always been animals in my analysands' dreams, but this process lately seems to be allowing them to come forward more actively to teach.

I seem increasingly to attend to the relationship between energy and image. Sometimes one is more predominant, sometimes the other is. In my own shamanic work, Rosie or the bear interact with me through both image and energy. With my analysands the image may come through dreams or active imagination. This involves my attending to my own energy and helping them locate and work with theirs. I may pay attention to where energy is in my body, how strong it is, and what it is directing me to see or do. I check with my analysands about where the energy is strongest in their bodies and what it feels like. Sometimes we just attend to it quietly for a while and see if it changes and if so, how. Sometimes it relates to childhood experience or may even have a name. Then we can talk to it and find out what it is holding for the adult and what it needs to let go. Thus we work with energy on a personal level.

Energy can be a powerful indicator of an active shamanic state as well. Recently an analysand felt the strength of the energy between us and shrank back, saying he felt too small to handle it. My voice came forward as though from someone besides me. It was deeper and louder and firmer than usual, and "I" said, "Make yourself bigger!" We both immediately knew we had experienced a shamanic energy speaking through me.

Throughout this process with Rosie, it has been hard to believe this is happening to me, and harder to believe that I have something to offer her. The sense of where Rosie's teaching will lead me is not yet clear, but I have no choice but to continue on this path. Rosie continues to make that clear. The message I passed to my analysand is also the message for me, and perhaps for many of us in Western culture: to be receptive to the world of beings like Rosie, "make yourself bigger!"

NOTE

1. Active imagination is to be distinguished from more conscious work with dreams, such as lucid dreaming, where a suggestion is made from the conscious mind for a dream ending in a form more satisfying to the conscious ego. When successful, the person sleeps and dreams again, with a more positive or powerful ending to the dream. Active imagination emerges from the unconscious, and the work of the conscious ego is not to direct but to be receptive to what comes up.

Chapter 15

Shamanic Dismemberment

Steven H. Wong

There are dreams and then there are Dreams. What Steve Wong describes here is a big Dream—the kind that comes like a thunderbolt out of the blue and changes your life. This one presents the archetype of shamanic initiation. Like shamanic dreams from all over the world, it sets forth a grizzly dismemberment scenario as a prelude to the shamanic vocation.

Old snow, crusty and black from the exhaust and grime of cars, caked the streets. It was bitterly cold, and a light snow had begun to fall. My body was fighting a cold that alternated between chilling me and feverishly heating me.

I had signed a lease for my new office to begin my career as a psychotherapist. While pushing a sofa across this new office, I suddenly fell unconscious.

It was dark and cold. I must have lain there for hours until I felt a shift out of my body. It was odd seeing myself shivering and sweating, rolling on the carpet.

A soft light permeated my mind when I realized I was in another world. Standing in a valley, I saw the sunlight slowly gliding across a landscape laden with steep cliffs and arching rocks. It felt like the beginning of the world; the first time the sun had kissed the earth with its luminosity. I watched the sun's rays climb a huge cliff until they reached the top and entered a small cave. In a flash I found myself floating in the air as I noticed an eagle on the sill of a window in the cave looking in. On the floor of the cave was a man lying on animal furs. A young woman kneeling beside him was crying. He looked ill and frightened. The eagle fixed its eyes on him and suddenly swooped down onto his chest. With its sharp beak glinting in the sun, the eagle tore into the man's chest, ripping it open from neck to navel. He screamed as his blood and innards flowed out of his gaping chest cavity. Arching its back while lowering its head, the eagle began pecking away at the man's chest. It pulled out diseased organs and slung them to the side. The young woman sobbed softly, helpless as she sat and watched the spectacle. Quickly the eagle placed quartz crystals into the now empty cavity. Soon the chest was full, and the eagle pushed the skin together until the folds overlapped.

For a moment the eagle twitched its head left and right, looking curiously at the man. Without any warning, its beak shot into the man's eyes and plucked them out. Blood oozed from the empty sockets. Suddenly I could not see and felt warm liquid in my eyes. I realized then, that it was I who was lying on the animal furs, waiting in the darkness, stones in my chest and my head floating in warm blood. I reached over and felt the warmth of the woman's knee, which reassured me that I was not mad. She reached down and held my hand firmly and lovingly. At that moment something fell into my eye sockets.

My vision began to return, and I saw white lines forming different shapes in the air. As I saw my face fading away with quartz crystals in place of my eyes, I awoke confused.

The sunlight was streaming through the office window. My wristwatch showed three in the afternoon, January seventeenth. January seventeenth? It should have said January fourteenth. Somehow three days had disappeared. How could that be? Had I been out for three days? I ran out of the office looking for someone to verify the date. A person was coming up the stairs with a newspaper; it was dated January seventeenth! Rushing back to my office, I checked my appointment book to find that I had missed two clients and still had an appointment with my Jungian analyst at four o'clock that afternoon.

In my analyst's waiting room I was depressed, anxious, and worried that I was going insane. It was so good to see a familiar face, and I told him about my vision. After a short pause he said it was a "shamanic dismemberment." My curiosity piqued, I asked him what that was. I knew about the dismemberment of the ego that leads to a new personality in Jungian psychology, but what did he mean by shamanic? He then explained that the shaman embodied the archetype of the wounded healer: a person who can cross between the worlds to acquire ally spirits, power and knowledge to heal the sick. He then recommended that I read Mircea Eliade's *Shamanism: Archaic*

Techniques of Ecstasy (1972). I was also reminded of my childhood experiences of seeing golden light and spirits. The reason the dismemberment experience had happened at this time in my life was because my practice was starting and the other world was teaching me a way to heal.

That evening I read the book my analyst had recommended. I discovered Australian Aborigines' stories of shamanic initiations in which quartz crystals are used:

> Among the *Wiradjuri* the initiatory master introduces rock crystals into the apprentice's body and makes him drink water in which such crystals have been placed; after this the apprentice succeeds in seeing spirits. (Eliade 1972, 135)

A few months later, during a session with one of my clients, I spontaneously went into an altered state. I saw a heart bleeding from its cracked center. Moments later, an exploding volcano, spewing its red and orange lava into the sky, emerged from the center of the heart. The room was filled with red and orange lights fading in and out. During this visionary state, I talked to my client about the terrible pain and suffering and seething anger and resentment experienced from rejected love. My client began to sob and confessed that her boyfriend had left her to return to his wife. I reached out and touched her arm to make sure she was all right and asked her if she had a dream for me to interpret. She was startled at my request and hesitated for a moment. Looking curiously at me, she told me her dream of a bleeding heart and an angry, exploding volcano. I sat back in my chair, felt warmth in my eyes, and remembered my dismemberment vision. "How odd," I thought. "This power to see has so many permutations."

At first I was frightened of this power to see because it made me different from other people. I felt the loneliness of being out of place and was afraid that I would be ridiculed and rejected, and so I hid it from others and, worst of all, from myself. The more that I rejected this power to see, the more I became ill. Soon I realized I had to accept it and develop it. What I learned was that the power to see had its limits and that the mastery of it required more than willpower. To my surprise, I discovered that tenderness and love were essential. Consequently, the power to see became more than an instrument. Rather, it was a spirit or a being with a purpose and meaning with whom one could relate. It seems to me that the mastery of this power, or of any power, requires a lifetime of care and tenderness of heart.

REFERENCES

Eliade, M. 1972 [1951]. *Shamanism: Archaic Techniques of Ecstasy.* Translated by Willard R. Trask. Bollingen Series LXXVI. Princeton: Princeton University Press.

Chapter 16

Coyote Attends My Surgery

Norma Churchill

Not all visionary experiences are deadly serious. Norma Churchill, a practicing psychic and visionary, contributes this short vignette in which Coyote helps her through an unsettling time.

I was faced with the unsettling experience of the possibility of breast cancer. From all the indications (mammogram, sonogram, and so on), I didn't think I had it, but of course I did not know. The next step was a biopsy.

On the appointed day, I decided to walk the two miles to the medical center. It was a glorious day and I was in good spirits. About halfway there I suddenly sensed a presence near my left side. Turning slightly, I saw Coyote loping alongside me. "What's this rascal doing here?" I thought. "Is he going to play a trick on me? What's he up to?"

He seemed very real and even nonchalant as he trotted along. "Why is he here, on this day?", I thought, knowing his reputation as a trickster. I mused, "Well, at least it's not Bear or Snake," both powerful medicine animals that would have indicated the need for strong medicine, foreshadowing a serious illness.[1]

I turned my attention to Coyote. The suddenness of his appearance and his apparent steadfastness signaled that he was not in his trickster mode, but rather had come as a protector. (He *is* one of the gods, after all.) My sense was that he had not come to play a trick on me but rather that he was alerting me to a trick or some sort of intrigue that day. By his presence, he also made me aware that I did not need serious medicine. This had a quieting effect on me.

We arrived at the radiology department for the first stage of the procedure. A doctor and nurse were waiting to insert a thin wire into my breast, they would take X rays before and after to help guide the surgeon to find the mass. Coyote trotted to a corner of the small room and flopped down, keeping an eye on everything.

They completed the first X ray. listening to them, I understood that the guide wire needed to be inserted very deep, near the chest wall and straight up about halfway into the breast so that the tip would rest exactly on the mass the surgeon would remove in the second state of the procedure. They consulted the X ray throughout the procedure.

In order to insert the wire the doctor had to get on his knees and twist his body like an acrobat. The nurse also had to be somewhat of a contortionist to assist him. It struck me as funny, and I suppressed a giggle. Maybe Coyote had come just for the fun. I glanced his way and saw that he was watching intently and thumping his tail in the telling way of one who knew a joke was to be played out down the line.

Through clenched teeth I couldn't help thinking what a tricky business this wire procedure was as they struggled to insert it in the correct place. After laboring for about twenty minutes, they sprang to their feet, jubilant that they had placed the wire and had done it in such a short time. Evidently it usually took forty-five minutes to an hour. They were pleased with themselves even though they had overshot the target area a smidgen; but they would inform the surgeon and send along the X rays.

While they were congratulating each other, I glanced over at Coyote. He gave me a memorable look, raising his eyebrows as if to say, "I don't think so!" (It would turn out that the smidgen by which they had missed was the problem.). I finally understood why Coyote had come—not to play a trick but to inform my conscious mind that something would go awry. This felt like *it*.

Coyote had a calming effect that soothed me. I knew from my spiritual practice and experience that this was a shamanic happening. A crack in the veil had opened to let Coyote through, and I was grateful. I was fully open to the experience, and I understood the nature of the animal that had appeared. I was exceptionally calm.

You can guess the rest, I'm sure. Coyote followed me upstairs to a small room used for minor surgery, where I was laid out on a narrow table under bright lights with the X rays clipped to a lit screen. I could see the line of the wire in the breast tissue. I marveled that anyone could "read" X rays. Coyote trotted off and made himself comfortable, all the while keeping a watchful eye.

First, I was given lots of Novocain. The surgeon began to work in earnest, using a laser to cut a precise line around the areola. (Later I would be grateful to see the scar disappear.) I was startled to smell the seared flesh, and I remarked that it smelled like a barbeque. The nurse cracked up. Coyote waited.

The surgeon worked for nearly an hour, struggling to spot the mass the wire was supposed to be resting on. We chatted; they worked; time passed. He mentioned that the wire was placed in a patient's breast while she was in a sitting position and that the X rays were taken in a sitting position also. The surgery was done with the patient lying down, however, and the breasts took on a slightly different shape. He evidently had tried for years to solve the difficulties that arose from this but had had no great luck.

Finally he threw up his hands and said, "I can't find the damn thing. Take her back down to radiology for another X ray." There followed a scene right out of the film M*A*S*H*. I was now sitting up on a gurney, clutching a bloody sheet with bloody towels surrounding me, a scissor-type clamp dangling from my breast, and heading full speed toward the back elevator. The nurse seemed to be going a hundred miles an hour, but for me it was like a dream. Coyote stood and watched silently as we raced by. I smiled.

Down we flew to the bottom floor, where a flurry of action began as the elevator door opened. Attendants moved desks and chairs and other objects out of our path as we sailed down the narrow corridor toward the radiology department. Everyone looked alarmed and worked furiously to get me quickly into the room I'd been in previously. Now the self-congratulations and hoopla had been replaced by appalled faces and grave apologies. They appeared chagrined to have to put me through another X ray, but it didn't bother me to endure the pressure of the mammogram machine, as my flesh was by now completely numb. I was even amused to see in the finished films not only the wire but also the dangling scissor clamp, like something out of a horror movie. I nearly laughed out loud, but they were all so serious and anxious. I could hardly tell them about being visited by a god in the form of Coyote, who had prepared me for this completely. I was the only calm one in the room. They took two films from different angles, which made it possible for the surgeon to read them more clearly.

The nurse put the X ray films on the gurney with me, raced me back down the corridor to the elevator with attendants running interference, and whisked me back upstairs to the operating room, where the doctor was waiting. The surgery was completed with good results. The tumor was benign, and I noticed upon my return that Coyote had departed, his job done. I marveled at the gift he had brought and smiled secretly as I was being sewn up. I silently said a prayer of thanks to Coyote, the trickster, who traveled across the worlds to serve me that day. I have honored him by setting out a prayer stick in his colors of white, blue, yellow, and black (Reichard 1950, 426).

NOTE

1. Donald Sandner explains that Coyote is the embodiment of the trickster principal. Paul Radin presents evidence that the trickster cycle is one of the oldest and most persistent myth cycles among the American Indians. Coyote is one of the most enigmatic figures in North American mythology, yet as the trickster he has counterparts everywhere such as Raven, Spider, Fox as well as the Greek Hermes and others. He is difficult for the rational intellect to grasp, but he enchants the imagination (Sandner 1979, 154).

REFERENCES

Reichard, G. A. 1950. *Navajo Religion*. Princeton: Princeton University Press.

Sandner, D. 1979. *Navajo Symbols of Healing*. New York: Harcourt Brace Jovanovich.

Chapter 17

The Dark Feminine: Death in Childbirth and Entry into the Shamanic Realm

Janet Spencer Robinson

Janet Robinson vividly describes her feelings, dreams, and visions during and after her terrifying experience of abruptio placenta in childbirth. This condition is extremely serious and life-threatening for both the mother and the fetus. In this case the fetus died, and the work Janet did then gave her an opening into the shadowy, hidden dimensions of a woman's life, and a firm connection with the Dark Mother.

At my first Symposium on Shamanism and Psychology, in May 1992, while trudging through the snow with some women to gather branches for a sweat lodge, the question of childbirth as a shamanic experience for women came up. Together we freely talked about the painful, dismembering, and numinous experiences some women have in childbirth and how this goes unrecognized in our culture. Nothing more was said at the time, but once again I found myself reflecting upon one of my experiences of giving birth, which resulted in stillbirth and my near death. Although this had been the most significant experience in my life, I had kept it hidden for the most part, as it was clouded with guilt and shame. At the same time I realized that my life as I now know it grew out of this crisis, and this essay is the culmination of what I faced in my early encounter with death: the wisdom of the Dark Feminine.

Death in childbirth brings up images of the terrible and devouring aspect of the mother in the archetype of the feminine. Images of Kali,

Coatlicue, Lilith, and Hecate come to mind. Ajit Mookerjee writes of a vision of the divine Maya as described by Ramakrishna, which is rather horrifying to our Western mentality.

> He saw an exquisitely beautiful woman heavy with child emerge from the Ganges, give birth, and begin tenderly to nurse her infant. A moment later, she had assumed a terrible aspect, and seizing the child in her jaws, crushed it. Devouring her offspring she entered the water. Mahamaya is the all-creating, the all-nourishing, the all-devouring. (Mookerjee 1988, 83)

Thirty years have passed since my encounter with death in childbirth, and I have spent much of that time in Jungian analysis, in practicing psychotherapy, and in facing my own four children in an attempt to understand both the creative and destructive aspects of the archetypal and personal mother. I have wrestled with the concept of the dual mother archetype, which contains the opposites of good and evil, as an adequate definition for women. Although the archetype is defined as holding the opposites, our cultural experience of the feminine is split. As a woman, I have experienced my cultural identity of the archetypal feminine from the perspective of a patriarchal anima projection that has been rooted in the body/mind split of Western dualism. Images of the good (light, the spiritual, madonna) associated with the rational mind, are on the one side, while images of evil (dark, whore, witch), associated with the body, are on the other. All women have received some aspects of these projections. At one time in my life, I aspired to carry the image of the idealized woman and good mother. I lived denying the evil or witch mother and was haunted by it when it erupted in rages, psychic and bodily symptoms, and illnesses. Since the terrible or death-wielding aspect of the archetypal feminine is not adequately honored in our culture, it is difficult to accept its dark side as something numinous, wise, and intrinsic to our human nature. Like many women, in order to find my Self I have been forced to go underneath the patriarchal projections to the dark regions of death where the archetypal feminine seems to remain whole and inclusive of its body, soul, and spirit nature.

Shamanism casts another light on death, and from its paleolithic origins allows us to look at the Dark Feminine as death in life, one inseparable from the another. This has enabled me to consider my experience of death in childbirth within the context of a shamanic event or crisis and has brought another level of meaning to it in my life.

The following Navajo chant is from Judith Savage's book *Mourning Unlived Lives*. She used this chant in a discussion of how the color black is associated with Mother Earth or nature, and how it relates to a "dark shame" that is rooted in the somatic dimension of childbirth loss.

I am ashamed before earth;
I am ashamed before heaven;
I am ashamed before dawn;
I am ashamed before twilight;
I am ashamed before blue sky;
I am ashamed before darkness;
I am ashamed before sun;
I am ashamed before that standing within me which speaks with me.
Some of these things are always looking at me.
I am never out of sight.
Therefore I must tell the truth.
I hold my word tight to my breast. (Savage 1989, 59)

In the summer of 1964 I was a young wife, mother of two little boys, and in my third pregnancy in three years. I was deeply depressed, with the problem centering around issues of failure and loss in my life. Physically this pregnancy had been different and difficult, and I had grown increasingly impatient with it and myself as the due date neared. Active during my previous pregnancies, I decided that even more activity might facilitate this birth. On a day in late summer, with a pickax in hand and an intensity my frustration was inclined to take, I chopped up a plot of hardened clay soil in my backyard, where I hoped one day to plant a garden. That night I experienced a major contraction that did not end. It was unusual, but reacting out of a stoical masochism learned from my mother, I waited for the typical signs of spotting and water breaking before contacting my doctor.

By the following afternoon, when my arms and legs were becoming increasingly numb and my vision blurred, I called my doctor. He advised me to go to the hospital. I was quickly admitted, and a nurse arrived promptly. She placed a stethoscope on my abdomen, listened briefly, then looked up at me with a frown and immediately pushed me off in a wheelchair to a labor room. She helped me onto a bed, where I lay in an acute state of awareness while my body took me into itself as if into a pressure chamber. Pain was filling my body. With a pensive look on her face, the nurse left the room, soon returning with a doctor. I was told they were waiting for the bag of waters to break and to "just hold on." They left, and I sank back into the pressure chamber of my body. The pain continued to eat away at every part of me. From time to time the nurse or a doctor appeared. Never had I felt such pain and I didn't know how much longer I could hold on. The pain was consuming me when suddenly the waters broke and blood washed over and around me. I was immediately surrounded by the nurse, doctors, and more medical staff, wiping up the blood spilling everywhere. Finally my doctor, who had been absent until this time, came into the room and took my hand. I started to cry, apologizing for the pain I could no longer bear. Pain was screaming down the walls inside me, and I saw red everywhere. He told me I was losing too much blood and that he was taking me into surgery to do a caesarean section. I lost consciousness, slipping out of the bloodbath and into darkness.

At the time I didn't know I was near death, but my experience took me into another level of consciousness where,

> *I found myself out of the operating room and in the foothills. Dawn was just breaking, and I was standing on a path under a large oak tree with a blanket around my shoulders. I was freezing cold and permeated by a loneliness I hadn't known before. A light at the other end of the road pulled me toward it. As I drew closer to the light, feeling that it was going to engulf me, I heard sounds of moaning coming from either side of the road. The sounds seemed to have an energic pull to them, as though they were coming from some kind of spirits or ghostly figures.*

> *The moaning on either side of the road and the light in the distance ahead were like two opposing forces of energy pulling at me. This went on for a while until the moaning grew louder and louder, and I awoke in the intensive care unit of the hospital. When a nurse appeared, I asked about my baby and was told that my doctor would be in the next day. I slipped back into a dark, silent stillness.*

The following day I learned from my doctor that I had almost died from abruptio placenta a separation of the placenta from the uterus. I had lost eleven pints of blood as a result of the internal hemorrhaging, which had been concealed until the bag of waters broke. My baby, a daughter, had been stillborn.

My life began to change significantly, but only years later would I begin to understand it as an initiatory experience. Facing death in childbirth had been an event that was both brutal and humbling.

> Something is "hewn" down in death, is "cut." Death is always a brutal event . . . and it is brutal not only as a physical event but far more so psychically: a human being is torn away from us, and what remains is the icy stillness of death. (Jung 1965, 314)

Also brutal was my first experience of analysis with a psychoanalyst who told me in the second or third session that I had killed my baby. A voice from within, similar to his own, was already screaming at me. I did not continue with him, as I knew my situation was not as simple as his reductive interpretation, although I didn't understand why. Intuitively I knew that there was a larger meaning and purpose to this event in my life and that my guilt and shame were parts of it.

Most significant, my near-death experience affirmed that life was more than one-dimensional. Prior to this time I had agonized over living in what felt like two disparate worlds: the outer one, a persona created to meet others' expectations, and the inner one, a secret chamber of intensity, feelings, images, and emotional turmoil. I sometimes wondered if I were mad or "interiorly autistic." Returning to life after nearly dying, I realized I had crossed over into another reality and back. In the other reality, I had been confronted with the powerful forces of darkness and light. In my return to ordinary reality, I experienced a heightened sensitivity and an intense desire to understand the meaning of my life. My world view shifted from a static cosmology to an evolutionary one. The writings of Teilhard de Chardin, scientist and mystic, came into my life. His finding that spirit was embodied in matter—what he referred to as "the divine principle inherent in reality" (Teilhard de Chardin 1959, 19)—dethroned the idea of a judging God. The darkness and the hauntings of my inner world opened the way to Carl Jung. His writings and analysishelped me to make sense of my tormented soul. In time, as I grew to understand the reality of the psyche, the unconscious, I became more comfortable with my own personality and its multidimensionality

Aspects of shamanism that relate to my experience and provide a framework are the shamanic crisis, soul loss, dismemberment, sacrifice, and transformation, and the returning to the community with a healing vision. Vicky Noble, in *Shakti Woman*, describes the shamanic crisis as one that is "frequently accompanied by illness, depression or injury that causes us to face death as a real possibility and to encounter life as a potential choice" (Noble 1991, 5).

Abruptio placenta, the medical term for the condition that caused the death of my baby and my near death, is significant physically and symbolically, and is central to my initiatory experience. The placenta is the site of metabolic interchange between the fetus and the mother, and *abruptio placenta* means the separation of a formerly normally implanted placenta prior to the birth of the fetus. When the placenta is completely torn from the uterine wall, the mother suffers life-threatening hemorrhage and the fetus is cut off from its essential supply of oxygen and nutrients.

The causes of abruptio placenta vary. One cause is a short time between pregnancies, which may result in chronic malnutrition. The most common symptom is vaginal bleeding, with only about 10 percent of women experiencing concealed hemorrhage, as I did. Abruptio severe enough to kill the fetus is less common, occurring in only a small minority of cases, and usually occurs within twenty-four hours of the precipitating event. Abruptio placenta may be seen as a final and dramatic expression of a difficult fetal-maternal relationship.

Symbolically, the placenta, which serves as the site for the exchange of oxygen and nutrients between mother and fetus, could be seen as the archetypal mother. It can also separate itself from the mother and fetus and cause death. The separation of the placenta from the uterus, that is, the tearing away of the blood life from the uterine wall which contains the developing self/Self, is dismemberment. The short time between pregnancies with resultant chronic malnutrition may be likened to the environment of Catholicism, in which I lived at the time, which valued the idea of life but not the reality of the body of the woman that bears life.

In the context of a shamanic crisis or illness, the placenta may be seen as the organ of dismemberment and the pickax as the instrument of dismemberment. The moment I grabbed the handle of the pickax to "fiercely chop weeds pounding / the dry barren soil to make a flower grow" (as I put it in a poem), the Dark Feminine (may have) entered.

At a psychological and symbolical level, the dismembered placenta may be seen as the site where the negative mother complex manifested in my body. Abruptio placenta resembled the relationship I had with my own mother, who dramatically separated herself from my need for her nurturance when I went away to boarding school as a freshman in high school. Within the first few weeks I became very sick, and my parents were called to the school. I had been brought there by a college student who was an acquaintance of my parents, and I found the "correctional home" environment alien to my background and wanted desperately to return home to attend high school. My mother refused to let me, and although my father agreed with me, he did nothing to help. My mother's abandonment of me in a time of emotional and physical illness was a cruel blow, and something in me died. My spirit was broken, and at age fourteen I entered into one of the darkest periods of my life. A compassionate nun, Sister Christella, helped me hold on, as did my identification with the image of the suffering Christ. In analysis many years later I learned that I had suffered from an anorectic break precipitated by abandonment.

Similarly, after the birth of my first daughter, I was an abandoning mother for not having protected the environment in which the placenta (and the pregnancy) could thrive. The placenta (the food supply) separated itself from my uterus (the containing space of the good mother), abandoning us both to death. In this context, Marion Woodman would see abruptio placenta as the negative mother complex embedded in the body. In *The Owl Was a Baker's Daughter* she writes:

> Where the primal relationship is disturbed, the child blames itself, and being unloved becomes synonymous with being abnormal, guilty, alone. Later, a girl's own Self becomes the Terrible Mother, whose rejection denies her child the right to live. (Woodman 1980, 95)

Haunted by my feelings of responsibility for having had a hand in causing the abruptio placenta, I felt like a lost soul living in the *mortificatio* (the alchemical term for psychological death) of guilt and shame. This wound has been a core of darkness and suffering out of which I continually try to sort out where the negative mother complex begins and the divine power of the Dark Feminine enters.

In my experience, the deeply wounded core in women often lies in what has been both rejected and repressed, and it manifests itself in bodily and psychic symptoms. The double wounding occurs when the repressed contents emerge, often in Kali fashion, through mental or physical illness, suicide and death. Jung refers to it as being possessed by a complex.

> All these states are characterized by one and the same fact that an unknown "something" has taken possession of a smaller or greater portion of the psyche and asserts its hateful and harmful existence undeterred by all our insight, reason, and energy, thereby proclaiming the power of the unconscious over the conscious mind, the sovereign power of possession. (Jung 1966, para. 370)

From the shamanic perspective, possession would be considered soul loss, and "is regarded as the gravest diagnosis in the shamanic nomenclature, being seen as a major cause of illness and death. It is becoming increasingly clear that what the shamans refer to as soul loss—that is, injury to the inviolate core which is the essence of a person's being—does manifest in despair, immunological damage, cancer and a host of other very serious disorders" (Achterberg 1988, 121).

Blood as sacrifice and mystery was another aspect of my initiatory experience. The loss of blood through hemorrhage and the massive blood transfusions that followed left a deep impression on me physically and psychologically. A few years later my uterus was removed at the birth of my youngest child. At age twenty-six I saw the end of my menstrual life and felt a loss in my bodily connection to the feminine mysteries. Blood and death and life had become intimately connected.

In *Blood, Bread, and Roses,* Judy Grahn traces the history of blood as a symbol. She shows how women's rites carry the mystery of life and influence the creation of societal "metaforms." By this she means generally "that all metaphor and cultural forms, if traced back far enough, should lead to menstruation and menstrual rite" Grahn (1993, 20). Out of these metaforms the part of the shamanic tradition for women that pertains to the blood mysteries of menstruation and childbirth was created. In regard to the numinosity of blood, "taboos all over the world indicate that in childbirth rites the point of awe and fear was woman's blood, not the birth of the baby, so that a woman who miscarried was just as feared as a woman who delivered a live child" (Grahn 1993, 124).

Life asked of me sacrifice, and the blood of it became the elixir that continues to define my life. In *Ego and Archetype* Edward Edinger writes, "Understood psychologically, blood represents the life of the soul, of transpersonal origin, exceedingly precious and potent" (Edinger 1972, 228).

A dream I had in my early period of analysis is significant to the initiatory process I was taken into through childbirth:

> *I am standing at the door of a small, stark white-painted room that is brightly lit like an operating room. In the center of the room is a woman lying on a gurney. She is pregnant, and a white sheet covers her body. The color red begins to bleed into the white sheet like a wave breaking onshore. I realize she is hemorrhaging. The woman is deathly still and pale, yet gives birth to what appears to be a bloody blue stone. Then I see it is a stillborn baby.*

At the time of this dream I was immersed in issues of abandonment, loss, and identification with the negative mother complex in my analysis. My ego was still involved in culpability, and I was stunned at having to witness the images of the vivid blood loss and stillbirth again. Although I associated the stillbirth to a blue stone that may have something to do with my individuation process, I looked at it primarily as a way of giving meaning to my vulnerability around my dead baby daughter.

Stillbirth also became a metaphor for my own creative process, which often ends abortively in frustration, self-hatred, and depression.

The dream images hold even deeper meaning today. Beyond my personal associations to the dream, I wonder if the image of a woman in childbirth isn't closer to women's shamanic and psychological processes of initiation (if not indigenous to them) than is the image of the alchemical laboratory that is more familiar to us in the Jungian world. I realize now that the image of a woman in childbirth contains the stages of an initiatory process that is familiar not only to the shamanic realm but also to the alchemical process of transformation and its elements.

Pregnancy, dismemberment, blood sacrifice, death, transformation, and birth are present in what might be considered a mandalic form with the alchemical colors black, white, red, and blue. Around the central image of a woman about to give birth is black: the darkness of the unknown, and the "dark shame" she experiences when closest to her bodily animal nature. There is red: the hemorrhage from her womb, the blood sacrifice, and dismemberment. There is white: the sheet that covers her body and acts as a veil between what is dark and hidden below (the body) and what is above (the bright lights of the spirit). It is the veil of transformation from girl-hood to motherhood. And there is blue: woman's bodily spirituality, the blue of her red blood, and the pain of her labor, which brings about the capacity for reflection. "Blue," as James Hillman explains, "is darkness made visible" (Hillman 1993, 136).

The blue stone (baby) is symbolic of the philosopher's stone, "the lapis or the child, the immortal one born out of the womb of fire" (Franz 1986, 80). This stone originates out of the *nigredo*, the black earth or *prima mate-ria*, and carries the transpersonal aspect of individuation.

The amplification of these dream images gives meaning and purpose beyond my ego's identity to the traumatic event in my life. The lapis, as stone and child, was familiar to me, but I did not make the connection to the stone as the Dark Feminine until I came across a reference to the dark blue stone in *Kali- The Feminine Force.* I was deeply moved.

> In her archetypal form, Mother Kali often has no iconographic image but is represented by a stone block or even mound. The Chinese pilgrim Hiuen Tsang who visited the Ghandara region of the North West Frontier in the sev-enth century described the image of Bhimadevi as a dark blue stone. (Mookerjee 1988, 71)

China Galland, in *Longing for Darkness, Tara and the Black Madonna* (1990, 120), an account of her search for the dark side of the feminine in Nepal and Czechoslovakia, finds the color blue-black painted on most of the fierce deities of Asia. Kali corresponds to the Tibetan goddess Palden Lhamo, a wrathful form of Tara. In Mexico we find the goddess Coatlique, her power and awe represented as a great stone statue with a head of twin serpents, a necklace of human hands, hearts, and feet, and a skirt of writhing snakes.

Jung also relates the stone to the Dark Feminine. He sees it as tran-scending Christian and alchemical symbolism and explains how alchemy was an attempt at the symbolic integration of evil. Although Jung has helped us pull back the projection of evil from nature and instead face it in ourselves, it remains crucial for women that the evil projected onto the feminine be differentiated from the true nature of the archetype. Jung's comment about the "stone" is important:

> The very concept "stone" indicates the peculiar nature of this symbol. "Stone" is the essence of everything solid and earthly. It represents feminine *matter*, and this concept intrudes into the sphere "spirit" and its symbolism. . . . The stone was more than an "incarnation" of God it was a concretization, a "mate-rialization" that reached down into the darkness of the inorganic realm or

even rose from it, from that part of the Deity which put itself in opposition to the Creator . . . because . . . it remained latent in the panspermia (universal seed-bed) as the formative principle of crystals, metals, and living organisms. (Jung 1970, para. 643)

Ultimately, the purpose of the shamanic illness or crisis is to carry another perspective into the culture. Parallel to this is the goal of individuation in analytical psychology whose purpose is to bring consciousness into the collective environment. Through my encounter with the Dark Feminine in childbirth, I feel I have been asked to recognize the emergence of this image and its energy in our culture.

An example of this is the experience of Susan Smith in South Carolina in November 1994, the anguished young woman who confessed to drowning her two young sons. I was working on this essay at the time the incident occurred and was sickened by the cover of *Time* on November 14, 1994, which carried the headline "How Could She Do It?" I heard myself say, "I know how she could do it." At one level, she could have been in a negative mother complex, cut off from any source of internal nurturance, feeling desperate, abandoned, and suicidal. On another level, she could have become possessed by the Terrible Mother archetype, whose rage at what had been done to the Feminine could no longer be contained; she became That Terrible Mother and ended her children's lives as if they were her own. She could have identified with being a good mother until this time.

Judith Savage tells us that "these archetypal forces are not within the realm of personal responsibility" (Savage 1989, 13), and she quotes Polly Eisendrath-Young:

> The negative mother complex is organized around the archetype of the "Terrible Mother." This complex expresses the instinctual-emotional responses to the negative aspects of nurturing and attachment. Incorporation, suffocation, [and certainly death], define her character. When the complex is attributed to a woman, or when a woman feels identified with the complex, she experiences herself as having more power than she rationally knows she has. She condemns herself for flaws which are exaggerated and beyond the responsibility of human beings. (Savage 1989, 13)

This is not to deny moral responsibility in such matters as the Susan Smith case, but it might point to an appropriate psychological attitude that can facilitate healing. "How Could She Do It?" might better be read as "How Can We Understand Why She Would Do It?" It seems that in our culture we fail to understand that what continues to be rejected as evil rises up as evil.

The identification with the negative mother complex for generations of women seems to be the result of our cultural perception of duality.

Through my own experience, and from the lives of other women, I am convinced that the nature of the archetypal Dark Feminine holds another perspective we need to experience in order to understand the archetype's presence and meaning in our lives.

This essay presents that other perspective, one that has been made known to me through my encounter with death in childbirth and my own near-death experience. Born from the initiatory experience that my pick-ax-wielding fury took me into at age twenty-three, a child of death was transformed into a child of reflection. I turn to her for vision, guidance, and the way to work with the dark, hidden, painful dimensions of life that pertain particularly to my life as a woman. She, in turn, has taken me back to our Dark Mother.

The following is a poem I began working on in 1979. It evolved as a result of using images from my dream in active imagination. The poem, like my own process, is the soil that I am always re-working:

Blue Sapphire Baby
you came to me
From the dead
no longer a baby
but a little girl
dressed in red
You took my hand
and pulled me
through the door
of the oak tree
where I'd been sitting
waiting for you.
In that hallowed space
you showed me your mother
the white sheet
over her body
turns red
from the blood
of her torn womb.
In silence
we watched her give birth
to a blue sapphire
stone.

It grew dark.
You took my hand and
we spiralled downward,
slowly, quietly

through the tree
trunk of musty smells and wet
wood onto the dark earth.
You left me
sitting alone
at the roots
of the Mother
where the river flows
over the blue sapphire baby
you were
and
I
weep.

REFERENCES

Achterberg, J. 1988. The Wounded Healer: Transformational Journeys in Modern Medicine. In G. Dore, ed. *Shaman's Path.* Boston: Shambala.

Edinger, E. 1972. *Ego and Archetype.* Baltimore: Penguin.

Franz, M. L. von. 1986. *On Dreams and Death.* Boston: Shambala.

Galland, C. 1990. *Longing for Darkness: Tara and the Black Madonna.* New York: Penguin.

Grahn, J. 1993. *Blood, Bread, and Roses.* Boston: Beacon.

Hillman, J. 1993. Alchemical Blue and the Unio Mentalis. In *Spring*, 132–46. Dallas: Spring Publications.

Jung, C. G. 965. [1961]. *Memories, Dreams, Reflections.* New York: Vintage.

———. 1966 [1953]. *Two Essays on Analytical Psychology.* Bollingen Series XX: The Collected Works of C. G. Jung, vol. 7. Princeton: Princeton University Press.

———. 1970 [1955–56]. *Mysterium Coniunctionis.* Bollingen Series XX: The Collected Works of C. G. Jung, vol. 14. Princeton: Princeton University Press..

Mookerjee, A. 1988. *Kali: The Feminine Force.* New York: Destiny.

Noble, V. 1991. *Shakti Woman: The New Female Shamanism.* San Francisco: Harper.

Savage, J. 1989. *Mourning Unlived Lives.* Willmette, Ill.: Chiron.

Teilhard de Chardin, P. 1959. *The Phenomen of Man.* London: Collins.

Woodman, M. 1980. *The Owl Was a Baker's Daughter.* Toronto: Inner City Books.

Chapter 18

Trapped Souls: A Passage to the Spirit World

Lori Cromer

Some few persons have the ability, probably inherited, to have visions and to see and converse with spirits, animated images of persons who have died. Lori Cromer is one of these psychic mediums. Much argument has been waged over the truth or reality of these mediumistic visions. What kind of reality do they reveal? How does one explain the many times mediums seem to receive information from the other world that they have no other way of knowing? In my analytic practice I have heard of many incidents of this kind. It will be a long time until we have definite answers to these questions. Meanwhile, most communities have their own psychics whom they consult in case of need or in unusual situations. Here we have the story of one medium's response in such a case. Mediums do not perform the more dramatic rituals of the tribal shaman, but what they do is so close to shamanism they are often called urban shamans.

It was a blustery February day, and I was full of anticipation. I was meeting my long-lost friend and kindred spirit, Sarah. After hours of talking, Sarah asked me if I would like to look at the upstairs apartment in her house. It was a rental apartment that she had just refurbished. We walked up a beautiful wooden stairwase, and Sarah began our tour in the kitchen. While she was explaining about all the kitchen refurbishing dilemmas, I looked out the kitchen window. As I was mesmerized by the beauty of the mountainside, Sarah's voice became fainter and I heard a woman's soft voice say. "Isn't this view beautiful? I have looked out this window for years, enjoying the hillside." I stood there agreeing, and then realized that this was not my friend's voice. So whose voice was it?

Confused, I asked Sarah if she had ever heard a spirit's voice in the apartment. She told me that she had never seen or heard a spirit but had for years heard footsteps at night coming from the upstairs. Sarah also recalled that a woman tenant moved out because she kept hearing a ghost yell out her name. Although bewildered, we continued our tour. As we stepped into the bedroom feelings of anger and fear overwhelmed me. An image surfaced of a slim black woman wearing a flowered dress, her hair up in a bun. She was prostrate on the bed, being beaten and raped by a black man. Frightened, I ran out of the room.

Sarah followed me to the living room. I was scared and breathing heavily. She asked me what was wrong. As I told her about the image I had seen, I could see shock and fear mirrored in her face. A thousand questions— Was this real? Where did the image come from? Who were these people?— bombarded my mind. Then suddenly one thought came into focus: I had to help this spirit in some way. She was trapped, and I did not know why.

As Sarah and I walked down the narrow staircase, another horrible image came to me. The black woman was standing at the top of the stairs with the same black man. He was sturdily built, dressed in work pants and a soiled white T-shirt. Sweat dripped from his brow, and a layer of dirt covered his arms. They were having an argument. The man appeared very angry and began to hit the woman. She struggled to get away, but he pushed her down the narrow staircase. I could feel the sensation of pain in my back and neck as her spine broke against the edges of the steps. She collapsed at the end of the stairs, broken and lifeless—murdered.

I had a rising sense of panic, and wondered, "Why can't Sarah see this? Why me?" When I regained my composure I told Sarah I would seek advice from my therapist and return the next day. I drove home in a daze, not sure whether to be excited about the journey unfolding or to commit myself to a psychiatric hospital. I called my therapist, and after a long conversation I was instructed to meditate, center myself, and call on my spirit guides for protection and guidance. After hanging up the phone, I reluctantly sat down and closed my eyes to meditate. Immediately I had to cope with incessant internal chatter: "What are you doing? Are you crazy? What's happening?" Finally, after what seemed an eternity, the internal chatter stopped. A sense of calmness enveloped me, and a strength entered my body. I felt ready.

The next day I arrived at my friend's house late in the afternoon. It was snowing, and I remember the silence of the falling snow. For a brief moment I was taken back to the best part of my childhood—playing out-doors. It was when I felt a sense of being alive, calm, and self-assured. I was not quite sure why these memories were coming back to me, but I decided not to block them. I allowed them to calm my uneasiness.

Sarah had been waiting for my arrival. We sat on the couch in her home to meditate and find that quiet place inside to connect with our spirit guides. My deer/panther spirit appeared before me. This particular spirit was one of my first acquaintances when I started connecting with the inner world. She had two sides. Her deer side was more docile and agile. The deer taught me the comfort and support of unconditional love and the importance of playfulness. Her other side, the panther, was more aggressive and fearless. She taught me how to hunt, to be steadfast, and to utilize incredible strength. Her appearance gave me courage, and I hoped to draw on her diverse strengths for help.

The time for us to go to the upstairs apartment had come. We walked up the stairwell, went to the bedroom, and sat at the foot of the bed. Sarah and I were side by side. I closed my eyes, and the image of the black man appeared. I spoke to him sternly. My words seemed to be guided and to come from a place deep within me. As I talked to him about the situation that was unfolding between the two spirits, he ran toward me with his hands raised and clenched poised for attack. By the time he reached me, however, his image had turned to mist, drifted up, and vanished.

I heard a faint whimpering at the edge of the room. I glanced over to the corner of the bedroom and saw the black woman spirit. I walked over and embraced her as she cried. I could feel her suffering. A great sense of love and compassion developed between us as we sat there together witnessing her life of fear and abuse. She said her name was Michelle Thomas and her husband's name was Tim. The feeling of compassion intensified as a whirling, healing energy unified us. A bright light shone through the ceiling and into the center of the whirling energy. As the light brightened, the image of Michelle faded and a spirit force came from the whirling energy and shot up through the light.

I opened my eyes and saw my friend sitting next to me. I was curious to know if she had experienced anything. Sarah said she had felt this incredible sense of power and protection just before I said it was time to go upstairs. At the same time, Sarah noticed that her cat's eyes grew to be three times their regular size. When we were upstairs and in the bedroom, she felt we were consoling the soul. Her eyesight was hazy, but then she saw an undefined image leave through the ceiling. I could not believe my ears. Her experience had been similar to mine. What did this all mean? I shared my own experience, and we sat quietly for a long time together.

Three months later I revisited Sarah. We talked about our shared experience. She told me that she had felt different, physically and mentally, since the release of the spirits. Specifically, she had not experienced as much back pain or the unexplainable depression spells. She thought that perhaps these physical and mental manifestations had been triggered by the pain of the trapped woman's soul. I did not know if it was true, but it seemed possible, considering the remarkable timing of the experience and the decreased symptoms. Even with these positive signs, she expressed concern because she continued to hear footsteps late at night in the upstairs kitchen and living room. Also, her cat, which previously had spent a great deal of time upstairs, hissed at seemingly nothing in the upstairs kitchen and then refused to ever return to the apartment.

I decided it would be a good idea to go upstairs. I happened to have my drum in the car, so I took it with me for protection and support. I went to the downstairs kitchen and did not feel, hear, or see any spirits. I turned around and reluctantly entered the downstairs bedroom. As I stepped into the room I immediately felt the anguish and terror again. I continued on into the living room and sat down in the middle of the room. I shut my eyes and began to drum. I asked for help from the spirit guide that I was currently working with, the dragon. His image appeared, dancing to the beat of the drum. His dance was a familiar ritualistic one that enabled me to unite with him. We danced in unison facing each other. I turned around, and the dragon followed me up the stairway to the upstairs apartment. As we approached the top of the stairs, I entered into the dragon and we became one. Now I was able to look through the red eyes of the dragon. My visual acuity and perception became very clear and precise, increasing to a point where I could view objects and people suspended in the dimension of trapped souls. As the dragon and I entered the living room I could see clearly that this was the same spirit, Tim, that I had seen three months earlier. He was cowering in the corner. As the dragon and I got closer to him I told him that he had committed terrible acts of violence and that to be released he needed to forgive himself and make amends to his wife. I turned and realized that the other spirit, Michelle, was standing across the room. I told her she needed to forgive her husband to be released. The male soul walked over to the female and they talked quietly in the corner. After some time they hugged and began to cry. Then the two spirits joined. Their forms became hazy and escaped up through the old stovepipe. Even though the spirits had disappeared, I could still feel a presence. I walked into the bedroom and heard a child's voice crying, "Mommy, Mommy, where are you?" I quickly transformed back into human form so I would not scare the child. He told me he could not find his mommy and that she had been gone for a long time. I took his hand and guided him to the living room and told him that we would find her. We called for Michelle, and she appeared. I could see only the outline of her figure within a mist. She swept the child into her arms and went back up through the stovepipe. Both of them were gone.

During the next year Sarah and I discussed ways to honor the released spirits and to welcome a new beginning for Sarah and her house. We chose a traditional way of cleansing areas and/or people called smudging. When smudging, you burn sacred material such as sage in the area that you want cleansed.

Because I was eager to see Sarah, I arrived a bit early for the smudging. Sarah excitedly told me that since the releases of Michelle and Tim Thomas, her back pain and unexplained episodes of depression had subsided even more. We decided to go to the upstairs apartment. Stashed on the floor in the corner of the living room was a group of pictures. We were engrossed in conversation when all of the sudden the pictures at the bottom of the stack began to rattle against each other. I thought, "It must be Sarah's cat." But the cat was not in the room. The window was shut, and I could not detect any drafts from doors or windows. The unexplained rattling startled us. I then became aware of the presence of another spirit.

We began the ritual cleansing, smudging ourselves and the room with sage and cedar. As I began to drum, I could feel more clearly the presence of a new male spirit. He came into sharp focus. He was standing at the side of the room, looking angry and feeling disgusted. He felt we were intruding. He appeared to be English and was impeccably dressed in a black linen suit with a patterned silk vest that had a gold pocket watch in the pocket. The drum discovered its own rhythm, and I began to beat faster and louder. I heard myself telling the Englishman to go past the light and leave the apartment. We argued back and forth. He told me that he did not need or desire to leave. I told him that it was time and that nothing existed here for him. Finally, although I was not sure why, he reluctantly disappeared into the light shining from the ceiling.

That night I was in bed at home reading a history book about Sarah's town when I saw a picture of a prominent town founder. It was the Englishman I had seen in Sarah's home! His name was Dr. Stephen Mountain. He had been a medical doctor specializing in homeopathic medicine. I was ecstatic. I had proof that I was not crazy or imagining the experience. But in my moment of exhilaration, I heard a male voice with an English accent. It was the spirit from Sarah's house. He wanted me to go on a walk for him in the morning. He wanted to experience his favorite mountain jaunt one last time vicariously through me. Reluctantly I agreed to go, wondering if I had gone crazy.

The next day I took the walk with him, and it was magnificent. The trail meandered easily up the mountain leading to a hillside of delicate bloom-ing wildflowers of all colors, shapes, and sizes. I could smell and feel the clear crisp air on my cheeks and arms. It was as if I were in a haven. Stephen told me he would miss the mountains and his town. At the end of the trail the mountainside and valleys were silhouetted against the backdrop of majestic peaks that surrounded the small town. It was a view I will never for-get.

When I arrived at the top of the mountain, Stephen related why he was trapped at Sarah's house. He had covered up Michelle's murder because he did not want violence to tarnish the reputation of his town. This unre-solved and unfair situation had trapped him at Sarah's. I asked why he had not left after the other trapped spirits had been released. He told me that he had grown fond of Sarah and felt he protected her. Suddenly the mood shifted to an even more serious tone. He asked in a very low and cautious voice, "May I stay with you for two weeks? Then I promise to leave." I was stunned. What do you say to a request like that? I mulled it over and replied, "I will allow you to stay with me under one condition: I must have complete authority over my body, mind, and soul. If you try any kind of control, I will set you free immediately." Even as I was saying this I was thinking, "Do I know how to do this? Can he read my thoughts before I speak them?"

Despite my concerns, the next four days were remarkable. Having anoth-er soul hanging around was an experience that is hard to describe. While I was gardening, he enjoyed the sensations of the cool earth on my hands, the hot sun on my face, and the perspiration on my forehead. These sen-sations were new to him because he was from a wealthy family and had never been allowed to become dirty and sweaty. However, on the fourth day I realized I had not had contact with Stephen for about two to three hours; usually we were in constant contact. I called for him, and he appeared, but he was old and fragile-looking. I asked in horror, "Are you dying?" He replied, "Yes." Fear and anguish began to torment me. What should I do? Who could help me? Would I die also because he was connected to me?

I immediately contacted my therapist. I was frantic and could barely tell him what was happening. He calmed me down and told me that it was time to witness Stephen's death. My therapist suggested that I drum for Stephen and just be present. So I began drumming. I closed my eyes and immedi-ately saw Stephen. We joined hands, and I led him into a room that had a large natural bath. The room was underground; love radiated from the earthen walls. Cleansing his body calmed him, and he began to look peace-ful. I then carried his fragile slim body down a stone and dirt tunnel into another room. Candles placed around the room illuminated a tomb. I placed him in the tomb and smudged his body and the area with sage and cedar. I stood there for a long time and witnessed his soul departing. After the soul was gone, I wrapped the body in cloth and carried it down the stairs into the center of a cavern, where I then burned it. As I looked upon this burning body I felt no grief, only calmness and serenity. I had never felt this peace before during a dying process. When the burning subsided, I walked up the stairs knowing I had honored someone's death.

A death passage ritual might seem to be a strange way to end this story, but death is a transition. My own transition began when I allowed myself to override my doubts and in some cases the intellectual voice. Trusting and honoring these other kinds of nonordinary experience has allowed me to accept a new aspect of myself that feels wise and centered. I do not know what is in store for me, or whether or not I will encounter any more spirits, but I do know that once you open and accept your soul, you start on an unusual adventure.

Part IV

THE NUMINOUS WEB:
CULTURAL CONNECTIONS

Chapter 19

Lakota Teachings: Inipi, Humbleciya, and Yuwipi Ceremonies

Pansy Hawk Wing

Pansy Hawk Wing is an authentic pipe carrier and spiritual leader in the Lakota (Sioux) culture. In this essay she describes traditional Lakota rituals in which old shamanic principles are firmly embedded. The experience of Inipi (the sweat lodge ceremony), Humbleciya (the vision seeking ritual), and Yuwipi (a traditional curing ceremony) are of special interest to analytical psychologists because they bring vision-seeking, which is also characteristic of active imagination, into a cultural setting in which the visioner seeks and experiences his visions with the full support of his community. Pansy Hawk Wing has won the heartfelt gratitude of our Denver group because of the many times she has shown us with great integrity and dignity the beauty and power of the Lakota sweat lodge ceremony.

Mitakuye oyasin to each of you. The literal translation is "to all my relatives," and the phrase is used to convey the sentiment that we are all related to each other.

In recent years, many people have returned to the way of the Sacred Pipe and many young people hunger for the teachings. Many tribes, or nations, have lost their ceremonies through assimilation and so look to the Lakota people to learn the ceremonies. The Lakota culture is preserved in oral history form because it was disguised and hidden from outsiders. Many writings have been published in an attempt to capture the richness and quality of the ceremonies, but it is not the same as the stories being told and sung in our own languages, the Lakota, Nakota, and Dakota dialects. In much of today's writings the interpretations are not quite the same as they are in the oral tradition because the authors of the writings are not speakers of the language. Our culture, our spirit, our songs, and our names are spoken in a language we believe is ancient, full of wisdom, and rooted in the way of the Sacred Pipe, the way of life given to our nations.

In recent history, the Lakota teachings went underground to prevent the U.S. government from annihilating the Lakota culture and language. Those of us who speak our language know that much has been lost in the resurgence. We have no way of knowing how much was lost, but today we give *wopila* (thanks) for that which we have, that which is rich in pomp and circumstance. *Mitakuye oyasin.*

INIPI CEREMONY

The Inipi, is the sweat lodge ceremony. The literal translation of *nipi* is "to live." The first letter, *I* comes from the root word *un*, meaning "through this" or "with this." Inipi, as passed down from generation to generation, is the first ceremony taught to the o*yate* (the people). I will attempt to describe the Inipi, but this is difficult for me to do because I have to visually place myself in the ceremony.

The Inipi structure represents the rib cage of the Mother. This is a dome-like structure built with chokecherry bush branches or willow branches and covered with a tarp, blankets, and utility plastic (W*opila* (thanks be) to modern technology). The idea is to have the structure completely dark and the covering dense enough to retain the heat and steam.

The ceremony is a return to the womb of the mother in order to be reborn. In so doing, we become grandchildren of the Great Grandfather, Tunkasila. As grandchildren, we become childlike in our wisdom, acknowledging we know only a little. No jewelry or ornaments are allowed during the Inipi so that we may be humble and present ourselves without the many faces we put on when we wear jewelry and ornaments.

During the ceremony, when others are speaking or praying, the rest of the people allow the speaking to happen without interruption. The leader of the Inipi ceremony is called "the one who pours water," "the leader," or "pipe carrier," and this person is the keeper of the discipline.

The sweat lodge is built with two poles facing each of the four directions of the wind; poles are also added to the diagonal positions. Two rows of poles run parallel to the ground, encircling the structure. The west direction will have a doorway built for entry and exit. The reason the door faces west is that the spirit guides enter from the west. A pit is dug in the center to hold the heated stones upon which water is poured to create the purifying steam. The dirt from the center of the inipi is placed outside of the dome structure, directly to the west, halfway between the outside fire pit and the door.

On the altar is a buffalo skull and the Sacred Pipes that are being offered in ceremony by those present. A staff may be placed on the altar, representing the sacred pathway for a particular individual; this same staff can be used during other ceremonies that he or she participates in, such as a Humbleciya (vision quest).

The fire pit is located directly west of the altar. To build the fire, four logs, each a yard in length, are aligned in an east-west direction, lying parallel to one another. The second layer of logs is placed in a north-south direction, again parallel to one another. Upon these two layers of logs, to the west is placed the first stone, to the north the second, to the east the third, and to the south the fourth. One stone is placed for Earth Mother, one for Heavens, and the seventh for the man's/woman's altar. A total of twenty-eight stones are used. The ceremony begins when the wood is arranged, the stones placed, and the fire started. In addition, someone must always tend to the fire when it is lit.

After eighteen months of learning the ceremony, I was approached by my mentor-interpreter (commonly called a "medicine man" in the Western cultures) to lead an Inipi. I was afraid I was not ready for such an important job, but he assured me that I was prepared. I did, however, need to seek guidance from the spirit guides and Tunkasila to perform the ceremony. Reluctantly I did as I was told. The ceremony was well received; I felt that I had accomplished a great task, and I was anxious to learn more. Since then, I've learned that whenever I have been approached to do a ceremony, I have never felt totally ready.

As mentioned before, the dome structure is heavily covered to retain heat and block out the light. The inipi is completely darkened, which helps me to focus inward and be able to connect with the spirit within. In one of the first Inipi ceremonies that I participated in, I saw an infant child in my mind and reached out and took the child into my arm and rocked the baby. This happened almost immediately during each Inipi I took part in. Through the years this child has grown older, and the one image that has been fairly consistent is that of a four-year-old hiding away in a corner who needs coaxing before she will permit herself to be hugged by me. I later found out that this was my age when my father and mother separated. Today when I am faced with a painful situation, be it loss or separation, this my inner child needs me in the Inipi, and I coax her into my arms to nurture her.

The prepared stones need to be heated for one and a half to two hours before they are ready for the ceremony. The leader prepares to make an offering of his/her Sacred Pipe to the spirits that will be utilized during the Inipi ceremony. All others who wish to make offerings of their Sacred Pipes for personal reasons may also offer and fill their pipes and place them on the altar. When the stones are ready, everyone is purified with smoke and enters the inipi in a clockwise manner. The first seven heated stones are brought in singly, and then the remainder are brought in. Cedar or sage is placed on the heated stones; the aroma is part of the purification. After all the stones are brought in, the door is closed, water is poured on the stones, and the purification ceremony takes place. Each subsequent opening of the door has a special meaning and is accompanied bu special songs and prayers.

Healing at the emotional, physical, spiritual, and communal or universal level can take place during an Inipi ceremony. I have personally experienced healing at all of the levels and feel that, healing deep in my being, as I walk the path of the Red Road, the Native American spiritual path.

People involved in the teachings of C. G. Jung appreciate the time and extensive learning involved in working with a mentor and in connecting with the spirit world to complete the circle of healing, the Sacred Hoop. It is "unconscious" to take only portions of the ceremonies and use them for the so-called healing practices of the New Age movement today. One needs to seek inwardly and to heal one's own spirit in addition to working with a mentor for a period of time, all the while helping to teach others and working with others utilizing ceremonies, before one is ready to perform such a ceremony properly oneself. I understand that it takes a minimum of seven years to begin to think of stepping into the world of Jungian teachings, and it takes at least that amount of time to learn the discipline, ritual, ceremony, and healing of the Lakota Way, the walk of the Sacred Pipe. *Mitakuye oyasin.*

HUMBLECIYA CEREMONY

At the age of twenty-four I began to fall into the world of alcoholism and other substances used to medicate oneself. Those things helped me run from facing myself. In Lakota this is called o*nuniyata un* (one who walks in darkness in the lost world). The last time I was partying with a group of friends, at the age of twenty-eight, I went outside very early in the morning and sat there as the sun came up. As I watched the sun beginning to warm the heavy early morning dew, I knew that this was a very significant turning point in my life. In front of me I saw a forked road. One way led to a life unknown to me, and the other showed me a road of self-destruction and the destruction of the people I loved, especially my children. I became afraid, shook, cried, and asked, "What do I do now?" Then I reached into my purse, pulled out the bottle of bourbon I kept there, and threw it as far as I could. At that point my body still shook, yet I had a knowing that everything would be all right.

A few weeks later I heard that an elder who was a mentor-interpreter for many people had returned from the Northwest Coast to conduct Humbleciya ceremonies at Bear Butte. I took some tobacco and went looking for him. He asked me to state my purpose, and I did. He told me to prepare and return to the site the following day when the sun was at the same place. I already had a Sacred Pipe. The mentor's female helper had explained to me all of the things I needed, so I went and began my preparation, which took all night. At sunrise the following day I had everything ready and returned to the site. The Inipi fire was lit, and we sat around the fire and began talking, sometimes about ceremony and other times about other topics.

When the fire was nearly ready, the mentor told me to fill my Sacred Pipe to be presented to him so that he could be my guide and interpreter-teacher for the ceremony. I was very frightened throughout much of this time. I filled my Sacred Pipe, the c*anupe*, while appropriate songs were sung. I extended the c*anupe* to him four times; he took it the fourth time. He prayed with it, made references to my being new in this ceremony and the fact that I needed guidance, and then he smoked the c*anupe*. Then he announced it was time to begin the Inipi ceremony in preparation for the Humbleciya.

During the Inipi ceremony for the Humbleciya, the door is opened only once, (in other Inipi ceremonies there are four openings). During the Humbleciya ceremony and the Wiwayang Wacipi (Sun Dance), there is only one door opening for each ceremony and only seven stones are used. The one door opening may last anywhere from one to two hours, depending on the situation. I was asked inside the inipi about my reason for participation in this ceremony. I was given further instruction. Then we came out of the inipi and in silence prepared for the trek up the mountain.

I announced that I wanted to be placed at the summit of Bear Butte; later I learned that usually only veteran Humbleciya people went to the summit. The instructions were to not touch anyone (the hugging and asking for prayers took place before the Inipi ceremony) or speak to anyone. People carried what I had prepared for the *Hochoka* (Mystery Hoop) and the blankets I had brought. One blanket was new and to be given away, and one was to keep. I carried my *chanupo* and altar stick. To the altar stick was tied a red cloth and on the red cloth was tied an eagle feather on a medicine wheel. Spirit food was prepared in a small wooden bowl, and I wore humble garb—a plain dress made of calico and a shawl. Beaded moccasins were optional, but no jewelry was to be worn.

We began the ascent of Bear Butte and were not to look back. We stopped four times on the climb and prayed at each stop to ask the spirits to relieve us of our bondage to material things: possessions, community, friends, immediate family, and other relatives. We were on the way to an altar where we would relate and communicate with the spirits, and the path was a relationship between me and the spirit world. I was afraid. At the summit they prepared my altar, and then I stepped inside while prayers were spoken and the sacred songs sung. Then the supporters left me in communication with the spirit world.

That night, once I got past my fear, I was completely tuned in with everything around me. Every sound and every movement became magnified. I was instructed to speak with spirits in the first person addressing them directly. This I did. Soon the fear dissipated and I calmed down. Then I began to drum and sing. I asked for help to learn songs, to pray, to learn ceremonies, and to learn about who I was. I began talking to Tunkasila and Ina Maka (Father and Mother), telling them about my past and asking how I would go about changing my life. Daylight came, and in front of me I saw there was a cedar tree that had no leaves but was rooted solidly into the ground. I began to realize that this was a symbol of my past. I was overcome with feeling and began to cry and give *wopila* (thanks) for the lesson I learned.

Toward late afternoon, I saw a movement to my right; when I looked, I saw a man who had no shirt. His shoulders were covered with a gray blanket, and his upper arms had the design of a yellow streak of lightning. He had long straight hair and was muscular and wiry in build. He came and danced in front of me. This image later became my Internal Warrior, the one who steps forward during times of hardship and gives me courage to continue and to not give up.

The image of the *wanbli* (eagle) came frequently and was very active during my first Humbleciya. Later this represented my faith and trust that all things have a time and a place. This image of the eagle became my foundation. Throughout the years many spirits, images, and symbols connected to the eagle have come my way. The image of the eagle has become a symbol of my spirit circle, my prayer circle.

My brother, six years my junior, had been involved with the Sacred Pipe long before I came to the Path, and in the beginning he advised me on many aspects of my journey. He once told me, "With these ceremonies, put much pomp and circumstance into what you do. Honor the spirits and honor the people by ritualizing and carrying yourself proudly in your best regalia whenever you take part in these ceremonies." He also advised me one year, "Do not wait for a man or woman to tell you when it is time for you to lead a ceremony or ritual. Look into your heart and you will know."

To this day, this has been a guiding influence in the rituals and ceremonies I do. I look inside and ask the spirits, and my heart gives me the answer. One of his favorite sayings was *hecetu Ktaca hecetu* (what is meant to be will be). My brother died at the age of thirty-two, at the height of his ascension to the position of ceremonial leader. He refused to allow surgery to save his life, and he died from a kidney disease he had had since childhood. He was one of my first teachers.

Dawson Has No Horses and Martin High Bear, now both deceased, both great ceremonial leaders, exemplified the walk on the Red Road. These two elders also influenced me—Dawson prodded me when he felt it was time for me to move beyond my comfort zone; and Martin intuitively knew when it was time to have high expectations of me and would settle for no less. Both were well respected, strong, and gentle men. *Mitakuye oyasin.*

The Humbleciya (Vision-seeking) ceremony is revered among the Lakota people. They look in awe at those who participate in this ceremony. Many of them feel they are not capable of completing this ceremony, so they serve in the capacity of supporter and seem to gain from this way of helping others. When one returns from the vision-seeking ceremony, others partake in the Inipi ceremony to hear what message for the people the participant returned with.

YUWIPI CEREMONY

The *Yuwipi* ceremony is a ritual in which the interpreter intercedes between the people and his spirit beings. This ceremony is the most difficult to explain to others in lecture form or written form. In the participation portion of the ceremony, all activities are interconnected and follow a very specific form, and the feeling and teachings all seem to pull together of the various parts of the whole. Dawson Has No Horses, an interpreter-intercessor who was most influential for many people, performed this ceremony. Dawson is no longer in this world, and to honor his spirit I will attempt to interpret my perceptions of what takes place in these ceremonies.

The ceremony I participated in is only one of many I took part in during the early days of learning about the Sacred Pipe. Participation in this ceremony is through invitation only. It is against tradition to show up uninvited. During the preparation for a Yuwipi, often an Inipi ceremony is readied for those who are able to participate. Many elders, invalids, terminally ill people, small children, and those who are troubled attend these ceremonies. It is believed that these ceremonies, Inipi and Yuwipi, are powerful and that the presence of the spirits will heal those who take part in them. Emotional, spiritual, physical, family, and relationship problems are brought to these ceremonies. All who are present pray with one mind and one thought, and participants are admonished to pray for healing for all present in the room.

These ceremonies are held in houses or structures specifically built for ceremonial purposes. Meals are prepared by the families of those participants who specifically request the Yuwipi ceremony. A specific number of tobacco ties (small ceremonial bagas of tobacco as offerings) and clothes (representing the six colors) are prepared by the family or families sponsoring the Yuwipi ceremony. The food is brought into the ceremonial house, and the altar for the interpreter is prepared.

After all is in place, the interpreter is brought to the center wrapped in a blanket, hands tied behind his back. As nearly as I understand, this is performed to allow for astro travel, shape changing, and spirit connections within a specific boundary. The binding of the interpreter is done to demonstrate the power of the spirit that enters and/or communicates with him. At this point, after the intercessor is wrapped and laid face down on the floor within the bounds of the altar, the singing begins. The intercessor begins talking aloud, asking why he has been asked to be an intercessor, acknowledging fear, and singing songs given to him that tell of his journey and how he became an Interpreter for the people.

The lights are turned off, and the drumming and songs begin. The songs are sung in a certain order: Sacred Pipe Offering songs, Four Directions songs, Honoring the Spirits songs, Sacred Pipe songs, Sun Dance songs, Healing songs, and Sending the Spirits Back to the Spirit World songs. The intercessor, whose voice is muffled because he is facedown, asks the people what it is they are there to ask. In the room there may be fifty to a hundred people praying for whatever reason they are there. The Intercessor listens to the people and speaks with the spirits.

During the prayers the sounds of the eagle-bone whistle and the rattle can be heard. It is said that these are the voices of the spirits that the intercessor interprets. He is simultaneously listening to the people and acknowledging what he is hearing in the whistle and the rattle. Sometimes he asks for a specific song and announces that a certain spirit is now present in the room. The people are in awe of the presence of the spirit. During this portion of the ceremony one can hear the heavy walking of the buffalo in the room, feel the wings flapping of the eagle, and see sparks and lights in the darkness, like lightning. This ceremony is most intense and powerful, building to a crescendo.

The people are all praying, giving thanks, and asking for forgiveness, knowing that the spirits can see right through to whether we are speaking the truth or not. When all the people have prayed, more songs are sung, and the intercessor announces that each person will be given a response to their prayer. Sometimes probing questions are asked of certain individuals for clarity, while others are given a sense of trust and hope, and yet others find the responsibility for their problems laid back in their own laps. The intercessor responds to every individual who prayed or was present in the room.

During the next-to-last songs, the mood in the room is one of being of one mind, a connectedness to the other world (the spirit world), a calmness and renewed hope, and a deep sense of being connected to oneself.

It is said that the intercessor's life is not his own. His family takes second place because the spirits use him as a channel for all people. Intercessors have a peaceful feeling about them; they are neither driven nor materialistic. They have the capacity to nurture and restore very gently and yet have the ability to reprimand or chastise with what feels like an eagle plume. They represent balance.

Being a Yuwipi intercessor is the highest form and level of connection with the spirit world. This is done in a collective setting in which collective healing takes place. This is both good and bad. The spirits channel healing through the intercessor for the people. What is dangerous is that some of the mental, physical, and spiritual ills of the people stay in the channel. We must continually pray for the intercessor and his family because we are taught that he cannot (use *he* because as of yet no woman has been given this power) pray for himself and cannot use the powers to heal himself or his own family. It is the responsibility of the people to pray for him and his family.

Dawson Has No Horses, the most powerful of such persons, contracted cancer and died from his illness. He was instrumental in helping many of us who worked with him and were witness to his healing power. We felt the compassion of a person who laid his heart, body, and soul on the line for the people. He knew the dangers of being a channel, and he talked to the people about this often, sometimes expressing fear. He had a passion and feeling, a sense of what he needed to do for the people. He died carrying the problems and woes of the people. His wife, Emily, and his sons and daughters still live in the same homestead on the reservation. They are a living tribute to this man who brought healing to many, many people in this country.

Dawson Has No Horses was a traditional dancer and Sun Dance leader. He was also a lay reader in the Episcopal Church. This is a man who walked more than one world—the white world and the Lakota world, the spirit world and the earth. Many of his students, including myself, have learned to walk in more than one world from him and others, while others are still looking outside themselves. Dawson Has No Horses was the only interpreter-teacher I have worked with. I worked with him for only three short years, but I still apply what he taught me.

During the ceremonies he talked often about his vision, the medicines that came to him, and the songs that were given him. He lived in a balanced way, and he had no need for being glorified. At the same time he did not keep his spiritual connections hidden. He had the grace to make people feel at ease, and he had a no-nonsense way that gave him the air of being real. He represented to me the pulling together of spiritual powers with the physical self. Many spiritual interpreters today have a gap that separates the spiritual from the physical; they talk one thing but live another. It is sad that this is so, for if they would merge the two, they would be powerful.

All the ceremonies and rituals represent a healing journey for the Lakota people. For me, I have observed that in the Inipi (sweat lodge ceremony) we each suffer the physical discomfort of the steam while praying for the circle as a whole. In the Humbleciya (vision quest), an individual ceremony, the person prays for a vision for the people. In Yuwipi, we pray for healing and in the Wiwayang Wacipi (Sun Dance) ceremony, a collective ceremony, we give thanks and offer all we have which is symbolized by our flesh, and pray for ourselves and our community.

For me, these ceremonies represent a major shift in myself from a person with a painful past who, in turn, created pain for others, to one who utilizes the ceremonies for inner healing. For my mental healing, I use what is available in society today to heal my relationships with people and with myself, but the ceremonies heal my spirit. When a new spirit comes to me, I know that is the direction in which I need to look for healing. The spirits come in their own time, not mine. These spirits form a circle, and I go inward to seek guidance and direction. My spirit is with you. *Mitakuye oyasin.*

Chapter 20

Buffalo Vision

Norma Churchill

This is a report of a single vision from a visionary in our own American middle-class culture, in which there is no community support for such visions. It is powerfully poignant, and it contains a warning for the whole culture. Such visions are ignored at great peril. They reach far beyond the individual who has them, and they are meant to be heard by all.

The Buffalo Vision occurred in the usual place of meditation on December 5, 1990.

After many months of absence, my splendid Elk of past visions appeared next to me. He then lay down beside me and put his great head in my lap. I clearly saw and felt his large body next to me as he tucked up his hooves and curled his great bulk, adjusting his antlers this way and that, like a large dog getting comfortable. I noticed the lovely patterns of his coat and could feel the flesh, viscera, and bone within as he moved beneath my hand, which rested upon his neck. I looked into his beautiful eyes and was struck by the poignancy I saw there—such anguish and rapture.

We remained with his head in my lap for some time, letting the serene energy wash over us, filling the gap of lost time together. Suddenly he was up on his feet, standing across the room and waiting for me to mount him. As usual, he was patient with my clumsy attempts to leap up onto his back. After several attempts I was up and felt the thrill of an impending journey, especially as he had come so unexpectedly and so intimately.

I was not prepared for the sorrow to come.

THE JOURNEY

We went slowly out onto the plain, sniffing the cool air and feeling the soft breezes dance against our skins. The great plain stretched out before us and I understood that, as in other visions, it stood for middle America or the heartland. We journeyed on and came upon an area with distant mountain ranges on the horizon. Clumps of trees dotted the landscape, as did shrubs, tumbleweeds, and rock outcrops. Above us strings of white clouds trekked across the vast blue sky. The pungent odor of discovery enveloped us as we made our way into the scene. In a curious way it was bleakly beautiful. The great open plain filled me with the wonder of its space, and the scene came inside my body as part of my psyche, where it seemed to belong quite naturally.

Without warning we came upon a devastating scene: a great, noble buffalo, dead, its face lying on the edge of a small water hole. It had been poisoned by the groundwater that filled the pond, the life source of this place. The great beast's mahogany-hued body looked as though it could suddenly jump up, be filled with life, and prance away. But no, it was quite dead, with its tender lip touching the water's edge. I gazed at its large wooly head, so lifelike, so recently alive, and was struck with sorrow that filled my whole body. I felt as though I were suddenly leaden and dead myself. A deep dread welled up in me as I realized that these poisoned waters also represented our spiritual life.

The Great Elk moved on, and I could see the hardship of the creatures that lived in this place. The Elk stopped many times, and I witnessed and endured all he showed me.

I felt the sorrow of our negligence toward the land, our land, for which we have had so little sympathy and less honor. We do not shine as caretakers of our sacred land, as did our red brothers and sisters, who kept it in trust for all generations.

We have poisoned it. We are dying at the water hole—for America is the buffalo! The Buffalo represents the instinctual part of us as a nation—now lying dead, poisoned by our wrong attitudes and deeds of the past. Even our spiritual life is threatened.

I was shocked to see the state of the land. The aquifers, our underground waters, are being poisoned by our hands, our inattention, our stupidity and our greed. Our cavalier attitudes of the recent past are close to killing us. The animals first, then us—our nation's short history passed before me, its promise diminished by the fouling of our deep waters, the rage of our children, the anguish of our fellow creatures.

I clutched the rough fur of the Great Elk and wept.

COMMENTARY:

As a visionary person living in our modern society, I have dealt with mythic themes arising from the depths of the psyche (collective unconscious) through Jung's idea of active imagination. My visions have been concerned with the rise of the feminine principle; I have done this mostly through the auspices of the Great Serpent, who has become a guide and mentor. Although my visions point toward collective changes that are not yet manifest in the mainstream mind, we can observe the hints pushing up slowly through dreams, art, and politics.

There is a continuous debate as to whether these images are inner visions that are projected into the outer world or whether they are really out there as spirit manifestations that are perceived by the inner eye. The psychologists favor the former view, and the dedicated spiritists champion the latter. Since no proof has ever been discovered, we are free to choose according to our inclinations.

Chapter 21

The Sun Dance: Wiwayang Wacipi

Steven H. Wong

The Lakota quest for a vision is paralleled in Jung's psychology by active imagination—a technique in which the analysand seeks a direct and reciprocal relationship with the unconscious. Steven Wong brought both of these methods to a peak in his courageous participation as a dancer in a Lakota Sun Dance. As you will see, this involves severe deprivation and physical pain. He was successful in tearing himself from the breast skewers that tethered him to the sun pole only because of his unwavering focus and unshakable intent. This is a very transforming experience, but it is not for everybody!

> *O Wakan-Tanka, be merciful to me, that my people may live!*
> *It is for this that I am sacrificing myself.*
>
> *—Black Elk*

In August 1992, Pansy Hawk Wing, a Lakota shaman (*winyan wakan*), invited myself and some friends to a Sun Dance ceremony in Porcupine, South Dakota.

It was dark, but the full moon and distant stars shed enough light to allow me to pitch my tent. Bo, Pansy's son, came up the hill overlooking the Sun Dance arbor to ask me to go pay my respects to her.

As I approached Pansy's campfire I noticed a group of people around the fire in deep but there was occasional nervous laughter. Standing before Pansy, I bowed and expressed my gratitude to her for permitting us to be on their sacred land and to witness the Sun Dance. In this solemn moment of reverence, Pansy giggled. Sitting on a worn-out patio chair, she pulled out a red piece of cloth with a sun disk in the middle and, with her face silhouetted against the campfire, said, "Do you want to dance?"

At first I was in shock. It takes years of spiritual and physical preparation to endure and survive four days of dancing without food or water. How could I possibly accept the Sun Dance skirt?

People around the campfire were laughing and teasing me. I quickly regained my composure and asked, "How much time do I have to make my decision?" Pansy replied, "Half an hour." I bowed and said I would return with my answer. Beneath all the laughter and sarcasm coming from the others, I sensed their fear and doubt mixed with reverence and terror.

Walking into the South Dakota hills, I thought seriously about whether to dance or just be an observer. As I do with all major decisions, I consulted my inner wife. In shamanistic traditions, each shaman usually has a spiritual spouse in addition to a human spouse. The inner wife or husband serves as a pyschopomp or guide in both outer and inner events. In Jungian psychology, the anima is the psychopomp for the male and the animus plays that role for the female.

The moon held a special luminosity, for it held the light of my inner wife. As a warrior, I asked her if I could do the Sun Dance, but as a spirit, she said, "What is your intention?" I searched my heart and replied, "The pain is deep in me. My wound is old and I hunger for healing. You have always touched me deeply. The Sun Dance is only a moment in time, but it is a moment for realization. I am ready. Please give me your permission to disfigure my body. I will abide by your decision."

I continued up the hill, wandering aimlessly, looking into the starry sky and waiting. A warmth began to envelop me, and a distant voice chimed in my ear. Softly and ever so gently, she said, "I am ready, my husband. We shall dance in pain and ecstasy."

The laughter and sarcasm grew louder as I approached the campfire, and the fear was more palpable. I became solemn and lost in my bond with my inner wife. With my bedroll over my shoulder, I stepped into the campfire circle and said, "I am ready!" Everyone was suddenly quiet. Pansy reached up, gently touched my arm, and gazed tenderly into my eyes.

Other women were quickly enlisted to help Pansy make sage anklets, wristlets, and crown, all wrapped with red cloth, for my Sun Dance. I was then taken to a large tepee on the west side of the hochoka (Mystery

Hoop), the dancing area about fifty yards in diameter with an arbor surrounding it, where I would share a space with the other dancers.

A sweat lodge was being prepared for the dancers. I counted six other men and five women (the women had their own quarters and sweat lodge, and Pansy was their leader). All the men, wearing loincloths, gathered together in the sweat lodge as the male shaman (*wicasa wakan*) stressed the seriousness of our commitments. We then prayed to Tunkasila and *Wakan-Tanka* (Grandfather and the Great Spirit) for blessings, protection, and courage.

We finally went to sleep at one in the morning, tired, excited, and scared. We were awakened brusquely at four A.M. by a crusty old ex-paratrooper who was one of four assistant shamans. "Get up, get up, get up, you lazy dogs! This is not a hotel! This is not the Holiday Inn!" He ran around the tepee, beating the walls, yelling and pleading with us to move, pulling some of us out of our warm bedrolls. The air was so cold that I could see my breath suspended in space. After another sweat lodge, I put on my skirt, crown, wristlets, and anklets and ran into the darkness looking for my position in the line.

There was frost on the grass, and my tender feet began to grow numb as we stood waiting for the drumming and singing to start. "*Ho ka hey*! *Ho ha hey*!! It's time to dance!" shouted the shaman. Six to seven men beat their drumsticks on a kettledrum and sang, their music blaring out of old speakers with broken woofers and strained tweeters.

We positioned ourselves at the northwest side and had to circle around the outside of the arbor to enter from the east gate. The *hochoka*, with its sacred tree, (also known as the sun pole) in the middle, was marked off by four gates to indicate the powers of the four directions. Each gate had two flags: yellow for east, white for south, black for west, and red for north. Once the flags were set in place, the mystery began.

The dancers, as a group or individually, always moved within the *hochoka* in a clockwise direction because in Lakota culture this indicates movement into good. A shade structure was built all around the circle for the onlookers to dance under and give support. They are not required to go without food or water for four days and nights, but they are invaluable, as they give the dancers courage and meaning.

The drumming and singing had now started, and we shivered as we entered from the east gate. We danced for about an hour, line dancing in different formations. Facing each direction, we lifted our legs, blew on eagle whistles, and raised our arms to appeal to Tunkasila, *and* Wakan-Tanka. In four consecutive lines we moved forward three times toward the sacred tree, and on the fourth time we finally touched it. I had gotten so cold at this point that part of the skin on my abdomen had frozen. It was excruciatingly painful. As I raised my arms the flesh cracked and droplets of blood spilled and froze on my skin.

Finally the dance was over. We exited through the south gate and made a beeline to the huge fire pit to the west of the *hochoka* where the sweat lodges, tepees, and rest area were located. The sun had risen and its rays gently warmed our bodies while the blazing fire scorched us. After resting for half an hour, we went back into the *hochoka* through the west gate. From that point on we would exit and enter the *hochoka* by the west gate until the ceremony ended, four days later.

The day grew long as the summer heat pounded on our bodies. We continued to dance in exhausting rounds from dawn to dusk, following the path of the sun. We would dance for an hour, then rest for twenty to thirty minutes. My legs and knees, high-stepping to the drumbeat, felt reduced to two hooves pawing at the parched ground. Heads and shoulders slumped, begging a respite from the continual movement. My pale body grew redder and redder; nausea welled up in my throat, and sweat seeped out of my pores. When the dances ended for the day, I collapsed on my bed.

The following day, during our afternoon break, a Sun Dancer invited me over to share the shade with his Sun Dance brothers. The shade was cool, and I fell into a deep sleep. When I was gently awakened by my friend, I found that my energy had returned and I was now extremely focused.

During the late afternoon some dancers chose to sacrifice their flesh by piercing their chest with skewers. The rest of the dancers took their positions at the four directions, facing the sacred tree. There on a buffalo robe, the sacrificing dancers pierced their skin and were then tethered by a long rope to the sacred tree. Silence blanketed the *hochoka* as dancers and supporters, who stood barefoot surrounding the *hochoka*, wept. The piercings seemed to go to the very core of human suffering. I was moved to tears, not so much by the suffering but by the humanity that suffering brings out in people.

As each day began and ended we had sweat lodges to purify us and to encourage and affirm our commitments to dance again for the ill, crippled, and aged and for the betterment of the community. Inside the sweat lodge, the shaman poured water onto hot stones. The steam permeated our bodies and souls. We pursed our lips and sucked the moisture out of the air and into our throats, which were parched from the heat and from blowing on the eagle whistles.

At the end of each round, four rows of dancers faced the south gate. Two rows of women behind and two rows of men in front danced with their cupped hands raised to Wakantanka. Each dancer's *chanupa* (Sacred Pipe) was brought to them from the sacred altar at the west gate, where the painted green and red buffalo skull sat. After three symbolic movements between the dancer and the shaman, each finally received his or her *chanupa* on the fourth gesture. A supporter was chosen to receive one dancer's pipe to smoke, and another pipe was given to a singer so that the drumming and singing would stop.

On the morning of the third day a dream came to me. A woman came before me and touched my naked chest. As I awoke, Wanbligleska appeared. "The eagle power has come," I thought. Rushing to the *wicasa wakan*, I asked for permission to pierce. Usually the decision is left up to the Sun Dancer, and it is based on a prior commitment—for example, he or she plans in advance to dance for an ill relative. The decision is also based on personal dreams or visions coming before or during the Sun Dance. Bo, in his role as the lead assistant to the *wicasa wakan*, used pipestone paste to draw two circles, one on each pectoral, to indicate the place for the piercing. To my surprise, I was more eager than fearful and seemed to have gained a more intense focus and strength during my days of fasting and dancing.

The summer sun was beginning to drop, and a cool breeze churned the dusty ground. The sun dancers who were to be pierced lined up along the west gate. In the past two days more dancers had come into the *hochoka*. There were forty of us now. The dancers not piercing supported the others with hugs, handshakes, and tears. Some dancers chose to be strong without tears and even seemed distant. This expressed to the ones to be pierced that the others understood how great the sacrifice of the flesh was and that it was death and resurrection. In this way, respect and affirmation of the participant's actions were conferred.

I lay on the buffalo robe beneath the sacred tree, my head aligned to the north with the buffalo's head. All I could hear in the silence was my heart pounding away. An eagle wing brushed over me and Pansy's face appeared. She was crying. Gently taking my sage crown and placing it in my mouth, she said, "Bite down!" I relaxed completely as Bo rubbed my chest. As he pulled up my skin a searing fire shot through me. The surgical steel did its work, and the cherrywood skewers followed the scalpel. Both sides were quickly done, and a thirty-foot rope that belonged to my Sun Dance brother was hooked to the skewers.

Immediately they brought me to my feet and handed me the rope, which was secured fifteen feet up in the sacred tree. Stepping to the tree, I touched its skin and prayed for the crippled and old who couldn't dance, prayed for my loved ones, prayed for myself, and appealed for pity. It hurt so much.

"*Ho ka hey!*" shouted the shaman as he looked up to Tunkasila and Wakan-Tanka and waved an eagle wing overhead. "*Ho ka hey!*" I backed away from the sacred tree. As I leaned, the skin pulled forward, and blood trickled from the wounds. I danced, lifting my knees high, raising my arms skyward and making the rope dance, appealing, "*Wakantanka unsimala ye. Wani kta ca lecumeun welo (Wakantanka, pity me. I want to live, that is why I am doing this)*."

"*Ho ka hey*!" I moved back to the tree, almost running while I wound the slack of the rope in my hand. I touched the tree as tears streamed down my face. A pair of hands reached from behind the tree and touched mine. I was startled to see a Sun Dance brother crying for me. I gazed into his eyes, and at that moment we were one.

Three times we prayed at the tree and four times we backed away. On the fourth round we had to break, tearing the flesh. "*Ho ka hey*!" As I moved back I remembered Pansy telling me, "You have two ways of breaking, Steve. The first way is that of the warrior. You use your will to break. The second way is that the visionary, where you give your will up to Tunkasila and Wakantanka. They decide when you break."

As I looked around, some of the Sun Dance brothers chose the warrior way. They leaned against the rope and threw back their shoulders to rip the flesh; if the flesh is too strong, they ran from the center and throw themselves into the air, screaming as the skewers ripped their chest.

I chose the visionary way. "*Ho ka hey! Ho ka hey*!" Drums beat—singers sang—I lifted my knees high—I lifted my head skyward and danced backward until the rope was taut. I heard some of my flesh beginning to rip, and I threw my shoulders back and danced. As seconds turned into minutes and minutes into pain, I began to doubt. The pain was shooting throughout my body, and my tears were drying up. Doubts flooded my mind, and I thought maybe I would be there for hours or even days. I said to myself, "Just pull. I've done enough. I'll be respected as a warrior. Just lean back, throw the shoulders hard, and I'll be released. No more pain. No more pain." A sea of faces looked on as I whirled in pain and confusion. "I'll just pull! End it!" But suddenly a huge bird dropped from the treetop. Its talons reached out and grabbed my wounds. "Wanbligleska! Wanbligleska!" I yelled in my mind. The eagle had come. It was pure white, with a twenty-foot wingspan, sharp talons, and piercing eyes. Its talons pulled my limp body up as it looked into my eyes and said, "What is your intention?" At that moment I remembered that it was the vision that I was seeking, not the respect that clouded my mind. I surrendered at that moment, and the pain then changed to an ecstatic dance with Wanbligleska. My chest was pulled upward as his wings came forward and was released as his wings went back. The dance was timeless, and we were held in perfect harmony.

Suddenly I flew into the darkness, which opened into millions of stars. Wanbligleska's soft downy chest caressed my back; his wings folded to the side, holding my arms as I looked through his eyes and we flew into the unknown.

Rings of different colors appeared, millions of them, each with a distinct image and feel, like a snapshot. A green ring opened up into a bathroom where a crawling baby stood, dropped his diapers, and defecated while watching the light emanate from the green walls. A red ring brought the smell of food cooking in a wok and the light from a setting sun streaming through red plastic partitions. A brown ring showed rolling dirt engulfing a boy hitting a fence. The faces of friends, relatives, and enemies dotted in rings of passion, love, hate, apathy, kindness, and fear. Then came the slamming of two spinning cars, with metal crushing, twisting, and bending; and then I saw the wing of a white eagle flicking the nose of a baby.

More and more images came faster and faster. I did not need to remember, analyze, understand, or process. I needed only to absorb and let go. The feeling was one of total contentment and knowing—ecstasy. A gold ring tinged with red appeared, and I felt that were I to pass through it I would never return. Suddenly everything was in slow motion. I felt the skewers ripping from my chest, blood shooting out, ropes coiling back like snakes, and dirt flying everywhere as I hit the ground. A huge roar came from the supporters as men whooped and hollered and women ululated. I was back. Pansy and others lifted me up. Bo grabbed my left wristlet and we ran around the arbor. It was strange to be back; everything was so physical, so ordinary. Then they took me to the sacred tree, where the wicasa wakan cut the small flapping pieces of skin from my chest. He wrapped them in a piece of red cloth and offered them up to Tunkasila and Wakantanka. Then he tied the cloth to the sacred tree with the other flesh offerings. Meanwhile, Bo placed a piece of mushroom on my wounds to help the healing. After the round of dancing was over, I was given raw buffalo kidney. The taste was very sweet and wet. It was primordial; not primitive but new and vibrant.

The last day was a day of healing. Over a hundred people, both people from the reservation and outsiders (including Europeans and Canadians), lined up for the healing power. Four days of dancing, fasting, prayers, and sacrifice of the flesh had brought power to the Sun Dancers.

The Sun Dancers were lined up according the number of Sun Dances they had performed and the days spent dancing. I was placed seventh, since I had danced four days. In all, forty dancers lined up; twenty-five men and fifteen women, with the men's line going first.

In an altered state, I saw a hole in the heart of the man who stood before me. I thrust my hand, which was holding sage, into his heart and began to sing and pray. He shook and cried as I pulled my hand out. His eyes were wide open as I blessed him. Later, at the conclusion of the Sun Dance, he told me that he had had open-heart surgery and had been released from the hospital only a week before. An old woman bowed her head as I blessed her. The years, the hard weather of Lakota country, and alcoholism had taken their toll; so many wrinkles, so many years of pain. I prayed hard with all my heart, dancing in place and calling for the power. Suddenly she swung around and lifted up a child in front of me. I took a step back and saw a Down syndrome child with arms and legs crossed and twisted, eyes staring at me out of a large head. I arched my neck back and cried. I put my hands on his head, brushing his eyes with sage while I prayed. Soon the child began to cry, and at that moment he became aware of his own suffering. Next was a young man who stood with pride and integrity; he bowed his head for the blessings and thanked me with his proud eyes. A shy girl looking at her fidgety feet held her hands out for blessings, and after I touched her forehead with my hands she smiled and barely glanced up. All afternoon we prayed and blessed the hundred or more people. All afternoon I danced and prayed in unison with the people. All afternoon I loved and felt love from the people.

The pinnacle of the Sun Dance was the healing of the crippled, ill, and aged and the general blessing of all people. From the Lakota perspective, the flesh is all that they own; they are born with the flesh and they die with it. Therefore it is the ultimate and only thing of material value. The flesh also symbolizes ignorance, and the sacrifice of the flesh is a transubstantiation of ignorance into healing and thanksgiving.

For me the ordeal and ecstasy of being a the Sun Dancer brought me not only prestige but also mana—power from the other world, to do good for people—as well as a deep experience of compassion for human suffering. *Mitakuye oyasin* (to all my relations).

Chapter 22

Renewal of the World Tree: Direct Experience of the Sacred as a Fundamental Source of Healing in Shamanism, Psychology, and Religion

Margaret Laurel Allen and Meredith Sabini

This chapter presents a magnificent dream received by a contemporary woman that illustrates the timeless archetypal meaning of shamanic visioning. Beginning with images of the spiritual poverty of our era, the dream describes an archetypal process of transformation which brings renewed vitality and greater individuality into forms of worship that have lost much of their healing power through institutionalization.

Were we tribal people living through a time like this, a time of intensive change, we would be gathering together regularly to hear the dreams of the elders, the shaman, and anyone else to whom guidance for the group had come. In this essay, we invite you to join us in a contemporary version of the clan circle to hear a "big dream" that describes the spiritual dilemma of our era and suggests what can be done to restore our connection with the sacred.

We could say that the spiritual crisis of modern times is that we are suffering from collective soul loss and a dismemberment of body, mind, and spirit. Where are we to turn for healing when the rationality we so highly value has itself severed us from the healing grace of the numinous? Our desacralized institutions cannot offer restoration of wholeness because there is no culturally cohesive foundation of belief in—much less knowledge of—the reality of the psyche, or soul, and the healing potential of the sacred. Attempts to treat our modern malaise are made by three disparate professions, each focusing on only one part of the dismembered self: medicine on the body, psychology on the mind and emotions, and religion on the soul.

We seem, however, to be in the midst of a major paradigm shift, as boundaries between these healing professions open up and interconnections are explored. The current resurgence of interest in shamanism and tribal spiritual practices is an integral part of this shift. Shamanism, which is not a religion but an ancient mode of experience still alive today, is a model for direct personal perception of spiritual reality. Because the transcendent dimension is unitary, not dismembered, the knowledge gained through this mode of perception is inherently interconnected, affecting mind, body, and soul as a unified whole.

More akin to the shamanic world view than any other psychological orientation, the approach of C. G. Jung is likewise able to guide us toward natural healing experiences and renewed contact with the numinous without imitating or robbing existing tribal practices. Jung's understanding of the collective unconscious was broad enough to include the transpersonal as well as the personal, the sacred as well as the instinctual. The primary way that Jung offered for renewing one's contact with the numinous, sacred, or spiritual dimension was through dreams and spontaneous visions.

In 1934 Jung analyzed the spiritual crisis of the twentieth century in terms that are still keenly relevant today:

> Modern man does not understand how much his "rationalism" (which has destroyed his capacity to respond to numinous symbols and ideas) has put him at the mercy of the psychic "underworld." He has freed himself from "superstition" (or so he believes), but in the process, he has lost his spiritual values to a positively dangerous degree. His moral and spiritual tradition has disintegrated, and he is now paying for this break-up in world-wide disorientation and dissociation. (Jung 1964, 94)

A condition of genuine healthiness—being able to naturally live out one's full humanness—is rare in our hectic and stressful society. Most of us struggle daily to cope with a range of "dis-ease" and ills; at one time or another, we are vulnerable to feeling alienated, disoriented, or in despair.

Through his own personal experience of confronting spiritual disorientation and through working with clients, Jung came to trust that the psyche, both the individual and the collective, does try to restore balance and heal itself; he found that this process can be observed through the symbolic representations generated by the creative unconscious. Jung came to realize that the libido, or life energy, originally held by these sacred healing images is never lost, but tries to return:

> Since energy never vanishes, the emotional energy that manifests itself in all numinous phenomena does not cease to exist when it disappears from consciousness. . . . It reappears in unconscious manifestations, in symbolic happenings that compensate the disturbance of the conscious psyche. (Jung 1961, para. 583)

The most common "symbolic happenings" that compensate for disturbances at a conscious level are symptoms, dreams, and spontaneous visions. In this essay, we are going to witness a dream that compensates for the disturbance in the field by returning the energy of ancient images of the sacred. The dream we will present portrays an individual and cultural process of renewal by showing that we do not have to abandon old forms of spiritual practice; rather, we can allow them to be revitalized.

A visionary dream such as this is known as a "big dream" in folk tradition, a "culture dream" in anthropology, and an "archetypal dream" in Jungian psychology. From all three viewpoints, it is recognized as being primarily for and about the group or tribe, although it does have some personal elements. Dreams and visions of this kind do not reflect the wishes of the ego or personal unconscious, but might be said to reflect the wishes of the Self. Jung referred to this type of dream when he said:

> A good dream, for example, that's grace. The dream is in essence a gift. The collective unconscious, it's not for you, or me, it's the invisible world, it's the great spirit. It makes little difference what I call it: God, Tao, the Great Voice, the Great Spirit. (Jung in McGuire and Hull 1977, 419)

The central figure in the following dream is Christ, who assumes the role of universal spiritual teacher or master shaman. The central symbol is the cross, in its universal aspect as the world tree. Christ comes down from the cross and explains that he will no longer be enacting the role of the divine scapegoat who suffers for others' sins and carries their hopes for salvation. He indicates that this is a time of historic transition in all religions, away from dependence on collective intermediaries so that individuals are more able to be responsible for their own sins and work toward their own redemption. At the end of the dream, Christ shows a group of contemporary seekers how renewal of the cross/world tree will take place and how religious experience can be mediated more directly and personally in the future.

The cultural context of the dream is the spiritual crisis of our time. The personal context of the dream, which came to Margaret Allen in 1989, was an individual version of the cultural dilemma. The dreamer, although raised in a Christian Protestant tradition, was not a practicing Christian. This dream came during a crucial period of midlife when she was struggling with some difficult choices regarding the proper way to integrate a lifelong interest in the healing power of visionary experience into her professional development as a psychotherapist. The dream presented a meaningful picture of the value of an individually defined spiritual orientation, and was one of several that helped illuminate the direction of her life's work. Our preference here is to let the dream speak for itself. We invite you to apprehend it as you might a meditation, perhaps even read it aloud, so that it can be felt with body and soul. It is a living thing, and comes to life again each time it is heard and felt.

I am with a group of friends who love Nature as a sacred place. We plan to climb a mountain in the High Sierra, as a spiritual adventure rather than as a physical challenge. We will spend the night together near the summit. Any potential danger would come from too much exposure alone to the numinous dimension, which is why we have come on the trip together.

In the next scene, we are in an old, ill-tended church. We are supposed to perform some act of spiritual service, but it isn't clear what. In trying to make a space in one corner for us to meet, we accidentally disturb an abandoned altar, a lop-sided old cross of dark wood with some illegible writing on it, not a fine and carefully finished piece, but crude and rough. It has a worn look and feel to it as I take hold of the cross to straighten it up, as though despite its inelegant appearance, it has been the focus of intense devotion for many years. The cross won't straighten up and is unstable, leaning sideways, and nearly falling over. Despite its wobbliness, I can feel the mana in it and treat it reverently.

The cross is stuck unceremoniously in a bucket of white ashes. These make me think of Christ's death and seem an appropriate holder for the cross. But the ashes are too loose to hold it up securely. I try pushing the cross farther in, like trying to firm up a wobbly plant in a pot of loose soil, but that doesn't work either. The horizontal axis of the cross is too low this way to convey a spiritual presence. So I put it back the way it was. I can't figure out how to solve this problem, so I content myself with cleaning off the lop-sided cross, removing some odd pieces of junk that have gotten stuck to it in the years of neglect, such as a cash register receipt.

As I'm working, I see an old priest with a sour face. He is watching me with a very critical look and tells me I'm being sacriligious to attempt to renew the old altar. I tell him, "No, I am not being irreverent. Restoring this altar is in fact the spiritual service we have come here to do." He accepts this, quieting down when he realizes I am not an impious infidel out to destroy his religion.

Then I look up and see a young man in workman's clothes just disappearing out the front door. He is hidden behind my group of friends. I have a sudden intuition, when I notice that there is no figure crucified on this cross, that this young workman is Jesus the carpenter. I call out to him, "Jesus, come back!" We need his help to solve this problem of the unsteady cross. He turns and looks at me, slowly shakes his head, and vanishes. I am disappointed and confused.

But then some mysterious process of renewal starts to unfold. It is happening on its own and not under our direction, and I settle back to watch in amazement. The old church building disappears and with it the sour-faced priest and the neglected cross also vanish. My friends and I are now standing in a wide valley at the site of the old altar. Independently of the now vanished church, this area has its own spiritual mana. We see a long white object moving toward us down the valley, heading for the altar site where we stand waiting. It is a tall tree with all the limbs intact, made of some white wood, polished so that it has become a sculpture piece without its natural form being altered. There are long cords fastened to the base of the trunk and to the limbs, and evidently some autonomous force exerted through these cords is moving the tree toward where we wait. At the end of every cord is a human figure in a white gown. They are singing and walking along the hill ridges on either side of the valley.

At first it seems logical to assume that the robed figures are moving the tree along by pulling on the cords. But then I realize they are walking in back of the tree, and it is coming toward me trunk end first with the cords stretched out behind it. Some unseen force is moving the tree so that it is pulling the robed people, who evidently, like our group, are among the witnesses of this marvelous event.

As the tree approaches, I realize it is the new centerpiece for the altar! When the movement stops on its own, the tree sculpture is firmly standing upright, planted in the ground, just where the old unstable cross was before. With the tall, vertical trunk and outstretched horizontal limbs, it looks like a natural, organic form of the vanished cross. The polished wood of the tree is gleaming white, like bone or marble, and I wonder if it is birch or perhaps ash, like an original form of the bucket of white ashes that held the old cross. The entire scene is deeply numinous and moving.

(At this point, I wake up part way but remain suspended in a deep trance between sleeping and waking, while the dream continues as a spontaneous vision, a vivid active imagination.) I see that Jesus has come back and is sitting near me, meditating on the tree-cross. I ask him why the new altarpiece does not have the figure of his crucified body hanging on it and ask how we are to worship it. He looks at me with kindness and replies that he will never hang on the cross again, that he has served his time as the Divine Scapegoat for our sins, and that he will no longer play this role. He tells me that the appearance of the new tree-cross means that this era of human history has to end if people are to see the numinous directly for themselves and not through his mediation. He explains that as long as there is a divinely ordained scapegoat-victim at the center of a religion, worshipped as savior, people will never be able to confront the consequences of their own dark sides, their own suffering, or the glory of resurrection and rebirth directly for themselves. He tries to make me understand that institutionalization of the scape-

goat-savior ritual in Christianity and its equivalent in other systems of world religion was a necessary stage in humanity's spiritual development, but this is now passing. Groups that still continue to place some one person concretely in this intermediary's position are blocking a necessary transformation.

I ask him again, "Then how are we to worship now in this new time with this bare tree-cross?" He answers that he cannot tell me in words, but, if I turn away from him and look at the tree-cross for awhile, I will have my answer, and then he will explain further. So I do this, and have a vision: I see the old Christian cross appear dimly along the trunk of the tree. In the place where the crucified Christ used to hang, a glowing circle of gold-colored light appears, so that the crosspiece area is encircled. The familiar figure of my ally, my guardian animal, appears within the image of the base and arms of the old cross with its head in the circle of light. It is not pinned against its will, suffering and dying, crucified there as Christ was. Instead, it positions itself there freely, glistening with life and full of vital energy, glad to be in the bright circle of light. With a glad rush of joyful feeling and awe, I recognize that my own ally is to be my spiritual guide.

When my vision ends, I look around to see others in our group also just stirring from their own contemplation of the new tree-cross. Though I already suspect the answer, I ask if anyone else saw the same creature that I saw. They all say no, and it turns out that each person saw their own ally and spiritual guide!

Jesus is smiling now and says, Yes, this is what he meant, this is to be the basis of a new way of worship. When no one culturally defined religious figure is collectively chosen to be the scapegoat-savior and there are no institutions of religion with codified spiritual instructions and principles to follow, each worshipper will have to study with a teacher who is personally meaningful in order to learn the course of religious development suitable for their individual nature. (Sabini and Allen 1994, 26–28)

The dream tells a stunning story and needs little comment. We would like simply to summarize it and amplify its central features. The beginning depicts our contemporary state of spiritual alienation, signified by the neglected altar, lopsided cross, and sour-faced priest. A group of pilgrims undertakes a classic quest, the ascent of a mountain, to prepare themselves for their spiritual task, which is restoration of the altar. Their efforts are ineffective, but their devotion to the underlying challenge is firm. An autonomous process of renewal eventually unfolds: some *unseen force* propels a magnificent, white sculptural tree-cross into place and secures it where the old cross once stood.

We need this larger perspective to sustain us through the intensely difficult time in which we are living, as the old religious containers fail to hold us and cannot escort us through life's passages. The sequence of events depicted in this dream follows the characteristic pattern seen when the archetype of death and rebirth is activated by a need for renewal. The famous religious historian Mircea Eliade identified this particular pattern in relation to the world tree, of which the cross is one version: "Its destruction is only temporary . . . the World Tree is destroyed only that it may be reborn" (Eliade 1964, 284–85). Apparently this time, the rebirth of the world tree will be from below out of nature, and not from the celestial realm.

Downton (1989, 73–88), in his article on shamanic initiation as a parallel to the process of individuation delineated by Jung, also focuses on the mythology of the world tree's renewal as central to the death-rebirth theme and its connection with initiation and healing. In ascending and descending the world tree, the shaman undergoes many stages of initiation, each time gaining more and more consciousness of the essentially unitary nature of all aspects of reality. The ordeal of dismemberment is central to shamanic initiation; Christ's crucifixion on the cross is one version of shamanic dismemberment, ascent, and descent of the world tree.

In this dream, Christ resigns his former cultural role as divine intercessor and becomes a shamanic initiator for the individuation process. The theological question as to whether there is evolution in the spiritual realm is answered affirmatively. Christ explains why this change is necessary: continued dependence upon collective figures and prescribed methods will block the individual and cultural healing that is needed. His new role, in his human clothing as carpenter, is that of a universal teacher for those seeking to develop a more direct and individual connection with the sacred. Christ's teaching is specifically not in words but in images and emotions: he invites the dreamer to contemplate the center of the cross, the axis point encircled in light. Within this circle, the dreamer and other seekers each see their own tutelary spirit animal. This is known as the ally in shamanic tradition, a spiritual being, often in animal form, who instructs and guides its human partner. (See Harner 1990, and Raff's paper "The Ally" in this volume.)

Raff proposes that the ally signifies the individual spirit of the Self experienced through the human psyche. We might say that Christ has served as a collective ally, a shared figure present in the psyches of many. He has also performed the function of a shaman, journeying as intercessor between the human world and the spirit world, bearing petitions for healing and redemption to the deity, and conveying comfort and guidance back to those in need.

It seems important that it is Christ who alters his own role and initiates a revised form of relationship between humans and the divine. He is like a master shaman, sending initiates out on a vision quest in search of the ally that will accompany them throughout life. This individual spiritual teacher, the ally, does not constitute a god nor is it to be worshiped, although one's relationship with it is certainly reverential. By inviting seekers in the dream to contemplate the center of the new tree-cross, Christ is making way for the Self image present in the individual psyche to be reflected within that circle of light, where it can be perceived; a dialogue with it can then begin and the course of personal development suitable to each person can be discerned over time.

The method that Christ teaches in this dream is essentially the ancient shamanic method called "journeying," which is similar to the process Jung termed "active imagination." By voluntarily entering an altered state of consciousness and allowing the ego's normal state to be relaxed, the mind can open to perceive the greater wisdom inherent in the spiritual dimension. Through such a method, the ally, the spirit of the Self, conveys the guidance and knowledge from the spiritual world to the conscious ego personality. A link between the conscious self and the larger Self, between the human and the divine, is established, and this relationship itself is healing to dissociation and dismemberment.

The original meaning of healing in both psychology and religion entailed the recovering of a felt sense of wholeness, a re-membering of the interrelationship of mind, body, and spirit. It is direct experience of the sacred, here pictured as the reverent contemplation of a numinous image and accompanied by a deeply felt emotional response, that transcends the separateness of body, mind, and spirit and allows a sense of unity—holiness—to return. This healing or restoration of wholeness does not necessarily result in afflictions being taken away, but enables them to be cared for, tolerated, and understood through the knowledge and wisdom available; this occurs naturally once the restored ego-Self connection allows for a flow of helpful communication between human being and spirit world.

The word *psychology* actually means "knowledge of the soul," and through the imaginal method that Christ demonstrates, the soul has a way of revealing itself to us. The shaman, by leaving the visible world and journeying into the nonvisible or spirit world, is able to perceive the soul, its wounds and its need for healing. Christ asks seekers to use this imaginal mode of perception—the "eyes of my eyes"—in order to see the soul image within the sacred center of light.

A shift in our attitude toward respect and reverence for the imaginal dimension is at the core of how contemporary spiritual deprivation can be healed. Many people today refer to images as "mere symbols," and this attitude betrays the lack of a vital emotional connection. Jung's concept of the imaginal was so organic that he actually referred to symbols as "organs" of apprehension:

> Our psyche is profoundly disturbed by the loss of moral and spiritual values that have hitherto kept our life in order. . . . Our consciousness has deprived

itself of the organs by which the auxiliary contributions of the instincts and the unconscious could be assimilated. These organs were the numinous symbols, held holy by common consent. (Jung 1961, para. 583).

At each juncture in the dream where a numinous symbol appears, the dreamer and others experience awe or some other intense emotion; the auxiliary contribution of the religious instinct is made powerfully present in consciousness so it can be assimilated.

This dream shows how shamanism and Jung's analytical psychology coincide in their valuing of the imaginal or spirit world and the importance of establishing a regular relationship with it. Jung spoke poignantly about the neglect of the soul by modern religious systems:

> The general undervaluation of the human psyche is so great that neither the great religions nor the philosophies nor scientific rationalism have been willing to look at it twice. (Jung 1961, para. 603)

Through the respectful empirical method of studying the imaginal world that Jung applied (and which is currently being used by Michael Harner's Foundation for Shamanic Studies to map nonordinary reality), we may one day know more about the range of Self and soul images, as seekers tell their stories.

This dream does not point to a new religion but to a shift in how experience of the sacred dimension takes place. Most major religious systems have actively discouraged direct contact with the numinous, reserving this for selected priests who follow prescribed patterns of worship. The mode of spiritual practice described in the dream represents a tremendous challenge and will require much of us as individuals: it asks us to "carry our own cross," meaning that we have to suffer the burdens of our own shadow side (our sins) and work toward our own redemption. But this goal is in accord with the original concept of a deity that is trying to incarnate in the human world; the sacred light encircles the point where the two axes meet—the vertical axis of the nonpersonal world of spiritual reality (upper and lower worlds, in shamanic terms) and the horizontal axis of the human world of ordinary reality (the middle, world in shamanic terms).

For some, conventional modes of worship may remain viable. The exercises of St. Ignatius, the Buddhist practice of zazen, the Tibetan meditations on mandala and mantra, and other methods of spiritual development may offer adequate containment the religious instinct. Like any general program of physical exercise, these culturally defined approaches will continue to be relatively satisfactory because they follow a universal, archetypal pattern. But they will also be limited in that they never quite correspond to individual needs nor do they encourage dialogue between the conscious self and a spontaneous Self-image. As Marie-Louise von Franz emphasized in her lectures on alchemy, "Normally, mankind has not approached the unconscious individually, but, with few exceptions, has related to it indirectly through religious systems" (Franz 1980, 18). However, those who have personally suffered alienation from the sacred, for one reason or another, may be called to heal that wound by entering into the kind of personal individual spiritual endeavor described in the dream. As the dream states at the beginning, it is important not to approach the numinous alone because of danger of inflation, but to have companions.

There is terrible suffering brought about by the belief that "God is dead" and that we are abandoned in a spiritual wasteland. This stage, however, may be a necessary precondition for the emergence of greater consciousness (see Edinger 1972). From this and other similar dreams, it is evident that Christ has not abandoned us but is encouraging us to continue the incarnation of the divine. The mythology of an incarnating deity seems to be alive and well and trying hard to communicate itself to us in the quiet grace of dreams and visions.

It may seem heretical to suggest that the inner life of the individual could play a significant role in remedying the spiritual crisis of the times. In a lecture called "Psychotherapists or the Clergy," given in 1932, Jung spoke to this peculiarity of human nature, namely, that the individual could be of such value:

> The modern man does not want to know in what way he can imitate Christ, but in what way he can live his own individual life, however meagre and uninteresting it may be. It is because every form of imitation seems to him deadening and sterile that he rebels against the forces of tradition. . . . He may not know it, but he behaves as if his own individual life were God's special will which must be fulfilled at all costs. (Jung 1958, para. 524)

Fulfillment of that will is a calling that has been blocked for many of us today. But dreams such as this inspire the resacralization of our individual lives. The spiritual service the seekers in this dream are to perform is restoring the altar. This is accomplished as the two sides, human and divine, work together: humans suffer the alienation, climb the mountain, ask the questions; and a mysterious, unseen force brings the altarpiece, the new tree-cross, into place and lights the sacred center.

We hope that part of the human service also lies in our sharing the gift of this unusual dream, in which Christ shows a way for our connection with the numinous to be restored, a way as old as the oldest human healer and as modern as the most sophisticated psychology: reverent contemplation of the sacred reality of the imaginal world.

REFERENCES

Downton, J. V. 1989. Individuation and Shamanism. *The Journal of Analytical Psychology.* Vol. 34, 73–88.

Edinger, E. 1972. *Ego and Archetype.* Baltimore: Penguin.

Eliade, M. 1964. *Shamanism: Archaic Techniques of Ecstasy.* Princeton: Princeton University Press.

Franz, M. L. von. 1980. *Alchemy.* Toronto: Inner City.

Harner, M. 1990 [1980] *The Way of the Shaman.* Third edition. San Francisco: Harper and Row.

Jung, C. G. 1958. *Psychology and Religion: West and East.* Bollingen Series XX: The Collected Works of C. G. Jung, vol. 11. Princeton: Princeton University Press.

———. 1961. Healing the Split. In *The Symbolic Life.* Bollingen Series XX: The Collected Works of C. G. Jung, vol. 18. Princeton: Princeton University Press.

———. 1964. *Man and His Symbols.* New York: Doubleday.

McGuire, W., and R. F. C. Hull. 1977. *Jung Speaking.* Princeton: Princeton University Press.

Sabini, M., and M. L. Allen. 1994. Christ Comes Down from the Cross: The Evolution of an Archetype. Chrysalis: Journal of the Swedenborg Foundation IX (1), 21–33.

Chapter 23

Beyond Tourism: Travel with Shamanic Intent

Pilar Montero and Arthur D. Colman

In the process of individuation, which is central to Jung's analytical psychology, it is necessary to build a personal myth that fits one's own life and facilitates its spiritual growth. In the previous essay Margaret Allen's dream, as recounted by her and Meredith Sabini, beautifully illustrated this process. Another way to do this is to travel with "special intent," as do Colman and Montero, in order to find and experience something in a foreign culture that focuses and amplifies one's own inner vision. In a certain sense, this is a larger use of active imagination—one involving a whole culture, its myths, and its rituals. I call this mythic imagination. The more closely and intensively one participates, the greater the rewards, although the immediate experience is not always pleasant. The trip portrayed in this paper is to the backcountry of Peru to witness a marvelous festival with strong echoes of ancient ritualized human sacrifice. It is a true example of a transforming experience.

Those of us who are interested in expanding and deepening consciousness are often inveterate travelers, for we have learned that the outer journey to another cultural landscape increases access to the inner world. But travel is usually synonymous with tourism, and being a tourist may not open the doors of perception in the way many would desire. Many tourist programs recognize this need by tailoring their offerings to particular interest groups, for example, they organize trips with a specific intellectual, aes-

thetic, or spiritual focus. This essay is our attempt to provide travel oppor-
tunities for individuals and groups in much the way the traditional shaman
"travels." We think of it as travel with intent, as consciously using travel as a
way to cross to an other world. Our trips can be very pleasurable, but
because of the serious intent behind them, we try to find venues where it
is possible to witness and possibly participate in rituals that most authenti-
cally evoke the divine spirit of that culture. We are also interested in facilitating a recrossing back to our own culture and helping travelers integrate
and transmit what is learned. In order to elucidate our vision, we will
describe the annual festival of Qoyllorrit'y in Peru and our preliminary initiation into Andean mysticism, which we participated in during the summer of 1994.

Human sacrifices are among the earliest form of ritual. Archeological
finds at a number of the highest Andean peaks have unearthed well-pre-
served children whose facial expressions suggest peaceful acceptance and
contentment despite their hideous deaths (Tierney 1989). The Qoyllorrit'y
festival captures the non-coercive surrender of human life typical of Peru's
ancient fertility rites and ensuing Inca sun worship rule. The festival took
place at the *Nevado de Qolqepunco*, a glacier seventeen thousand feet above
sea level, and concluded with the ritual death of a young man. For three
days and nights, accompanied by steady drumming, the music of flute,
harp, and trumpet, and the devotional energy of close to seventy thousand
Andean villagers, we camped in this icy environment. There we awaited the
dawn of the last day and the final sad and triumphant descent of all but one
of the hundreds of young male initiates.

The dramatic sacrificial ceremony in the snows of *Qolqepunco* was the cli-
max of our initiation, but just as pertinent were the preceding weeks, which
prepared us to partake in the ceremony. We learned an ancient meditation
method that has been part of the Andean priesthood's sacraments for centuries. These techniques are a portion of a very complex cosmology and set
of mystical and meditative practices constituting a remarkable tradition
that included an ecumenical ethos that allows for the reciprocal interchange of initiations between different mystical traditions. Persons who felt
themselves to be ready and who, in addition, were judged by the priest to
have achieved a high enough initiation level in their own path, either in a
formal religion or in a personal spiritual practice, could undergo a short
form of the initiatory journey created especially for this purpose.
Completion was tantamount to full initiation.

The trial informing the aspirant of his or her readiness to embark on this
venture took place on the first day of the initiation during a mass at the
cathedral in Cuzco. Each of us implored the Virgin for permission to proceed, and we repeated our request before the shrine of the highly revered

Crucified Black God of the Earthquakes. An inner experience of peace and joy and a sense of rightness and belonging suggested the candidate's readiness to face the powerful forces in the coming weeks; but if fear was predominant, then the initiation was annulled. During the initiation a few members of our group did feel fear, some in overwhelming amounts akin to a panic attack, and so they stopped. After three weeks immersed in the spirits of the Andes, the festival of *Qoyllorrit'y,* and its glacial sacrifice, we completed the circle by returning to the cathedral and the festival of Corpus Christi in Cuzco.

THEORY AND PURPOSEFUL INTENT

Jungian theory, shamanic practices, and the kind of travel we envision here coalesce around key motifs central to each framework. The one overarching principle is the establishment of a perspective larger than the one that typically encases the individual. The grip that ordinary ego awareness has on the psyche needs to be released in order to allow for something else to enter and affect the larger psyche. In Jungian analysis, the patient is encouraged to actively dialogue with dreams and other products of the imagination until these take over the work. The result is a lasting attitude change from the ego's more limited and constricting perspective to the more encompassing view from the Self, which can embrace the totality of conscious and unconscious possibilities. Shamanic healings parallel this process. Despite the huge variety in form, texture, and color, that characterize shamanic practices around the world, all shamans engage in healing ailing persons or groups. Typically the work begins with music's steady pulse via drumming, rattling, chanting, and so on and includes the presence or active participation of community members. The induced trance state both lowers regular ego consciousness and opens the threshold to the spirit realm. The encounter with the other world is the altering factor. In all healing systems intent is critical to the outcome which includes the capacity to integrate the other-worldly experience into the ensuing everyday life of its participants.

Our interest in using actual travel for this crossing is partly related to our long commitment to awakening collective as well as individual consciousness (Colman 1995; Montero 1992, 203–32; Montero 1995). To do this there must be development of a reflective organ of collective consciousness analogous to the reflective capacity in individual consciousness (Colman 1995). Consciousness of our collective identity is a psychological function that seems to be lagging way behind the steps taken this century to develop individual awareness; if this consciousness is not strengthened, the resulting imbalance may be the doom of our species and most life on the planet. The fundamental archetype in life is death and rebirth, but in our time the newly emerging archetype is death without rebirth (Colman 1995). The antidote is for groups to evolve the capacity to function with sufficient consciousness to support a larger-than-individual ecological perspective of sustainability while promoting a sense of oneness with diversity in a collective. We need to know more about how to stand firmly at the point of synthesis where material and mystical realms unite while holding in awareness the interconnectedness and interdependence of all life. Our mode of travel invites one to become a participant and observer in an unfamiliar culture, particularly at the level of underlying sacred structures.

THE JOURNEY AND ITS SETTING

Our exploration in the Peruvian Andes in May 1994 was our second trip to this area. We joined Juan Victor Nuñez del Prado, our guide and initiation master, Elizabeth Jenkings, his apprentice, and a group of ten people in the cathedral that dominates the main square in Cuzco, the ancient capital of the Inca empire. Cuzco, at 11,150 feet above sea level, was originally conceived in the shape of a puma. The surrounding ruins accentuate the jaguar's body parts; for example, the head is the majestic hilltop fortress of *Sacsayhuaman.* Peru is vertically divisible into three clearly demarcated regions: the coast, with its beaches, deserts, and valleys; the Andean mountain ranges, at the center; and the largely impenetrable Amazon jungle, to the east. The Andes offers the most viable environment for the development of an empire. Among the soaring peaks and plunging gorges nestle the fertile plains of large valleys through which meander rivers that eventually make their way down into the Amazon basin. It was in the impressive ruins surrounding Cuzco and dot the mountainous walls bounding the sacred valley of the river Urubamba, which connects Cuzco with the jungle, that most of our mystical training took place. On the way *Machu Picchu,* well known for its spiritual and ceremonial significance, was a key setting for our work.

The journey, most appropriately, began in Cuzco, for visually the city is an eloquent microcosm of the traumatic accommodation to, and assimilation of, Spanish conquest and its legacy since the sixteenth century. For example, most streets and buildings have at their base the exquisite stonework the aboriginal Peruvians are famous for. Rising on top of them are the sumptuous and also extraordinarily beautiful European architectural forms. Major local festivals manifest a similarly perverse overlay of cultures. The Spanish and the Andean submerge and influence each other

mostly in their shared love of the grand, the richly colorful, and the aes-
thetically opulent, no matter how meager the resources available or how
sacred the enterprise. For example, we witnessed the final initiatory extrav-
aganza the day we returned from Qoyllorrit'y. The festival of Corpus
Christi took place in the main square that day, and this major Catholic
occasion coincides with the most holy of festivals devoted to the sun by the
Incas and their descendants. Corpus Christi was celebrated by slowly parad-
ing a huge silver-plated limousine carrying the Eucharist around the main
square, followed by fourteen enormous bejeweled and gaudily dressed statues of Christ, the Virgin, and key saints. Appearances belie the fact that this
seemingly typical Catholic procession has been forcefully influenced in
structure and meaning by its Andean predecessor and is now one of a kind.

The Inca empire was a theocracy that imposed the worship of the sun
and its mountain-peak homes on the many prexisting ancient and highly
developed fertility cultures that worshiped the spirits in water and earth.
The Inca himself, therefore, was the deity incarnate, the ruler and the body
politic. In the festival to the sun, all the mummified bodies of previous
Incas were paraded around the main square after their vigil in the temple
of Viracocha, currently the stone foundation of the cathedral. For many
years after the Spaniards replaced the Incas with Mary, Jesus, and the saints,
during the procession the Andeans would hide the remains of the Incas
under the clothing of the Catholic statues and surreptitiously worship their
own gods simultaneously with, or instead of, the new ones. Similarly,
Viracocha was their first metaphysical god and the most powerful in their
pantheon, and the Inca Viracocha was one of their most renowned rulers.
Despite the paradoxes involved in joining such different religious and cultural traditions, the worship of Viracocha seems to have been transposed to
that of Jesus Christ, the son of God. However, a prominent visual image of
Christ has emerged as a very dark-skinned man on a cross. He is most
revered in the cathedral and reappears in Qoyllorrit'y as the apparition
emblazoned on the stone wall where the sanctuary stands. Appreciating
the ability of the Andean psyche to accommodate this divine amalgam and
their apparent capacity for simultaneous worship of two different kinds of
gods was a major dilemma and lesson for the Western initiates.

For example, we were troubled by the cultural tendency that we felt
demeaned the aboriginal and exalted the European import. With sadness
we noted that a large egg-shaped stone that once was reverd as Viracocha's
icon stood forgotten as a doorpost at the Cathedral's main gates, while the
Black Christ and the mass devoted to him were so obviously important. But
the mystical training we were engaged in deeply honored many of the
Christian modes while equally engaging in the old traditions and ways. So
we exchanged energy with this spirit of the stone at the beginning and at

the conclusion of our initiatory journey while simultaneously using the church and its symbols as part of the initiatory trial. Unlike most of us, our Andean priest guide seemed untroubled by the polarity between the two spiritual traditions of what from our perspective were conqueror and conquered cultures. In fact, he really did not seem to recognize the conflict despite our many attempts to draw him into our struggle. Gradually we understood that the system he was teaching held complementarity above polarity as one of its prime beliefs; later we took part in initiatory rites that were designed to help acolytes grasp this principle as deeply as possible.

OUR INITIATORY TRAINING INTO THE ANDEAN MYSTICAL PRIESTHOOD

The highly complex cosmic vision from which this Andean mystical tradition emerges is richly populated with spirits that inhabit and articulate the three worlds that comprise the Andean cosmos. As Nuñez del Prado describes, the internal world," *uyu pacha*, is inhabited by beings who live in caves, rivers, and waterfalls and have characteristics ranging from the murderous and bloodthirsty to the mischievous, witty, and inoffensive trickster qualities of a joker (Nuñez del Prado, 1993). This world, *kay pacha*, is made up of plants, animals, rain, hail, snow, wind, rainbows, lightning, and human beings. The generator of life is the omnipresent mother. Pacha Mama. She is accompanied primarily by Nusta, a lesser feminine spirit who lives in special rock formations, and her husbands, the *Apus*, who are the spirits of the mountains and who protect and guide human beings. The third world, *hanaq pacha*, is the higher world presided over by God the Father and integrated with Jesus Christ the Son, the Holy Spirit, the Virgin Mary, the saints, and the spirits of the dead. The three worlds are interconnected. For example, from this world it is possible to cross to the internal world through oceans, lakes, lagoons, and places of origins, and to the higher world via crucifixes, tombs, and religious icons. Communication between the three worlds is maintained by means of the supreme ethical principles of Andean existence, which are based on communal mutuality and reciprocity.

The priesthood is hierarchical, and the many levels of apprenticeship require training under the direction of a master. The focus at first is on learning the elaborate religious functions, offerings, and sacrifices until the capacity to communicate directly with the spirits is attained. The path culminates in the ability to see the higher world and call forth the Creator. A required step on the way is to attend, as a costumed dancer, one of the great religious pilgrimages, such as Qoyllorrit'y, and humbly request the permission of the deity of the sanctuary to follow this path. Also, the aspirant who wishes to ascend to the highest initiatory levels spends three days and nights in solitude at the top of a mountain, then participates in Qoyllorrit'y to conclude his rituals and be consecrated by means of visions uniting him to the spirits of the three worlds.

Our initiation roughly followed the pattern prescribed for the ascent of aspirants to the higher levels of priesthood except that it was highly condensed in time and learning requirements. Our apprenticeship lasted a few weeks instead of many years, and we relied wholly on our guide to make all necessary offerings and pace us through the rituals, which sensitized us to the experience of crossing to either of the other worlds. The training itself was highly experiential and largely consisted of the interchange of energy with spiritual beings at locations such as caves, lagoons, mountain peaks and passes, ruins, and Catholic icons where the inner and worlds connected with this world. Eating was both the metaphor and the actual practice through which energy patterned its movement. Typically, we took in through the *cosco*, the belly area, the more rarified spiritual energy of the sacred place, thus opening key centers in our body, and then we released into the ground the heavier residue in us. Many of the ruins had a designated area, near the most holy of spots, with a rock that had been carved as a seat or bed for just this purpose, to release heavy energy into the earth.

In this system, unlike in our polarized Western thinking, earth and sky gods had a complementary rather than an oppositional relationship, as did the fundamental tenets of the philosophy on which the religion rested. Even gender differences were based on principles of similarity and reciprocity. Also, both individual and group could coexist without conflict. The ritual form required a high level of meditative concentration on our inner experience, but its focus was the outer world, which included the group. We received and transmitted energy to each other as well as to and from the spirits of the place. We mirrored in our practice the priority of the groups what is part and parcel of the Andean perspective. For Andeans, even the spiritual realm is ordered in symbolic personifications of social groupings that correspond to the actual ones. The community, not the individual, is the unit; and in the end not only maintains a solid sense of belonging but also is provided with his or her own social cosmos.

THE FESTIVAL OF QOYLLORRIT'Y

Qoyllorrit'y takes place ninety miles from Cuzco, but hazardous road conditions and delays typically make it necessary to spend full day getting to base camp. From there villagers embark on their serpentine ascent toward the peak of Qolqepunco. The festival can draw as many as seventy thousand people from all over the land; the participants are mostly villagers, who walk over rugged mountainous terrain to get there. They are dressed in typical colorful garb, and many villages send groups of musicians and costumed dancing troupes who choreograph a symbolic enactment meaningful to them. This organic weaving of vernacular music, dancing, and drumming goes on incessantly for days and nights. We joined them and, like them, periodically interrupted our arduous climb to prostrate ourselves before the large stone crosses dramatically and strategically erected on the way. We paused before each of these shrines and, not unlike the bands of musicians playing first a slow, lugubrious tune followed by a bouncy or sparkling one, exchanged heavy and light energy with the god. We all replayed in Andean fashion Christ's agony at Calvary much as the twelve stations of the cross are trekked yearly in Jerusalem.

Qoyllorrit'y takes place on a peak considered a tutelary deity in pre-Columbian times, drawing animal and agricultural offerings. During Inca rule its cult was institutionalized and put in the service of the highest social caste, which displayed its power and wealth with sumptuous festivities. As mentioned earlier, the Spanish conquest, which introduced Christianity to Andean society, was modified by local practices and beliefs, and a pantheon of Peruvian deities and saints took their places next to the European imports. The dark skinned Christ of Qoyllorrit'y is one of these hybrids. The story explaining his apparition and crucified imprint on a natural rock follows a typical Catholic form. Briefly, Jesus came to a very poor, suffering, but obedient Indian boy. After many events came the final encounter, witnessed by a number of adults, when the apparition turned into the agonizing and bleeding Christ on the cross and the boy died. A very large but simple sanctuary was built on the mountaintop encompassing the blazoned rock. During the festival days, pilgrims crowd into it holding lit candles requesting health, money, or whatever wishes they hope to have granted. However, at the heart of the worship are the *ukukus*, the bear men. These personages are considered to be half divine and half human and those who play this role are selected from the best of each village's crop of young men. They have to excel in physical prowess as well as in goodness of character. They must be very agile and capable of withstanding the intense cold and thin air of high altitudes, for they are the ones who climb beyond the sanctuary to the highest glacier, where they spend the night challenging and surrendering to greater powers by doing the most daring of feats including handstands, jumping, and running on the glacier. Those who survive descend at dawn carrying a block of ice on their backs, which reflects the light of the rising sun. They are in charge of bringing down the stars, which, as semigods, they have grabbed out of the sky. The ice is delivered to the Christ in the sanctuary. We were shocked to hear that one of the young men died during the ceremony, and we learned that five men had died the year before; we were told this with equanimity by our guide and teacher of Andean mysticism, who also told us that someone dies this way every year. The eager, searching look in the eyes of the villagers who clustered halfway up the glacier at dawn, looking for the returning young men, belied the pose of acceptance. Their eyes clearly mirrored fear and hope for the life of a son, nephew, friend, or some loved one. Yet they offered them annually as transforming vessels in the hope of a better collective existence.

Almost as overwhelming as these deaths was the remarkable social order created in the festival community surrounding us during those three days. Men, women, and children of all ages and states of health somehow climbed this very high mountain, squatted at the foot of its glacier with no food, sanitary provisions, or facilities of any kind, and engaged in a multiplicity of religious and social exchanges in peace and harmony. This was a magnanimous group event defying most of our Western social psychological explanations. Obviously these pilgrims had the rhythm of centuries of custom and tradition to guide them, and it was grandly evident that their behavior flowed from the authenticity of their belief in their spirits and in the vessels that could mediate their prayers. Each individual and small group within the larger crowd seemed irrationally but intelligently linked by a web of invisible threads to the two interlocking spiritual centers. One was a pre-Columbian moving altar embodied in the *ukukus*, the costumed sacrificial bear men dancing the treacherous slopes of the glacier for the sake of one and all. The other was the crucified Christ, at once an image for the ubiquitous scapegoat victim and an emblem for the conquest and subjugation of human life and soul.

Yet a third center of energy captivated us and the pilgrims during this festival. Not far from the sanctuary, a mount consecrated to the Virgin Mary served as the center for a large area devoted to a very active, symbolic commercial transaction. There one could purchase with make-believe money a small model or facsimile of one's heart's desire. Simply built of clay or wood and colorfully decorated, small trucks, agricultural fields, baskets of fruit, human figures, and so on were sold at stone stands. It was a kind of sacred marketplace, a land of fantasies and dreams where the typical Western split between the sacred and profane, between worship and commerce, was most evidently absent. The game could become quite complex. As soon as we entered the scene, we were approached by excited villagers who wanted visas to go live in the United States. In notebooks fashioned to resemble passports we wrote visa entry messages with signatures notarized by yet another vendor at his post. In exchange, we were awarded a travel business on Sun Street and a University of Andean Mysticism. The rest of our money we deposited at the Virgin Mary bank, where we found numerous Indians who behaved like New York stock traders on a day of heavy trading. Good humor and hope permeated this commercial realm, but it also exhibited all the frenzy and seriousness that financial transactions foster.

THE SPIRIT IN CEMENT

In Cuzco the two of us parted ways with the other group members, fully cognizant of their reality in us but easily relinquishing the actual group ties that had held and shaped us through our shared initiation. Our enhanced sense of a communal bond with all of humanity greatly facilitated the release of personal connections. Here we can only try to speak briefly for ourselves; although our intense immediate responses to the experience in the Andes were different, the ensuing integration of the experience into our daily lives has been similar in effect.

Both of us were raised in the Judeo-Christian tradition, one a Jew and one a Catholic, but neither of us is currently an active worshiper in our faith of origin. However, each of us had faced in our personal and collective histories the sacrifice of family members and social groups to the political upheavals in Europe and Peru. Arthur, as a Jew deeply involved for much of his life in the death-rebirth saga of modern Israel and the Holocaust, was extremely sensitive to the Christian oppression of the Andean people. His initial outrage at the historic and ongoing role of the Catholics as conquerors and despoilers of the highly developed Inca culture was inflamed further by what he witnessed in Qoyllorrit'y. It seemed to him that Indian customs had been subsumed by Catholicism; a symbol of that domination was the surrender of the *ukukus'* hard-won star/ice treasures during Catholic Mass held by an Irish priest at the sanctuary. Yet ultimately he came to embrace a larger reality, one in which the Indians, however poor and downtrodden, have nevertheless effected a spiritual miracle: the marriage of Inca and Christian ritual into a new faith that worked for them and which paradoxically served his own development and those of his colleagues.

Pilar, for many years a resident of the United States, had been born an upper-class Peruvian, the descendant of the Spanish rulers of the land. During her childhood the racial and class barriers between rich and poor were impermeable. As part of that division Indians had been her servants, nurturing her body as if she were their own child, without question or even the right to complain. In their milieu she learned of powers at least as mysterious and enticingly strange as the aesthetic and intellectual gifts of her European birthright. While still a young woman she watched the military revolution of the 1960s transfer economical and politic power to the Indians and other, racially mixed lower classes while decimating the fortunes of her own class and family. Now, years later, her participation in an Andean initiation brought much-needed healing. The symbolic human sacrifice stood for her own symbolic sacrifice—the loss of her birthright and the personal suffering of herself and her family even as centuries of social abuses were redressed. The festival of Qoyllorrit'y purged her anger and deepened her compassion for all participants in the historical drama of her country.

Perhaps most critical was the way the events of Qoyllorrit'y deepened our relationship by providing a living mirror for the sacrifice and difference that lived in our dyad. We were able to witness our past worlds and our past and present prejudices in a sacred setting that transformed antagonisms into interconnectedness and polarity into complementarity, a gift that continued to have positive consequences in our relationship long after we left the high Andean glacier.

The call for all of us—as a group, as a pair, and as individuals—was for a deeper and broader understanding of the death-rebirth archetype, the repetitive demand by life to give itself up for its own renewal. At the center of our learning was the realized experience of the sacred and the profane, the individual and the collective, and matter and spirit as one undivided whole. The poverty we saw around us in the Andes accentuated our awareness of the sacredness of the material world we inhabit in California. We clearly realized that it was not just nature but also our technological superimpositions on it that are the face of God. Once back in the United States, we could more readily identify in our paved surroundings those threshold structures dedicated to our communion with the divine. For example, our supposedly secular therapy offices, where we participate in healing practices with clients and colleagues, are clearly altars not unlike the mountain peaks, caves, icons, and other places and means we used for crossing to the spirit realm in our Andean journey. In Jungian terms, the view from the Self had been affirmed and established in the ordinary reality of our everyday experience.

We have both worked for over twenty years with individuals and with groups to enhance a conscious dialogue with unconscious forces as they arise in the present or move through people's lives. Our decision to investigate travel as a "crossing" technique, one that will serve our mission to awaken collective consciousness, has been fueled by the rich journey we took and by the promise of other journeys to come. Ultimately the inner vision is not separable from outer reality, much as the body is not separable from the psyche. Travel in the mode we have described above is a powerful teacher about these inseparabilities, for in these experiences crossings are not only shamanic-like dreams, fantasies, and active imaginations but actual crossings of the entire organism into powerful other world settings in which coping is critical. Crossing through bodily presence in the actual physical, aesthetic, commercial, social, and spiritual aspects of a new place while participating *with intent* in the ecstatic rituals of a culture is an extraordinarily potent way to bridge the threshold to another world, learn and heal, and perhaps move closer to a unified vision of existence in which humans play their part.

REFERENCES

Colman, A. D. 1995. *Up from Scapegoating; Awakening Consciousness in Groups.* Wilmette, Ill: Chiron.

Montero, P. 1992. *The Imaginal at Crossings: A Soul's View of Organizational and Individual Analysis.* Willmette, Ill: Chiron Publications.

————. 1995. "The Altar in Human Groups: A Path to the Living God." In Proceedings of the Thirteenth International Congress for Analytical Psychology, Zurich, in press.

Nunez del Prado., J. V. 1993. "The Cultural State of the Inca Empire: The Andean Priesthood." Unpublished manuscript.

Tierney, P. 1989. *The Highest Altar: Unveiling the Mystery of Human Sacrifice.* London, Penguin.

Chapter 24

Firework: A Hawaiian Guidebook to the Goddess

Sara Spaulding-Phillips

This is a story about a *ho'oponopono*, a "setting-things-right" healing ritual, as directed by a Hawaiian *kahuna* for the benefit of a *haole,* a shamanic initiate. Called to the Big Island of Hawaii through her dreams of the Fire Goddess, Pele, and following a series of spiritual retreats there, the author/initiate returns from the deepest recesses of the cave of Koheleapele, "womb of the goddess Pele," to tell about her journey. Her experience vividly illustrates how the traditions of shamanism and contemporary psychotherapy may productively converge. We think this story is a fitting ending for the long, many-sided adventure of this book, with its alternating shamanic and psychological dimensions. We hope, in the many chapters presented here, the two disciplines have come to be reflections, amplifications and complements for each other.

The narrative following this introduction is an account of my psychological and spiritual development and my initiation into shamanism through the earth-centered spirituality of Hawaii—a world away from my training as a Western psychotherapist with a master's degree in counseling psychology from Goddard College in Plainfield, Vermont. I am a licensed marriage and family therapist and have practiced in Santa Rosa, California, for twenty years, seeing couples, families, and individuals. I see many women who come to be treated for depression, with quite a few experiencing a great spiritual emptiness or loss of soul. *Firework*, a work in progress from which the following two chapters are taken, is my story about soul loss, about a soul never wholly developed.

In the winter of 1983 I began having a series of dreams unlike any dreams I have had before. They seemed to be telling me a story. They were set in Hawaii. I traveled to Hawaii often to visit Jessie, my friend of many years. The dreams were telling of a spiritual retreat taking place on the Big Island, a retreat for the healing of the feminine and the earth.

Three years later I initiated such a retreat on the Big Island, following the instructions in my dreams. I entered into the mysteries of Hawaiian spirituality, which expresses regard for the holy predicated on a deep reverence for all living things and a special relationship to the Fire Goddess, Pele, who rules the islands.

To perform a ceremony or hold a workshop on her island without her blessing, however, is *kapu*—forbidden. So it was that I met several *kahuna*—the priests or priestesses of Hawaiian spirituality, the keepers of the secrets and the healers in the communities. One of these was Kalika, a *kahuna* dedicated to Pele.

The time was one of powerful transition for me. I was at midlife, at the onset of menopause, my children grown. I was still clinging to the last remnants of a patriarchal orientation and to an identification with masculine values such as heroic pursuit, domination, and linear and hierarchical thinking. I was deeply into Jungian analysis and was hungering for a spirituality and a connection with God that would feed my soul. I burned with a need to reclaim my own connection with my female authority. I didn't know the depth of what I had lost or had never had.

The first retreat, at the time of the 1986 spring equinox, began as my visions suggested. It was called "Who Heals the Healers?" and our chosen *kahuna*, Kalika, seized on our request that she preside as an invitation to take over. Where I wanted to create a sacred place for us all to forge our own paths to healing, her focus as the *kahuna* was on leading and controlling the retreat. Where I wanted a safe space for us to speak among ourselves, to stumble and work to come up with our own wisdom, Kalika talked at the women for hours. I wanted to create community; I wanted the leaders to facilitate, to listen, to model nonhierarchical organization. The *kahuna* wanted to run the show, to "give the women their money's worth."

It did not take long for the two of us to get into a power struggle. Kalika was stronger psychically than I. The Self I thought I knew dissolved, faded away. The loss of Self was also a loss of soul, and I became very ill psychically—I had two frightening suicide dreams—then physically with nausea, vomiting and diarrhea. A deep fatigue took over my entire being. My views of psychotherapy and healing underwent profound questioning and doubt as well. In my search for health I went from traditional Western physicians to homeopaths, then to a Chinese medical doctor and an acupuncturist.

The following year, as we prepared for the second retreat, I spoke of my concerns to the *kahuna*. She saw me questioning her system and beliefs, and she withdrew from any further work with me. It was her way or nothing.

Jessie found another *kahuna*, Auntie Mua, who, when told of our problems, gravely insisted we perform a *ho'oponopono*—a ritual for setting things right—before the second retreat was to take place. The following narrative relates those events immediately leading up to the *ho'oponopono* and the ritual itself, which took place in the sacred cave called Koheleleapele, the "womb of Pele." This is an ancient birthing cave deep in the earth, used before the arrival of the missionaries and then in secret for years following the westernization of Hawaii. It is very dangerous to enter; the Hawaiians do not even speak the cave's name.

The cave journey was such an integral part of my healing and my initiation into Hawaiian spirituality that I cannot remain silent; I must speak of it. Enter with me now, into the cave, into the story, and into the healing.

THE JOURNEY TO KOHELELEAPELE

The day begins early. The air is cool with a hint of breeze. Once again I awake in Jessie's ginger-scented room, the one with the peephole into the cane fields. Through it I can see the swaying sugar cane silhouetted against the first light of dawn. I feel urgent and expectant, and I cannot remain still. I jump out of bed, listening for signs that Jessie and Zeena are stirring. There are none.

We are headed for the volcano goddess Pele's home this morning to hold a dawn cleansing and a sacred blessing ceremony at the crater Kilauea's rim. Then the *ho'oponopono*, the special forgiveness ritual, will take place in the sacred cave of Koheleleapele. The new *kahuna*, Auntie Mua, is directing the events through her ability as a spirit guide. In order for our descent into the volcano to go safely, we must follow very specific instructions. Two parallel journeys are under way: one on a physical level, a frightening journey deep into a hole in the ground and another on a spiritual level, a journey to recover and heal my soul.

We all climb into my white rental car. I back out of the gravel driveway and nose the car onto the narrow lava-bed road that will eventually take us to the house of our guide, Gitta. Jessie keeps shifting around on the seat to get comfortable. She broke her leg falling down the stairs at her mother's home and is still healing. Even so, her weak leg isn't going to keep her from the descent into the sacred cave.

We drive without speaking. The car hums over the snakelike route through Volcanoes National Park and on to Kilauea Crater. My mind follows its own road, full of switchbacks, ruts and holes as old as my first meeting with Jessie—maybe older. I continue to go over and over the painful rift that has occurred between Jessie, the banished *kahuna*, Kalika, and me, and which threatens to cancel the healing spiritual retreat I am working so hard to produce.

The sequence of events leading to this moment flashes before my eyes. First come the awesome dreams that pointed me toward planning the first retreat. My mind then fast-forwards to the conversations with Jessie and Zeena about the preparations. I replay with a shudder the moment of inviting Kalika to join the retreat, then recall the terrible battle of wills that followed.

I could not work with the *kahuna*; I remember our struggle and her final withdrawal from the retreat. I feel again the sense of abandonment: by Kalika, by the participants, and by Jessie, who was so angry with me for chasing the *kahuna* away.

But mostly I feel my own betrayal of myself and my beliefs, dreams, and visions. I gave away my power, my voice, and my truth, and I psychically allowed myself to be killed off, to commit suicide. Mesmerized by the hum of the car and the curving mountain road, I remember a fragment of one of my suicide dreams, and I feel again the awful pall of the illness that almost killed me.

The first retreat—with the openness of its participants, the place that was Hawaii, and, yes, the spirituality of the *kahuna* Kalika—was a catalyst for many of the women, who subsequently underwent profound and deeply transformative experiences—marriages, births, divorces, and separations, life purposes clearly found. Yet while the retreat participants might now be hungry for more magic from the *kahuna*, to accede once more to her way would also result in our not pursuing our own way, our own spirituality—the healing retreat for women that I, not the *kahuna*, had envisioned.

My mind returns to a scene on the plane when Zeena and I were coming to Hawaii for this second retreat. She gave me a gift, a small black and white pewter pin of a lively flying lady. It is unlike her to give me a gift or make any special overture like this, so I knew that she was making it easy for me to talk about the rift with Jessie. I thought of a line from a favorite poet, Diane DiPrima: "With or without my broom, I will fly." My unspoken thought was that I was certainly flying on my own now into this Hawaiian venture, after all the trouble and my sickness of the last year.

"I've tried hard not to talk about what happened last year in a negative way, Zeena," I said, watching the clouds through the window. "I don't want to criticize my sisters." She was silent, watching me collect my thoughts. "I guess the crux of the matter is that my vision of the retreat is so different from Jessie's and Kalika's. Now I am trying to regain my soul. I envisioned this beautiful, safe, protected space where all women would come together in an egalitarian way with no defined leader to share our knowledge of women's mysteries. I wanted to work with the old tools—the chants, the magic, the tarot, the I Ching, the herbs and crystals—and remember the old stories, and tell our stories. Pretty idealistic, huh?"

Zeena nodded and I went on, caught up in the vision that had inspired and motivated this adventure. "I wanted to create the retreat together, experimenting in our deepest feminine ways of being, the Great Round Way. And I wanted to hold it in Hawaii, with the Hawaiian Mother Earth goddess reigning supreme in all her forms."

"What happened? Why did you let Kalika take over?" The plane dropped slightly in turbulence, mirroring my chaotic memories of the sharp interchanges I had with Kalika.

"I saw you lose your energy, Sara," Zeena continued. "You seemed to become a shadow of yourself."

"Exactly. I became my shadow. I allowed Kalika to eat me alive, to swallow me up. It felt like soul murder. Maybe a possession. Whatever it was, Zeena, I almost died."

I had not been prepared for working within the completely different cultural orientation and belief system as embodied by the *kahuna*. I ran up against this shamanism, and my Episcopal-Buddhist practices had not given me any preparation. I had felt as if beliefs and teachings were being rammed down my throat. It had been as if I were being pulled through a rent in the psychic world and into a foreign, alien world.

"How did you get rid of her?" Zeena asked.

"Well, it wasn't my intention in the beginning to get *rid* of her. I thought we could work things out." My voice lowered, and Zeena leaned forward to catch my words.

"After the confrontation, I had a dream," I said. "In the dream I am checking the rooms on the third day of this coming retreat, and I find Mary, the disturbed one from our first retreat, bleeding to death on the bathroom floor. She has slashed her wrists, and all the life is draining from her. I can barely see the thin silver cord connecting her to what life remained. I summon the hotel doctor. I awoke before it was determined whether she would live or die."

Zeena raised her eyebrows. "Well, that seems pretty serious. What did you do?"

"I called Jessie immediately and told her my dream. I just couldn't ignore it a second time," I replied. "Although Jessie laughed off the dream, I felt it was showing me how threatened I felt by Kalika's intensity and power. Being around her makes me doubt myself, and this feels like a death."

I drift into a memory of Jessie speaking on the phone after Kalika pulled out of the retreat, taking half the participants with her. "Sara, Kalika doesn't want to work with you again. She doesn't go along with all your psychology, the analyzing and mythologizing. She thinks it's bullshit. It's too much work. Half the women who signed up are coming because of her. I'm just furious with you.

"This is a powerful energy here in Hawaii," she continued. "You can't fool around, Sara; this isn't kindergarten. Madam Pele is a fierce and awesome force." I see myself psychically cowering, as if waiting for the hot lava of her words to come spewing up through the holes in the mouthpiece of the phone.

A rock in the rough road jolts me out of my reverie and back into the car driving over the volcanic landscape. My hands are cold and clammy on the steering wheel, and my eyes are staring into the darkness. I have an image of Kalika walking to the edge of the crater. Pele, dressed in a fiery red dress, waits with open arms. For a moment Kalika and Pele are one. Kalika's face looms before me with her condemning smile. While she carries my shadow, my dark side, all the attributes I don't want to own, Kalika also carries my powerful self, my shaman self come to claim me, to bring me home.

I shake my head to release the vision. I sneak a glance at Jessie, at this woman I have called friend for so many years. She sits staring out the window at the dark and melted landscape. In the past few weeks the silence between us has grown louder. We are communicating through Zeena. I am in my own psychological descent now, an inner peeling-away of layers of ideas about who I thought I was. I am alone and feel dishonored. I have never before felt so shamed and guilty, and I am not even certain why.

Suddenly I am jolted awake. I slam on the brakes so hard the sole of my foot burns. I have narrowly missed a woman dressed in white who had stepped in front of the car.

"What the hell are you doing?" Jessie screeches as she lurches forward, straining her seat belt to its maximum. "Why did you stop?"

"The woman. Didn't you see the woman? We almost hit her." I can hardly breathe. I turn around to look at Zeena. A look passes between Jessie and her, and they eye me strangely.

"I didn't see anyone," Jessie says curtly.

"Maybe it was Tutu Pele," Zeena answers lightly, referring to the legends about the goddess who can take different forms and appear and disappear. We had heard about one woman who said that once as a child she had been picking *lehua* blossoms to make a wedding lei. As she skirted each plant, picking only the prize blossoms, an old woman approached her with an outstretched hand. The young girl offered her the basket. When the girl turned back from summoning her father to meet this woman, the old lady and the basket of blossoms had vanished.

Our pace slows to a crawl. We are enveloped by *vog*, a gritty blend of volcanic ash belched up in nightly surges by the dragon in the volcano and mixed with the early morning mist. The sky darkens, and it is hard to breathe. It is as if the day has turned its back on our journey. Pele is very near. Her ominous presence seems to lure us to her. Is the descent into the cave our will or hers? I shudder with the cold. I feel afraid.

"Turn right at the next stop sign," Jessie says in a tone not unlike the sound of fingernails scraping on a blackboard. This disdainful tone takes me right back to a time when she scolded me before, this time concerning my profession: "You shrinks are all alike. You analyze too much, Sara. You read too much theory. As an intellectual, you don't have time to live your life. You sell all your hours to your customers. You 'the-rapist,'" she spat, carefully separating the syllables to convey her meaning. "It's so exploitative! How long have you been in therapy, anyway?" she asked me.

"Fourteen years," I replied quietly, closing my eyes.

"Fourteen years! That's like buying water by the river. I don't think it's cured you of anything, has it? Basically psychotherapy is a tool of the patriarchy and continues women's oppression. Psychology and shrinks make women crazy."

I had nothing to say. She doesn't understand. Our worlds are far apart. I can't argue with Jessie any more than I could argue with my father or my tyrannical grandfather or Kalika. All four of them seemed to be always right, never in doubt.

These days, I feel always in doubt and never right. I keep running straight into my shadow—into the Dark Goddess. What will I find in the shadows of her womb today?

"God, I wish I had brought a bottle of gin to offer as an appeasement to Pele, just in case," I hear myself say. Now that I am nearing Tutu Pele, I experience an urge to offer her gifts. I feel so strange here in Hawaii, thrust into the interior darkness of an earth culture where everything is alive and has a spirit of its own, and where a deity is responsible for every blade of grass, every tiny fish and every flower. In the very beginning, Kalika had threatened me with Pele's power: "If she doesn't approve of the retreat, she'll throw us off the island." Am I being thrown off?

As the car scrapes and jolts along the crater's road, Jessie muses blandly, "I thought fifty dollars was about right to pay Gitta. Actually, we're very lucky to have her as our guide today. She sees guiding people through Koheleleapele and instilling reverence toward the feminine and the earth as sacred and healing work." I am quiet, letting Zeena fill the space with her comments.

We travel into more and more isolated terrain. The air is much warmer than the cool jungle climate of Wood Valley. The *vog* is gone. Small, delicate orchids spring up among the hulking rocks on each side of the road, surprising me. An unexpected sign points us to the right. Gitta lives in Orchid Land. We have arrived.

The car doors spring open all at once, like a car full of clowns arriving for a performance. Zeena and I get out and hug the tiny German woman who comes out to greet us, while Jessie struggles to pry her great girth and weak leg from the car. She collapses in a lawn chair.

We sit in the shade of a tree and sip hibiscus tea. Behind our chairs are piles of hats and baskets woven from palm fronds, Gitta makes them to sell to the tourists. I watch Gitta sipping her tea and listen to her cheerful voice. I imagine her leading us through the dark corridors of lava. Very shortly, my safety is going to rest solely in her small hands, and this is the first time I've laid eyes on her. I have to trust Jessie's recommendation completely.

She is recounting an important Pele story, the story of the creation of Koheleleapele, the cave we will soon enter: "Tutu Pele's home is the Kilauea Crater, which you just drove through. The Goddess of the Volcano spews forth fire with her every breath. She is a consummate lover. Her man, Kama-puah'a, is a savage wild boar. Kama-puah'a has a fierce appetite for sex, and he enjoys chasing the nymphs. Pele is forever tracking him down, wreaking terrible damage among the nymphs who are his lovers and dragging him home. Finally she tires of his escapades and dreams up a divine solution to his philandering: she will create a flying *kohe*—a flying vagina. When Kama-puah'a becomes restless with lust, she will send her creation to lure her lover on a great and endless chase.

"She is so proud of this giant *kohe*! As she fervently admires her handiwork, strong stirrings and rumblings begin in her voluptuous body. Her enormous breasts and belly begin to undulate. Her eyes roll back, and a great and awful cry escapes from her gaping mouth . . . ahhhhhh!

"Her loins open. Fire and lava, birth and life erupt from her *kohe*, forging a great hole in the earth. A huge tunnel of massive proportion is created, through which flows a furious fire. The fire rushes on with wondrous force, sculpting an enormous underground cave deep within the earth: the womb of Pele.

"Days, weeks, and months go by. Pele cannot be seen. No one can get near her underground formations.

"When at last the roaring diminishes and the fire has burned itself out, Pele sits dazed, enveloped in her warm amniotic juice. She opens her eyes and sees deep within her earthy body a womb of great proportion—a perfect womb to house the great *kohe*. Spent from her earthly orgasm, Pele lies down. She see Kama-puah'a in constant pursuit, following her great creation but always just out of reach . . . and she is pleased."

I listen to the story. I think also of Zeus and Hera. It has the essential elements of the male-female myths—the never-ending story of man as the pursuer. But this story has an interesting twist: the man is the pursuer, all right, but the woman holds all the power.

Gitta's voice brings me back to the group. "Up behind the cabin by the water tank is a medicine wheel. Walk around the wheel and select something to offer Pele. We cannot enter the cave without asking her for safe passage and praying for our world to once more be right. We will leave an offering at the entrance."

The first thing that catches my eye is a beautiful sprig of orchids. I lean over and gently finger them. There are seven—each different but similar. They are the palest of lavenders with yellow and a speck of black. "Ah," I think, "these will symbolize my family." I smile at the thought of Jacob, Bret, Victoria, Ondrea, Amanda, and Eric. Silently I ask the spirits for permission to pluck the flowers and feel an inner affirmation. I gently pick the sprig and lay it to rest on a giant *ti* leaf.

My next choice is a beautiful black and white stone, round and smooth and strangely foreign in this place of lava roughness. As soon as I touch it, I hear the sound of Jessie's voice. I know immediately that the stone represents Jessie and her part in rubbing my edges smooth, like water rushing over jagged rocks. I add the stone to the *ti* leaf.

I choose another smooth, cylindrical stone—like a pestle to grind grain to flour. This is Kalika, another shadow woman. Both Jessie and she are guides to the underworld and my inner darkness.

I add some furry stuff from a weed—a soft cotton batting, protection from sharp objects and from sharp people and piercing situations. This would be for my vulnerable self, the part I call Mary, the Mary of the suicide dream. Mary will be protected by that which is overlooked, dishonored, like this weed.

I add a kukui nut, sacred to the Hawaiian *ali'i*, or royalty, to symbolize forgiveness. I add it as a prayer to heal myself and all my relations.

Zeena, Jessie, and I gather together in the *lanai*, where Gitta has laid out eight large *ti* leaves in a crisscross pattern on the table. She quietly asks that we put our symbols in the center of the *ti* leaves and she gives us each a thin reed to bind them. In silence and with reverence, we wrap and bind our *ho'okupu*, our ceremonial tributes to Pele.

Now we check our backpacks for our flashlights, water, a snack, and a sweatshirt for the cold. Shivers ripple through me. We all put on sturdy shoes for the strenuous hike over lava. The air is tense. We are in deep silence; it's as if we have wrapped all our words in our packets, along with our offerings.

We get into the car. Again we bump over the lava-strewn, potholed roads, silent but for an occasional comment in Gitta's sweet German accent.

At the end of the road, there is a broken old fence, a rusty fender, and a Coors can. We park, lock the car, and begin walking. We hike over the hardened lava and through a small dappled bamboo forest in the middle of nowhere. In front of us is a boulder-sized entrance into the dark, moist earth.

THE DESCENT INTO THE SACRED CAVE

We stop for a moment to gather at the cave's entrance. No one speaks. The moment is too sacred to be scarred with words.

The sun is a little past its zenith, and the air is warm and thick. As we huddle close to each other on the narrow, sloping rocky path, Gitta places her offering with great care against the hillside among other aging offerings of flowers and *ti* leaf packets.

"*E-Pele-e! Mahalo nui loa!*" she chants three times in a beautiful singsong. "Honorable revered Fire Goddess, grant us a safe and sacred passage. We thank you for all your great gifts to us!" We place our offerings next to Gitta's on the hillside.

Jessie, Zeena, and I follow closely as Gitta enters the cave, each praying in our own way for a safe journey into the darkest part of the earth. And then we begin going down, down, down—descending into the sacred womb.

The path is rocky and very steep. Gitta reports the terrain ahead, the beam of her small flashlight roaming over the dark walls, and we stay close to each other, touching. I am alert to helping Jessie in any way I can, knowing her leg is untried and unstable. The path takes us rapidly downward along a ledge. We have to duck to miss the low ceiling and the jagged outcroppings along the way. Our flashlight beams crisscross in crazy pinstripes across the cave walls and ceilings.

The ceiling of the cave is smooth and moist. As we proceed, the light from the entrance gradually narrows to a thin slit. In a few seconds it has disappeared altogether, and we are plunged into darkness. For a moment we stand stunned, our flashlights out.

My eyes grope frantically for something to fix on, but there is nothing lighter than the darkness. Never have I faced such an utterly lightless void. There is no sense of motion as I walk ahead into nothingness. Everything seems to stop. The sound of silence magnifies the slightest noise. My heart races with fear. I am in the Dark Mother, the mother with vacant eyes. I am in the part of me that says, "I don't know who I am. I don't know where I'm going. I am lost."

I am sweating with fear. The ground is precariously uneven. The thought that at any moment the old cave floor could give way and one or all of us could drop into oblivion through a deep lava tube sweeps through my mind like an icy wind. A tremor would bring the ceiling down, at best killing us or at worst trapping us forever in the dark birth canal to die by inches.

I reach for some support in my mind, but instead come the words from Inanna's poem:

> *Oh, Lady of the Great Below*
> *Hard are your lessons,*
> *I know your shadow falls beside me*
> *Everywhere I go.*

Inanna, another old goddess, entered the underworld and returned— small consolation to me now.

Gitta stops without warning, and Jessie, Zeena, and I bump into each other, Charlie Chaplin style. Gitta is poised on the edge of a huge hole, the entrance to an aberrant lava tube that drops bottomless into the earth. Shining our small lights into the void, we look into the nothingness with horror.

To continue our descent, we will have to find another path, since the ceiling now slopes to the floor. Utterly shaken, we watch Gitta climb down a six-foot drop to another floor of the cave, as unafraid and nimble as a Sierra mountain goat.

Zeena and I go next. When it's Jessie's turn, we all shine our lights on her and help her navigate her bulky body and her weakened leg down the slope. There is an instant when she is caught in the circle of our lights, backing down the rocks, one leg pawing wildly in the air for safe footing. "I'm scared to death," she whispers, releasing a small cry of terror like a child. Minutes tick by as she struggles and heaves. We reassure her, brace her, guide her. Finally, after reaching the next ledge safely, she breaks down and sobs.

I too am terrified. I'm so afraid that I can only hope that the Goddess hears my prayers for protection, and I plead over and over again, "I serve the Goddess. I serve the Goddess. I serve the Goddess." The only way I can bear to go forward is by renewing my trust and my commitment with every breath. I dare not dwell on the claustrophobic, dark situation. I am too far in now; there is no going back. I am reminded of those endless last minutes of my pregnancies, with the inexorable movement forward and no possibility of backing out. Like giving birth, this journey into the cave must be taken to the end.

I stare ahead into the void and try to push away the thoughts of earthquakes and collapsing vaginas as I remember the Pele myth that Gitta told us earlier. By a sheer act of will, I bring my focus back to the incredible structure of the walls and the drops of moisture that have collected along the formations. Touching the moist walls is strangely embarrassing, as if I am touching real inner tissue. Gitta seems to read my mind and explains:

"I brought a Western medical doctor here one time, and he commented that the structure, down to the textures, lines, and curves, is an exact replica of a woman's vaginal canal, cervix, and uterus. He was amazed at the accurate configuration." How does he know? I ask myself, and for a moment I am distracted from my fear by the old man-anger.

We advance further into the ancient pathway formed by Pele's white-hot menstruations. Gitta halts us each time on the edge of countless lava tubes. Pointing my flashlight into these infinities, my heart jumps into my throat and seems to stop and start with a primordial fear of its own. My heart knows that if I am to fall into the bottomless crevice, my body will lie there forever—a final and most precious offering to Pele. Shuddering, I hope she will not require such a sacrifice.

Miraculously, around a bend there is a small crack of light in the far distance. I am suddenly filled with deep gratitude for this renewal of light and hope. A new depth of meaning for the reverence we humans have for "the light" floods over me.

The ground approaching what Gitta calls the "womb room" is very rocky, and we have to use our hands to brace ourselves so as not to fall. In front of us is a ledge about breast high. We are on our hands and knees as we approach the "altar." Larger rocks are piled up on the right side of the ledge, and I scramble up them for a view of this magnificent cave. I stand in awe of the dramatic setting before me.

The crack of light has turned into a beam shooting through an opening. My eyes follow the beam down to where it lands on a large, flat stone the size of some gigantic ancient millstone. Instinctively I know it is a birthing stone. It is near the cave's sloping ceiling and is illuminated by a vibrant aura of colored rainbow lights.

It is stunning. I gasp, and tears fill my eyes. At this moment, I am All-Woman embodied, the eternal feminine. I feel whole and complete.

Near the birth stone is a rock shaped like a primitive throne, carved from a smooth piece of lava. Shaking badly, I am relieved to sit on it. The cave has become deathly quiet.

Gitta scurries off like a field mouse into another opening to the left. Jessie sits in the shadows, her breathing gradually quieting. Zeena sits near me, but I cannot see her. All of a sudden the events of the past few days pour into my mind: returning to Hawaii, facing the absence of the *kahuna* and spiritual direction, feeling alone and dishonored and unsure of my own spiritual leadership. It is as if I now have permission within this great, dark holding tank to confront the demons of my psyche, to give birth to the silent agony of an old friendship, a sacred sistership gone awry and taken over by the Hawaiian spirits, nearly costing me a huge ego loss. Beginning this journey into the dark, both inner and outer, my mind sees

Jessie, Kalika, and Zeena as three characters who have moved about on my interior and exterior stages and who are parts of me.

I remember the dream I had one night long ago of having a psychotherapy office in Hilo in which women were coming out of the walls. I hear them speaking to me from my dream again, their voices now coming from the cave's dark interior. In my mind's eye I see and hear a woman declare, "The problem is that our femaleness is not valued, and men see women as weak and dependent." Another one shouts angrily, "Women have sold out." A smallish woman says softly, "But we have to recognize our vulnerable selves first and pay respect to our undervalued parts."

"We are afraid to be afraid," a lively blonde in a pink angora sweater calls out, "so we are too competitive. We need to control others, the situation. Repressed male energy drives us on and makes us feel we have some personal power and self-esteem."

"And meanwhile our daughters don't get mothered," adds an older woman who looks worn and worried.

"I was never mothered myself," another woman says. "I only gave what I wanted to get. My children were my mother. I was never nurtured. I really don't know how to genuinely give, to be intimate."

"We must take a stand for the unmothered part of us now," proclaims the first woman. "Our strong, competent, vulnerable woman needs space to find her deeper spiritual self—to find her soul."

The ghostly chorus fades, and with a jolt my mind comes back to the present moment in the cave. The dialogues with myself, my past, my frustrations, and the conflicting systems and cultures fly back and forth in my mind like fireballs thrown by Pele and Kama-puah'a. My thoughts have worn me out. I am so tired. I am so old.

This dialogue within me is more an argument than an understanding, and in the silence of the cave the argument continues. My goal on this journey is to help women develop our own ideas, to remember our individual stories, and to connect us with humanity's creation myths so that we can remember who we really are. Is this possible? My idea is rooted in Western culture and its patriarchal practices, a culture that values logos, left-brain knowledge, and power over people, places and things—a dominator's model. We have been indoctrinated to value linear time, accomplish goals, earn money, and acquire possessions. Above all, we have been taught we can dominate nature, which includes our earth, all things that live on this earth, and our own bodies, souls, and minds. This model has led to great abuses.

Here in Hawaii, there is little recognized need to analyze feelings or to understand. Here people trust their intuition, trust synchronism (which we call coincidence), and trust themselves to be in the hands of their goddesses and gods. Here great value is given to the earth and all its creatures. Here people live side by side with nature. Here experiencing the interrelationship between all things is all-important, necessary for survival.

When I said to Kalika that I wanted to enact the descent myths at the spring equinox celebration, with the participants playing the goddesses Persephone, Demeter, and Hecate, or Inanna and Ereshkigal, Kalika had a violent reaction. "You cannot do this! It is wrong. When you play them, you summon them, and you cannot summon a god or goddess without their permission. You will bring their energy to the retreat, and you do not know what you are doing." She had been emphatically opposed, and her words felt threatening. I overruled her, but to what end?

I try to quiet my breathing. I close my eyes to feel this cool, moist center of the earth, and I think I hear faint voices again, the voices of other women in the shadows. What are they saying?

"Remember your body. Trust it. Remember you are nature. Your body is the earth. Trust it. Listen to your own voice." The shadows around me seem to take gigantic shapes as the voices continue, and I feel surrounded by a chorus of councilwomen, the elders. These are the giant warrior women I had hoped to meet, who I hoped would support and reassure me, those whose feet are firmly planted on the soil and in the soul.

Time passes. I have no idea how long I have been sitting here. There has been no other sound around me. I am immensely happy, full of peace. I see, out of the corner of my eye, a lone lizard, a *mo'o,* scurrying down the rock. This beautiful creature is said to be able to live through fire. My psyche grabs this image and sees Kalika perched there on the rock instead. She promised us she would come to the cave. She's here!

Seeing her here releases thirteen months of pain. I begin to cry, spilling tears across my knees, hunkering in the darkness with the echoes of my sobs. Through my skin, I begin to hear the awakened cries of hundreds of thousands of women, giving birth, burying loved ones, healing the sick, bearing all. The great wail of shared grief. Their cries create a channel for my connection to Kalika—my true connection to another woman. I love her. I am her.

I notice that the light that had been illuminating my head and shoulders is now flooding across my pelvis and hips. The light slips through my fingers like water, flushing out these strange thoughts and emotions.

Suddenly I feel that I must ask for forgiveness from all the women I have offended in my life—Kalika, Jessie, my mother, my daughters, my grandmother, women I envied, women I gossiped about, judged harshly, laughed at behind their backs, betrayed, abandoned, and hurt. I feel the greatest urge to set things in order. The shadow of Auntie Mua, our new *kahuna,* appears on the farthest wall. She is waving a giant *ti* leaf and chanting something I cannot hear. I feel moisture fall over me and around me. I am drenched. I feel cleansed.

I do not know how long I have been sitting here, but now all the others have come back from side caves and distant journeys, and without words we move in unison to the upper level. We sit in a circle and begin to chant a familiar chant that our mutual friend, Brooke Medicine Eagle, gave us in a circle years before.

I give away this blood of mine,
  for all my relations
And open my womb to the light.
I give away this blood of mine,
  for all my relations
And open my womb to the sun.
Give away, give away, give away, give away,
I open my womb to the light.

Over and over we chant, in and out of time. My eyes and heart fill with the energy of the cave, the swelling of birth, the smoke of fires, and the smiles of women. The faces of my friends shift and change, and all generations seem present at once. There is no separation from those who have gone before; my memories are their memories. I am flooded with the feel, the scent, and the image of first blood, menstrual blood, birth blood, miscarriage blood, blood from a tragic accident in Australia in which two children die, menopausal blood, and then no blood. My usefulness for birthing is gone. My womb is burned out, blackened, darkened like this cave.

The cave seems ugly now, shadowy, harboring unknown demons and dangerous spirits behind every boulder and in every crevice. It is dark and cold, and there is no meaning in my life. I am my useless mother, untrained for life without a family. What is my purpose now? We have no ritual honoring this time of life.

Earth cultures have rites and passages around blood and cycles. Blood is respected and has a special place, as do elders and crones. They are the storytellers around the fires. They carry in their hearts the knowledge of healing with herbs and ritual. They move freely within their tribal family. They teach the young ones. They tell their truth. They no longer compete to gain or hold. Who tells the stories in our culture? What wise women lead us?

The mood in the cave changes. There is a rush of air, a swirl of flashing light. We look at each other, and our eyes widen. Something is happening. Shadows of midwives, of birthing mothers nine layers deep, appear and flicker on the cave walls. I hear sound and wonder if the chants have led us back to the core of early ceremonies stored within this space. Gradually time returns and the sounds and shadows recede. We all sit stunned.

We trek out of the cave without conversation, without incident. The only challenge is getting Jessie back up the steep ledge. I push her rear end from behind while the others pull her from the front. She lands safely with a big cheer from all of us. Ahead is the welcoming light from the dwindling day. We are all exhausted.

The colors of the upper world are incredibly sharp and vivid. My eyes blink to adjust. Smells are pungent, and the air has depth and form and seems to encircle me, making a visible trail back to the car.

There is little conversation at dinner, and we scatter to our rooms early. The ginger blossoms are intoxicating as I sit here, tired to the bone, in my flannel nightgown and long underwear. This is my last night here. I slip into sleep.

I dream:

An old temple-keeper awakens me, touching me on the shoulder with extreme care. He beckons me to follow him. I pad into a solitary cell at Wood Valley Temple. It is the Tara temple, where we will hold the retreat, and it is also a cave. The candles from the altar are flickering magically. The spirit sits in meditation, still, a knowing smile emanating, a grandmother welcoming her grandchild. The temple-keeper hands me a broom, and I begin to sweep the temple-cave floor.

In the early morning, without a word, I pack up my belongings and take them to the car. I fix a cup of Kona coffee and sip it slowly on the porch, watching the awakening dawn until it is day. I leave a note for Jessie and Zeena. I drive slowly the two miles to Wood Valley Temple to prepare for the retreat, the retreat I will lead with Zeena, Jessie, and Auntie Mua. A great feeling of peacefulness floods over me, washing me new.

With or without my broom, I will fly . . .

Editors and Contributors

EDITORS

Donald F. Sandner and *Steven H. Wong,* who originated the Winter Park Conferences in 1990, have both had long connections with shamanism and psychology. Both have been in the clinical practice of Jungian analytical work for many years.

Donald Sandner M.D., University of Illinois, has been a practicing psychiatrist and Jungian analyst for more than thirty years and has had a lifelong interest in tribal healing throughout the world, especially shamanism. He has sited Navajo medicine men and studied their impressive healing system over a ten-year period, resulting in a detailed book entitled *Navajo Symbols of Healing* (Crossroad, 1991). He is now working on a book about worldwide tribal healing and its meaning for modern medicine, entitled *Sacred Medicine.*

Dr. Sandner has also been a lecturer and teacher of C. G. Jung's principles and works. He has put forth a theory that extends Jung's complex theory and its bipolar nature to make it more clinically useful. He has been resident of the C. G. Jung Institute of San Francisco and served on most of its training committees. He has lectured at that institute and at many Jungian training centers both in the United States and abroad. In all, he has published more than thirty book chapters and articles on Jungian psychology, Navajo medicine, and tribal healing.

Along with his clinical experience as a Jungian psychotherapist, Mr. Wong has since childhood had strong shamanistic leanings. In any tribal culture that included shamanism he would have been seen as one who had the call to the shamanic vocation, and he would have been apprenticed to a master shaman for intensive training. In our culture, where these qualities are not recognized, he has spontaneously been in touch with his deep psyche by means of intensive Jungian analysis including deep experiences of visions and Jung's technique of active imagination (the closest thing to shamanism in the spectrum of modern psychology). He has been interested in vision questing as it appears in the tradition of the Lakota Sioux and has studied with a Native American medicine woman of high renown, Pansy Hawk Wing. He has recently deepened his work by full participation in an annual Lakota Sun Dance ritual, which will be described in one of the chapters of this book. As a second generation Asian American, he is also interested in Chinese Taoism and its shamanic characteristics, as in Tai Chi Chuan and classical Chinese culture.

Mr. Wong is also a documentation film maker who has recently completed films on Rohert Johnson and Joseph Henderson, a leading Jungian analyst. He received his B.A. in History from The Colorado College.

CONTRIBUTORS

Margaret Laurel Allen, Ph.D., is a licensed clinical psychologist practicing in Berkeley. A poet and a student of shamanism with a lifelong interest in visionary experience, she is the recipient of the dream discussed in her essay.

Norma Churchill is a visionary and artist whose work depicts the mythic theme of her descent into the underworld (or collective unconscious). She uses both the models of shamanism and Jungian psychology to describe her work and experience. She has lectured widely since 1979 at conferences, institutes, universities, and colleges. She has had many articles, poems, and drawings published over the years.

Arthur Colman, M.D., is a Jungian analyst in private practice in Sausalito and San Francisco and, for the past several years, the chair of the Review Committee of the C. G. Jung Institute. He is also a clinical professor in the Department of Psychiatry at the University of California Medical School. In addition, he is an internationally known depth group consultant to health and governmental organizations and is a past president of the A. K. Rice Institute and editor of its Group Relations Reader Series. He is the author of several professional and general works on subjects ranging from love relations to group dynamics. He has a long interest in shamanism and most recently has traveled to Peru to study Andean mysticism.

Lori Cromer is an occupational therapist specializing in pediatrics in southern California. She recognized her paranormal abilities at a young age but hid them out of fear. Her search for understanding led her to a Jungian therapist a few years ago. Initially surprised by the interest in her experiences, she now shares her journey in her stories.

Patricia Damery, M.F.C.C., is a licensed psychotherapist in private practice in San Francisco and Santa Rosa, California. She is an advanced candidate in the analytical training program at the C. G. Jung Institute, San Francisco.

C. Jess Groesbeck, M.D., is an associate clinical professor of psychiatry at the University of California at Davis and the University of Utah College of medicine. He is also a training analyst in the Interregional Society of Jungian Analysts and Jungian Analysts, North Pacific. Dr. Groesbeck has ad a longtime interest in shamanic studies and research based on personal experience as well as study of traditional healers. He is the author of numerous papers and essays on the integration of shamanism with psychiatry and psychoanalysis.

Pansy Hawk Wing, C.A.C. III, a Lakota medicine woman, has worked as a substance abuse and addiction counselor within her tribe in Pine Ridge. South Dakota, and continues as a spiritual leader practicing the Seven Sacred Rituals of the Lakota Nation.

June Kounin, M.A., a certified analytical psychologist at the C. G. Jung Institute of San Francisco, has fifty-one years of clinical experience with both sexes and all ages from infancy to advanced age. She has lived many male roles, including daughter maiden, wife, mother widow, divorcee, mistress, Grandmother, and great-grandmother and was born with shamanic abilities.

Carol McRae, Ph.D., is a psychologist, Jungian analyst, and a member of the C. G. Jung Institute of San Francisco. She is on the faculty of the Jung Institute Analyst Training Program and teaches interns at the Jung Institute Clinic and graduate students at the California School of Professional Psychology about the sandtray. She has taught various courses, written on women in Jungian analysis, and co-directed a Ghost Ranch national Jungian conference on the body.

Pilar Montero, Ph.D., is a Jungian analyst in private practice in San Francisco at the C. G. Jung Institute. She has served as chair of the curriculum committee and as faculty and training analyst. In addition to her clinicial work, she is a social psychologist and has held academic appoint ments at the University of California Medical Center and San Francisco State c University. She has worked extensively as a depth group and management consultant to organizations in the United States and abroad. She of Peruvian origin and has recently broadened her interest in shamanism to include the study of Andean mysticism in Peru.

Jeffrey A. Raff, Ph.D., is a psychologist. Jungian analyst, and member of the International Association of Analytical Psychology. He has taught seminars, workshops, and classes on Jungian psychology, shamanism, mysticism, and related areas of study for eighteen years all over the United States. He has been in private practice as a Jungian analyst in the Denver area since 1976.

Janet Spencer Robinson, M.A., is a psychotherapist who draws from her background in Jungian psychology, art, and religious studies in her private practice in Palo Alto and San Francisco. She has served as clinical supervisor at Santa Clara University and the Institute of Transpersonal Psychology and is currently completing her certification in the International Society of Sandplay Therapists.

Meredith Sabini, Ph.D., has a blended career as a licensed clinical psychologist, dream researcher and writer. In private practice in Berkeley since 1979, Dr. Sabini taught Jungian psychology and dream seminars at the California School of Professional Psychology and worked as psychologist at Episcopal and Unitarian churches. Her own background combines a Jungian analysis and shamanic initiation and training that took the classic interior form identified by Eliade, beginning with illness and visionary dreams in youth. She designed the Dream Assessment Protocol and now specializes in consultation on dreams and spiritual experiences.

Dyane Neilson Sherwood, Ph.D., is a psychologist in private practice in Woodside, California, and a candidate in analytic training at the C. G. Jung Institute of San Francisco. Before becoming a therapist, she taught in the Human Biology Program at Stanford University and conducted and published research on the neurobiology of learning and memory and the cellular basis of behaviors in simple nervous systems. Dr. Sherwood has also been a consultant to the Hopi tribe and has taught workshops for attorneys and mental health professionals. She has a special interest in the healing potential of direct experiences of the deep unconscious.

Sara Spaulding-Phillips M.A., M.F.C.C., is a psychotherapist, a visionary, and a writer. Her articles on the psychology of current events and women's spirituality have appeared in many professional publications and newsletters. She gives spiritual retreats and teaches writing practice classes in California and Hawaii. For thirty years she has done cross-cultural training and consultation in a variety of settings, most recently at the C. G. Jung Institute in San Francisco. In connection with her writing, Ms. Spaulding-Phillips is working on her doctorate in contemporary spirituality at Union Graduate Institute.

Bradley A. TePaske holds an M.F.A. in printmaking from the University of Massachusetts, a diploma in analytical psychology from the C. G. Jung Institute of Zurich, and a Ph.D. in depth-psychology from the Union

Institute. He is a psychotherapist, a teacher, and a serious student of Gnosticism, Hinduism, early Christianity, and the relationship between sexlity, the body, and religious imagination. A native Iowan of Dutch ancestry and the father of two sons, he now lives in Santa Barbara, California.

Louis Vuksinick, M.D., is a psychiatrist, Jungian analyst, and a member the C. G. Jung Institute of San Francisco where he currently serves as chairman of the Certifying Committee. Trained at Stanford University in psychiatry, he has taught psychiatric residents at McAuley Neuropsychiatric Institue in San Francisco as well as serving as chairman of the department psychiatry at St. Mary's Hospital. Currently he is in private practice in San Francisco and Palo Alto and serves as a consultant to several religious communities and seminaries.

Index